PRAISE FOR ...

Java Reflection in Action

Java Reflection in Action is unique in presenting a clear account of all the cool things you can do with reflection, and at the same time providing the sound conceptual basis that developers need to create advanced applications. The book includes careful explanations of sometimes perplexing programming techniques along with enough background to understand how to extend and vary them. This book overcomes reflection's reputation as a mysterious and esoteric philosophical pursuit, or as a set of messy error-prone coding tricks.

As reflection becomes increasingly common and useful in all sorts of applications, it is great to finally have a book that features disciplined yet still creative and fun software engineering practices based on reflection. Even occasional users will immediately adopt the book's patterns and idioms to solve common problems. Many of the examples can be directly adapted for customized solutions in diverse areas such as XML processing, automated software testing, and program analysis tools. Readers will also find underlying rationales for code performing introspection, proxies, class loading, and so on, that are often seen but not often explained well in everyday Java programs. And even experts will find new ideas and well-thought out advice for using some of the more subtle aspects of reflection.

—Prof. Doug Lea, SUNY Oswego,
author of *Concurrent Programming in Java*

Java has brought reflection to the programming masses, but they're still struggling with it. The Formans turn struggle into adventure as they guide you through one compelling example after another, each one illustrating reflection's power while avoiding its pitfalls.

—Dr. John Vlissides, IBM
coauthor of *Design Patterns*

Java Reflection
in Action

IRA R. FORMAN
NATE FORMAN

MANNING
Greenwich
(74° w. long.)

For online information and ordering of this and other Manning books, please visit
www.manning.com. The publisher offers discounts on this book when ordered in
quantity. For more information, please contact:

Special Sales Department
Manning Publications Co.
209 Bruce Park Avenue   Fax: (203) 661-9018
Greenwich, CT 06830   email: manning@manning.com

Ⓜ Manning Publications Co.   Copyeditor: Linda Recktenwald
   209 Bruce Park Avenue   Typesetter: Dottie Marsico
   Greenwich, CT 06830   Cover designer: Leslie Haimes

ISBN 1-932394-18-4

Printed in the United States of America
1 2 3 4 5 6 7 8 9 10 – VHG – 07 06 05 04

To Janet/Mom
This project wouldn't have happened
without your love and support.

contents

preface xiii
acknowledgments xv
about this book xvii
about the title xx
about the cover illustration xxi

1   *A few basics 1*

   1.1   Reflection's value proposition   3

   1.2   Enter George the programmer   4

      Choosing reflection 5 ▪ Programming a reflective solution 6

   1.3   Examining running programs   8

   1.4   Finding a method at runtime   10

   1.5   Representing types with class objects   12

      *Representing primitive types 13 ▪ Representing interfaces 13
Representing array types 14*

   1.6   Understanding method objects   14

      *Using dynamic invocation 15 ▪ Using primitives with dynamic
invocation 16 ▪ Avoiding invocation pitfalls 17*

   1.7   Diagramming for reflection   19

1.8   Navigating the inheritance hierarchy   20

Introspecting the inheritance hierarchy   22 • Exposing some surprises   23 • Another reflective circularity   24

1.9   Summary   26

2   *Accessing fields reflectively*   27

2.1   Serializing objects   28

Serializing to XML   29 • Choosing reflection   30 Designing serialization with reflection   30

2.2   Finding fields at runtime   31

2.3   Understanding field objects   33

2.4   Getting and setting field values   34

2.5   Examining modifiers   35

Introducing Member   36 • Interface introspection pitfall   37 Introspecting for instance variables   37

2.6   Accessing nonpublic members   38

2.7   Working with arrays   40

2.8   Serialization: putting it all together   41

Serializing each component   43 • Serializing instance variables   43

2.9   Using reflective serialization   45

2.10   Summary   48

3   *Dynamic loading and reflective construction*   49

3.1   George's deployment problem   50

Designing with patterns   51 • Programming a reflective solution   52 Enhancing the factory method with reflection   54 • Combining benefits of delegation and reflection   54

3.2   Loading classes dynamically   55

Basics of forName   55 • Getting array classes   56 Primitives and forName   56

3.3   Constructing objects reflectively   57

Reflective construction basics   57 • Using constructor objects   57 Constructing arrays reflectively   59

3.4   Designing for dynamic loading   60

Disadvantages of reflective construction with arguments   61 Initializing through an interface   62

3.5   Implementing deserialization   63

*Initiating deserialization   64 ▪ Constructing the instances   65
Restoring the object structure   66*

3.6   George's serialization: limitations   69

*No interaction with readObject or writeObject   69 ▪ No handling of
final instance variables   70 ▪ Only no-argument constructors   70
No handling of illegal XML characters   70 ▪ Performance   71*

3.7   Summary   71

4 *Using Java's dynamic proxy*   73

4.1   Working with proxies   74

4.2   George's tracing problem   76

4.3   Exploring Proxy   77

*Understanding invocation handlers   79
Handling the methods of Object   80*

4.4   Implementing a tracing proxy   81

4.5   A note on factories   84

4.6   Chaining proxies   86

*Structuring invocation handlers for chaining   86 ▪ Implementing
a synchronized proxy   88 ▪ Chaining the two proxies   89*

4.7   Stubbing interfaces for unit testing   90

*Examining stubs   90 ▪ Design for stubbing with Proxy   91
Implementation of stubbing with Proxy   93*

4.8   Generating SOAP remote proxies   99

4.9   Pitfalls of using Proxy   103

4.10   Summary   105

5 *Call stack introspection*   107

5.1   George's logging problem   108

5.2   Performing call stack introspection   111

5.3   Logging with call stack introspection   112

5.4   Pitfalls   114

5.5   Class invariant checking   115

5.6   Summary   120

6 Using the class loader   121

6.1   George's test problem   122

6.2   Essentials of ClassLoader   123

Understanding the delegation model   123 ▪ *Programming a simple class loader   127* ▪ *Reinitializing static fields: a solution   128*

6.3   Multiple namespaces   130

6.4   Dynamic class replacement   132

Designing for replacement   132 ▪ *Implementing replacement   134 Simplifying assumptions   137*

6.5   Additional considerations   138

Security   139 ▪ *Don't reinvent the wheel   139* ▪ *Modifying bytecode in a class loader   140* ▪ *When not to invent a specialized class loader   140 Additional examples   141* ▪ *Endorsed Standards Override   142*

6.6   Summary   142

7 Reflective code generation   143

7.1   Reflective code generation   143

7.2   Generating HelloWorld.java   145

7.3   Class-to-class transformation framework   147

C2C   148 ▪ *Args   152* ▪ *C2CConstructor   154 C2CTransformation   157*

7.4   Example: extent management   159

7.5   C2IdentitySubclassOfC and its subclasses   168

7.6   UQueue   170

7.7   Using the framework   173

7.8   Relation to Aspect-Oriented Programming   175

7.9   Summary   176

8 Design patterns   179

8.1   Singleton   181

8.2   Decorator class-to-class transformations   187

8.3   Proxy (again)   197

8.4   Another composition feature   201

8.5 Problematic issues in writing
class-to-class transformations 201

8.6 Summary 204

9 Evaluating performance 207

9.1 Evaluating performance 207

9.2 Categorizing performance impact 209

9.3 Using microbenchmarks 210

9.4 Benchmarking two ways to use Proxy 214

9.5 Understanding Amdahl's Law 218

9.6 Applying Amdahl's Law 221

9.7 Summary 223

10 Reflecting on the future 225

10.1 Looking forward: Java 1.5 226

JSR 14—Generics 227 ▪ JSR 175—Annotation Facility 229
JSR 201—Language extensions 234
Impact of Java 1.5 on reflective code 235

10.2 Looking forward: competition for Java reflection 236

C# 236 ▪ Python 236 ▪ Smalltalk 236 ▪ CLOS 237
Ruby 237 ▪ Perl 237

10.3 Looking forward: Aspect-Oriented Programming 237

10.4 Looking forward: your career 238

appendix A **Reflection and metaobject protocols 241**
appendix B **Handling compilation errors in the
"Hello world!" program 253**
appendix C **UML 256**

glossary 258
references 260
index 267

preface

We wrote this book because reflection inspires us. It produces solutions so elegant that they elicit the same sense of wonderment that we often felt as children. It is this inspiration that has driven both of us in our study and practice of reflective programming over the last ten years.

In the early 1990s, Ira Forman was a member of the development team for IBM's SOMobjects Toolkit, generally known as SOM. It was not a programming language. Rather, SOM was an API to a highly capable and reflective object model.

For the second release of SOM in 1994, Ira and Scott Danforth wrote the Metaclass Framework, which used the reflective facilities of SOM to provide useful tools for the rest of the development team and the IBM customers. This may well be the first commercial instance of what has become known as Aspect-Oriented Programming. Included in the Metaclass Framework was a tool to dynamically create proxy classes. Another tool could wrap the methods of a class with code to execute before and after every method execution (this was the way the trace facility was created without modifying the SOM kernel). Yet another modified a class to be a singleton. In addition, there was a metaclass to support the conversion of plain-old classes into replicated classes (in the context of the SOM Replication Framework, which was programmed by Hari Madduri and Ira). These experiences convinced Ira that reflective programming is cool.

Despite all of its technical innovation, SOM was not a financial success.[1] In 1996, Java pushed SOM out of the marketplace. Allowing those innovations to be lost was unacceptable. So, while employed to work on other matters, Ira and Scott pushed on to write *Putting Metaclasses to Work*, which was published in 1999.

About that time, Ira's son Nate was looking for a topic for a master's paper at the University of Texas at Austin. Nate accepted Ira's suggestion: study the use of reflection to support the application of Gang-of-Four[2] design patterns. The resulting paper led to some interesting insights into both reflection and patterns. But most of all, it reinforced our conviction that reflective programming is cool.

Nate graduated and went to work as a Java developer, first at Liaison Technology and currently at Ticom Geomatics. Nate was able to leverage Java reflection to the benefit of his employers, producing flexible application frameworks and APIs. These experiences proved to us that reflection is more than cool—it's valuable.

With this value in mind, we teamed up to teach reflection. In 2001 and 2002, we taught a course titled *Software Patterns, UML, and Reflection* as part of the Software Engineering Program at the University of Texas. Also, each October since 2001, we have presented a Java Reflection tutorial at the OOPSLA Conference.

One of our OOPSLA traditions is to have dinner with John Vlissides. At the first dinner, John asserted, "You two should write a book," and went on to suggest a stimulating topic. This father and son team will be forever grateful for that suggestion.

We hope that, through this book, you will find Java reflection as cool and valuable as we do.

---

[1] SOM was IBM's product to compete with Microsoft's COM for control of the architecture of object-oriented programming. Both SOM and COM were designed on the assumption that the world needed a better C++. The world, however, wanted something else, as was evident by the astoundingly rapid rise of Java to preeminence in object-oriented programming. In 1996, SOM exited the marketplace, but, with its bigger market share, COM survived. Now, the battle for control of the architecture of object-oriented programming has moved to C# versus Java. Control of an architecture is where the big money is made in information technology. In the 1980s, IBM ceded control over the hardware architecture of personal computers to Intel; as a result, today we speak about "Intel inside" and not "IBM compatible." For more information about the importance of controlling an architecture, see *Computer Wars: How the West Can Win in a Post-IBM World* by Charles H. Ferguson and Charles R. Morris (Random House, 1993).

[2] This term refers to the four authors of *Design Patterns*: Erich Gamma, Richard Helm, Ralph Johnson, and John Vlissides.

acknowledgments

The first person we must thank is John Vlissides. At our first annual OOPSLA dinner, John suggested that we should write a book together. We are grateful for this suggestion and for John's encouragement over the years.

We are grateful to Dewayne Perry for giving us the opportunity to teach this material in the Software Engineering Program at the University of Texas. We also thank the students who persevered as we honed our explanations of reflection. In particular, we thank Chris Hamilton and Atif Saeed, whose master's papers started us on the road to chapters 7 and 8.

For their excellent reviews of our manuscript we thank Bill Alexander, Muhammad Ashikuzzaman, Walter Cazzola, Scott Danforth, Prasannavignesh Ganesan, Jim Heath, Stuart Halloway, Berndt Hamboeck, Jack Herrington, Lane Holloway, Michael Houghtaling, Norman Richards, Scott Shaw, Kent Spaulding, Bruce Tate, Luigi Viggiano, Rick Warren, and the set of unknown reviewers. Your detailed and helpful comments have made this a better book.

Special thanks to Norman Richards who reviewed the final manuscript for technical acurracy shortly before it went to press.

We thank the people with whom we consulted or who made memorable comments during our presentations: Craig Becker, Joshua Bloch, Neal Gafter, Jesse Gordon, Chance Harris, Doug Lea, Stuart McDow, Phil Mitchell, Stu Nickolas, Lance Obermeyer, Charlie Richter, Kim Rochat, Wayne Vicknair, and Lane Warshaw.

We are indebted to all of the hard-working folks at Manning Publications who helped bring this book to fruition. In particular, we thank

Marjan Bace—the publisher who recognized the importance of reflection and whose eye for organization and style was tremendously helpful.

Jackie Carter—our development editor, whose insights improved the manuscript dramatically and whose advice guided us through the process.

David Roberson—who arranged for manuscript reviews and provided comments.

Linda Recktenwald—who performed a really great editing job.

Dottie Marsico—who did the typesetting and the graphics.

Susan Forsyth—who ensured quality and did not falter during the last phase of production.

Mary Piergies—who managed the production team and got the book out the door.

Throughout this book, we follow a fictional character, George the programmer. George's situations represent hard-working programmers and the challenges they face. Sometimes these stories were from our own experience. Many other times, these stories were inspired by coworkers. We are grateful to Thomas Chen, George Copeland, Rick Efruss, Erik Kartzmark, Chaitanya Laxminarayan, Kevin Locke, Rob Ratcliff, Matt Sanchez, and Keith Yarbrough, for being George at one time or another. Your experiences have taught us—thank you.

about this book

How this book is organized

The ten chapters of this book are organized as follows:

Chapters 1, 2, and 3 introduce the basics of Java reflection: how to access class objects; how to dynamically examine classes, methods, fields, and constructors; and how to dynamically load classes.

Chapter 4 introduces the first advanced reflective feature: dynamic proxies. The chapter covers the facilities of the Proxy class and how to use them. There are several useful examples, including how to add properties to objects and how to create a test stub generator.

Chapter 5 covers the topic of examining the call stack. This is important for reflectively solving problems related to what a running program is doing.

Chapter 6 delves into customizing class loaders. This topic is necessary to reflective programming because some problems require the collection of meta-data that is available only when classes are loaded.

Chapter 7 begins a two-chapter sequence on reflective code generation. This chapter introduces a framework for class-to-class transformations, a particular kind of code generator that starts with a compiled class and produces a new compiled class, which usually has some additional property.

Chapter 8 continues the sequence by using the framework for class-to-class transformations to support implementation of designs that use patterns.

Chapter 9 presents performance-measurement techniques for making design decisions among reflective features.

Chapter 10 takes a look at the future of reflection in Java. This includes an overview of the impact of Java 1.5 on reflective programming, which other production languages will influence the future of reflection in Java, and the influence of Aspect-Oriented Programming.

Appendix A is a reprise of the introduction to reflection but with a more academic point of view. The appendix presents a brief history of reflection and the terminology that you are likely to encounter when reading advanced papers.

Appendix B explains how to handle compilation errors in the program that dynamically compiles the "Hello World!" program.

Appendix C summarizes the UML conventions used to diagram reflective programs.

Who should read this book

This book is a practical guide for intermediate programmers. The book has one goal: to make your programming job easier. We accomplish this in two ways:

- *Teach Java reflection*—The book concentrates on small teachable examples, mainly in the area of software development and test tools, a problem area common to all programmers. We describe the reflective facilities and also prescribe effective ways to use them.

- *Convey an understanding of reflection in general*—Reflection is much broader than what is incorporated in Java. We discuss the limitations of Java reflection and show techniques for working around them. This discussion furthers your understanding of Java reflection by using it in the techniques. It also motivates ideas about next-generation features, preparing you to use them.

This book is prescriptive. That is, it advocates techniques for using Java reflection that we have used and profited from in our jobs.

Source code

The examples in this book have all been compiled and minimally tested. Source code examples are available online from the publisher's web site: www.manning.com/forman. No warranty is implied as to the total correctness of the source code in this book.

A note about Java programming style

In order to make this book as readable as possible, we have adopted a style of Java programming that suits the static line size of the printed page rather than the dynamic interface of the program editor. With this style, we have succeeded in limiting almost all classes to no more than two pages. This style tends to reduce whitespace. We do not recommend this style, but we do hope you appreciate the readability of the book.

Author online

Purchase of *Java Reflection in Action* includes free access to a private web forum where you can make comments about the book, ask technical questions, and receive help from the authos and from other users. To access the forum and subscribe to it, point your web browser to www.manning.com/forman. This page provides information on how to get on the forum once you are registered, what kind of help is available, and the rules of conduct on the forum. It also provides links to the source code for the examples in the book, errata, and other downloads.

Manning's commitment to our readers is to provide a venue where a meaningful dialog between individual readers and between readers and the authors can take place. It is not a commitment to any specific amount of participation on the part of the authors, whose contribution to the AO remains voluntary (and unpaid). We suggest you try asking the authors some challenging questions lest their interest stray!

about the title

By combining introductions, overviews, and how-to examples, the *In Action* books are designed to help learning and remembering. According to research in cognitive science, the things people remember are things they discover during self-motivated exploration.

Although no one at Manning is a cognitive scientist, we are convinced that for learning to become permanent it must pass through stages of exploration, play, and, interestingly, re-telling of what is being learned. People understand and remember new things, which is to say they master them, only after actively exploring them. Humans learn in action. An essential part of an *In Action* guide is that it is example-driven. It encourages the reader to try things out, to play with new code, and explore new ideas.

There is another, more mundane, reason for the title of this book: our readers are busy. They use books to do a job or solve a problem. They need books that allow them to jump in and jump out easily and learn just what they want just when they want it. They need books that aid them *in action*. The books in this series are designed for such readers.

about the cover illustration

The figure on the cover of *Java Reflection in Action* is an "Arabe Petreo," an inhabitant of Arabia Petraea, the name given in ancient times to the region between Egypt and Mesopotamia. The capital city was Petra in what is today Jordan. Petra is famous for its rock formations and the city was built into the high cliffs surrounding it, making it the most impenetrable of ancient cities for centuries. The illustration is taken from a Spanish compendium of regional dress customs first published in Madrid in 1799. The book's title page states:

> *Coleccion general de los Trages que usan actualmente todas las Nacionas del Mundo desubierto, dibujados y grabados con la mayor exactitud por R.M.V.A.R. Obra muy util y en special para los que tienen la del viajero universal*

which we translate, as literally as possible, thus:

> *General collection of costumes currently used in the nations of the known world, designed and printed with great exactitude by R.M.V.A.R. This work is very useful especially for those who hold themselves to be universal travelers*

Although nothing is known of the designers, engravers, and workers who colored this illustration by hand, the "exactitude" of their execution is evident in this drawing. The "Arabe Petreo" is just one of many figures in this colorful collection. Their diversity speaks vividly of the uniqueness and individuality of the world's towns and regions just 200 years ago. This was a time when the dress codes of two regions separated by a few dozen miles identified people uniquely as belonging to one or the other. The collection brings to life a sense of isolation and distance of that period—and of every other historic period except our own hyperkinetic present.

Dress codes have changed since then and the diversity by region, so rich at the time, has faded away. It is now often hard to tell the inhabitant of one continent from another. Perhaps, trying to view it optimistically, we have traded a cultural and visual diversity for a more varied personal life. Or a more varied and interesting intellectual and technical life.

We at Manning celebrate the inventiveness, the initiative, and, yes, the fun of the computer business with book covers based on the rich diversity of regional life of two centuries ago, brought back to life by the pictures from this collection.

A few basics

1

In this chapter

- Reflection basics
- Class fundamentals
- Using methods reflectively

1

We are often faced with problems that could be solved simply and elegantly with reflection. Without it, our solutions are messy, cumbersome, and fragile. Consider the following scenarios:

- Your project manager is committed to a pluggable framework, knowing that the system needs to accept new components even after it is built and deployed. You set up some interfaces and prepare a mechanism for patching your JAR, but you know that this will not completely satisfy the need for pluggability.

- After months of developing a client-side application, marketing tells you that using a different remote mechanism will increase sales. Although switching is a good business decision, you now must reimplement all of your remote interfaces.

- The public API to your module needs to accept calls only from specific packages to keep outsiders from misusing your module. You add a parameter to each of the API calls that will hold the package name of the calling class. But, now legitimate users must change their calls, and unwelcome code can fake a package name.

These scenarios illustrate, in turn, modularity, remote access, and security—and do not seem to have much in common. But they do: each one contains a change in requirements that can be satisfied only by making decisions and modifying code based upon the structure of the program.

Reimplementing interfaces, patching JAR files, and modifying method calls are all tedious and mechanical tasks. So mechanical, in fact, that you could write an algorithm that describes the necessary steps:

1 Examine the program for its structure or data.

2 Make decisions using the results of the examination.

3 Change the behavior, structure, or data of the program based upon the decisions.

While these steps may be familiar to you in your role as programmer, they are not tasks that you would imagine a program doing. As a result, you assume that adapting code must be accomplished by a person sitting at a keyboard instead of by a program running on a computer. Learning reflection allows you to get beyond this assumption and make your program do this adaptation for you. Consider the following simple example:

```
public class HelloWorld {
    public void printName() {
        System.out.println(this.getClass().getName());
    }
}
```

The line

```
(new HelloWorld()).printName();
```

sends the string HelloWorld to standard out. Now let x be an instance of Hello-World or one of its subclasses. The line

```
x.printName();
```

sends the string naming the class to standard out.

This small example is more dramatic than it seems—it contains each of the steps previously mentioned. The printName method examines the object for its class (this.getClass()). In doing so, the decision of what to print is made by delegating to the object's class. The method acts on this decision by printing the returned name. Without being overridden, the printName method behaves differently for each subclass than it does for HelloWorld. The printName method is flexible; it adapts to the class that inherits it, causing the change in behavior. As we build our examples in scope and complexity, we will show you many more ways to attain flexibility using reflection.

1.1 Reflection's value proposition

Reflection is the ability of a running program to examine itself and its software environment, and to change what it does depending on what it finds.

To perform this self-examination, a program needs to have a representation of itself. This information we call **metadata**. In an object-oriented world, metadata is organized into objects, called **metaobjects**. The runtime self-examination of the metaobjects is called **introspection**.

As we saw in the small example above, the introspection step is followed by behavior change. In general, there are three techniques that a reflection API can use to facilitate behavior change: direct metaobject modification, operations for using metadata (such as dynamic method invocation), and **intercession**, in which code is permitted to intercede in various phases of program execution. Java supplies a rich set of operations for using metadata and just a few important intercession capabilities. In addition, Java avoids many complications by not allowing direct metaobject modification.

These features give reflection the power to make your software flexible. Applications programmed with reflection adapt more easily to changing requirements. Reflective components are more likely to be reused flawlessly in other applications. These benefits are available in your current Java development kit.

Reflection is powerful, but it is not magical. You must master the subject in order to make your software flexible. It's not enough to just learn the concepts and the use of the API. You must also be able to distinguish between situations when reflection is absolutely required from those when it may be used advantageously from those when it should be shunned. The examples in this book will help you acquire this skill. In addition, by the time you reach the end, you will understand the three issues that have thus far impeded the broad use of reflection:

- security
- code complexity
- runtime performance

You will learn that the concern over security was misguided. Java is so well crafted and its reflection API so carefully constrained that security is controlled simply. By learning when to use reflection and when not to, you will avoid unnecessarily complex code that can often be the result of amateurish use of reflection. In addition, you will learn to evaluate the performance of your designs, thereby ensuring the resulting code satisfies its performance requirements.

This introduction describes reflection, but scarcely reveals its value. Software maintenance costs run three to four or more times development costs. The software marketplace is increasing its demand for flexibility. Knowing how to produce flexible code increases your value in the marketplace. Reflection—introspection followed by behavior change—is the path to flexible software. The promise of reflection is great and its time has come. Let's begin.

1.2 *Enter George the programmer*

George is a programmer at Wildlife Components, a leading animal simulation software company. In his daily work, George faces many challenges such as the ones previously mentioned. Throughout this book, we will follow George as he discovers the benefits of implementing reflective solutions.

For one project, George is working on a team that is implementing a user interface. George's team uses several standard Java visual components, others that are developed in house, a few that are open source, and still others that have been licensed from third parties. All of these components are integrated to form the user interface for the team's application.

Each of these components provides a `setColor` method that takes a `java.awt.Color` parameter. However, the hierarchies are set up such that the only common base class for all of them is `java.lang.Object`. These components cannot be referenced using a common type that supports this `setColor` method.

This situation presents a problem for George's team. They just want to call `setColor` regardless of a component's concrete type. The lack of a common type that declares `setColor` means more work for the team. In case this scenario seems contrived, we invite you to explore the JDK API and see the number of classes that support the same method but implement no common interface.

1.2.1 *Choosing reflection*

Given a component, the team's code must accomplish two steps:

1 Discover a `setColor` method supported by the component.
2 Call that `setColor` method with the desired color.

There are many alternatives for accomplishing these steps manually. Let's examine the results of each of these.

If George's team controlled all of the source code, the components could be refactored to implement a common interface that declares `setColor`. Then, each component could be referenced by that interface type and `setColor` could be invoked without knowing the concrete type. However, the team does not control the standard Java components or third-party components. Even if they changed the open source components, the open source project might not accept the change, leaving the team with additional maintenance.

Alternatively, the team could implement an adapter for each component. Each such adapter could implement a common interface and delegate the `setColor` call to the concrete component. However, because of the large number of component classes that the team is using, the solution would cause an explosion in the number of classes to maintain. In addition, because of the large number of component instances, this solution would cause an explosion of the number of objects in the system at runtime. These trade-offs make implementing an adapter an undesirable option.

Using `instanceof` and casting to discover concrete types at runtime is another alternative, but it leaves several maintenance problems for George's team. First, the code would become bloated with conditionals and casts, making it difficult to read and understand. Second, the code would become coupled with each concrete type. This coupling would make it more difficult for the team to add, remove, or change components. These problems make `instanceof` and casting an unfavorable alternative.

Each of these alternatives involves program changes that adjust or discover the type of a component. George understands that it is only necessary to find a setColor method and call it. Having studied a little reflection, he understands how to query an object's class for a method at runtime. Once it is found, he knows that a method can also be invoked using reflection. Reflection is uniquely suited to solving this problem because it does not over-constrain the solution with type information.

1.2.2 Programming a reflective solution

To solve his team's problem, George writes the static utility method setObject-Color in listing 1.1. George's team can pass a visual component to this utility method along with a color. This method finds the setColor method supported by the object's class and calls it with the color as an argument.

Listing 1.1   George's setObjectColor code

```
public static void setObjectColor( Object obj, Color color )  {
    Class cls = obj.getClass();        ❶ Query object
                                           for its class
                                                          ❷ Query class
                                                             object for
    try {                                                    setColor method
        Method method = cls.getMethod( "setColor",  ◁──────┘
                                  new Class[] {Color.class} );

        method.invoke( obj, new Object[] {color} );  ❸ Call resulting method
    }                                                   on target obj

    catch (NoSuchMethodException ex) {  ◁──────❹ Class of obj does not
        throw new IllegalArgumentException(        support setColor method
                    cls.getName()
                    + " does not support method setColor(Color)" );
    }

    catch (IllegalAccessException ex) {  ◁──────────❺ Invoker cannot call
        throw new IllegalArgumentException(            setColor method
                "Insufficient access permissions to call"
                + "setColor(:Color) in class " + cls.getName());
    }

    catch (InvocationTargetException ex) {  ❻ setColor method
        throw new RuntimeException(ex);        throws an exception
    }
}
```

This utility method satisfies the team's goal of being able to set a component's color without knowing its concrete type. The method accomplishes its goals without invading the source code of any of the components. It also avoids source code bloating, memory bloating, and unnecessary coupling. George has implemented an extremely flexible and effective solution.

Two lines in listing 1.1 use reflection to examine the structure of the parameter `obj`:

❶ This line of code queries the object for its class.

❷ This line queries the class for a `setColor` method that takes a `Color` argument.

In combination, these two lines accomplish the first task of finding a `setColor` method to call.

These queries are each a form of **introspection**, a term for reflective features that allow a program to examine itself. We say that `setObjectColor` *introspects* on its parameter, `obj`. There is a corresponding form of introspection for each feature of a class. We will examine each of these forms of introspection over the next few chapters.

One line in listing 1.1 actually affects the behavior of the program:

❸ *This line calls the resulting method on* `obj`, *passing it the color*—This reflective method call can also be referred to as dynamic invocation. **Dynamic invocation** is a feature that enables a program to call a method on an object at runtime without specifying which method at compile time.

In the example, George does not know which `setColor` method to call when writing the code because he does not know the type of the `obj` parameter. George's program discovers which `setColor` method is available at runtime through introspection. Dynamic invocation enables George's program to act upon the information gained through introspection and make the solution work. Other reflective mechanisms for affecting program behavior will be covered throughout the rest of the book.

Not every class supports a `setColor` method. With a static call to `setColor`, the compiler reports an error if the object's class does not support `setColor`. When using introspection, it is not known until runtime whether or not a `setColor` method is supported:

❹ *The class of* `obj` *does not support a* `setColor` *method*—It is important for introspective code to handle this exceptional case. George has been guaranteed by his team that each visual component supports `setColor`. If that method is not supported by the type of the `obj` parameter, his utility method has been passed an illegal argument. He handles this by having `setObjectColor` throw an `IllegalArgumentException`.

The `setObjectColor` utility method may not have access to nonpublic `setColor` methods. In addition, during the dynamic invocation, the `setColor` method may throw an exception:

❺ The class containing listing 1.1 does not have access privileges to call a `protected`, `package`, or `private` visibility `setColor` method.

❻ The invoked `setColor` method throws an exception.

It is important for methods using dynamic invocation to handle these cases properly. For simplicity's sake, the code in listing 1.1 handles these exceptions by wrapping them in runtime exceptions. For production code, of course, this would be wrapped in an exception that the team agrees on and declared in the utility method's `throws` clause.

All of this runtime processing also takes more time than casts and static invocation. The method calls for introspection are not necessary if the information is known at compile time. Dynamic invocation introduces latency by resolving which method to call and checking access at runtime rather than at compile time. Chapter 9 discusses analysis techniques for balancing performance trade-offs with the tremendous flexibility benefits that reflection can give you.

The rest of this chapter focuses on the concepts necessary to fully understand listing 1.1. We examine, in detail, the classes that George uses to make it work. We also discuss the elements supported by Java that allow George such a flexible solution.

1.3 *Examining running programs*

Reflection is a program's ability to examine and change its behavior and structure at runtime. The scenarios previously mentioned have already implied that reflection gives programmers some pretty impressive benefits. Let's take a closer look at what reflective abilities mean for the structure of Java.

Think of introspection as looking at yourself in a mirror. The mirror provides you with a representation of yourself—your *reflection*—to examine. Examining yourself in a mirror gives you all sorts of useful information, such as what shirt goes with your brown pants or whether you have something green stuck in your teeth. That information can be invaluable in adjusting the structure of your wardrobe and hygiene.

A mirror can also tell you things about your behavior. You can examine whether a smile looks sincere or whether a gesture looks too exaggerated. This information can be critical to understanding how to adjust your behavior to make the right impression on other people.

Similarly, in order to introspect, a program must have access to a representation of itself. This self-representation is the most important structural element of a reflective system. By examining its self-representation, a program can obtain the right information about its structure and behavior to make important decisions.

Listing 1.1 uses instances of `Class` and `Method` to find the appropriate `setColor` method to invoke. These objects are part of Java's self-representation. We refer to objects that are part of a program's self-representation as **metaobjects**. *Meta* is a prefix that usually means *about* or *beyond*. In this case, metaobjects are objects that hold information about the program.

`Class` and `Method` are classes whose instances represent the program. We refer to these as *classes of metaobjects* or *metaobject classes*. Metaobject classes are most of what make up Java's reflection API.

We refer to **objects** that are used to accomplish the main purposes of an application as **base-level objects**. In the `setObjectColor` example above, the application that calls George's method as well as the objects passed to it as parameters are base-level objects. We refer to the nonreflective parts of a program as the **base program**.

Metaobjects represent parts of the running application, and, therefore, may describe the base program. Figure 1.1 shows the `instanceof` relationship between base-level objects and the objects that represent their classes. The diagramming convention used for figure 1.1 is the Unified Modeling Language (UML). For readers unfamiliar with UML, we will describe the conventions briefly in section 1.7. For the moment, it is important to understand that the figure can be read as "*fido, a base-level object, is an instance of Dog, a class object on the metalevel.*"

Metaobjects are a convenient self-representation for reflective programming. Imagine the difficulty that George would have in accomplishing his task if he had tried to use the source code or the bytecodes as a representation. He would have to parse the program to even begin examining the class for its methods. Instead, Java metaobjects provide all of the information he needs without additional parsing.

Metaobjects often also provide ways of changing program structure, behavior, or data. In our example, George uses dynamic invocation to call a method that he finds through introspection. Other reflective abilities that make changes include reflective construction, dynamic loading, and intercepting method calls. This book shows how to use these mechanisms and others to solve common but difficult software problems.

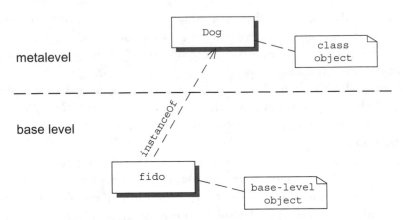

Figure 1.1   `Dog` **is a class object, a metaobject that represents the class Dog.
The object** `fido` **is an instance of** `Dog` **operating within the application. The**
`instanceof` **relationship, represented in this diagram by a dependency,
connects objects on the base level to an object that represents their class on
the metalevel.**

1.4 *Finding a method at runtime*

At the beginning of our example, George's `setObjectColor` method is passed a
parameter `obj` of type `Object`. The method cannot do any introspection until it
knows the class of that parameter. Therefore, its first step is to query for the
parameter's class:

```
Class cls = obj.getClass();
```

The `getClass` method is used to access an object's class at runtime. The `getClass`
method is often used to begin reflective programming because many reflective
tasks require objects representing classes. The `getClass` method is introduced by
`java.lang.Object`, so any object in Java can be queried for its class[1].

The `getClass` method returns an instance of `java.lang.Class`. Instances of
`Class` are the metaobjects that Java uses to represent the classes that make up a
program. Throughout this book, we use the term **class object** to mean an instance
of `java.lang.Class`. Class objects are the most important kind of metaobject
because all Java programs consist solely of classes.

---

[1]   The `getClass` method is final. This keeps Java programmers from fooling reflective programs. If it were
not final, a programmer could override `getClass` to return the wrong class.

Class objects provide programming metadata about a class's fields, methods, constructors, and nested classes. Class objects also provide information about the inheritance hierarchy and provide access to reflective facilities. For this chapter, we will concentrate on the use of `Class` in listing 1.1 and related fundamentals.

Once the `setObjectColor` method has discovered the class of its parameter, it queries that class for the method it wants to call:

```
Method method = cls.getMethod("setColor", new Class[] {Color.class});
```

The first parameter to this query is a `String` containing the desired method's name, in this case, `setColor`. The second parameter is an array of class objects that identify the types of the method's parameters. In this case, we want a method that accepts one parameter of type `Color`, so we pass `getMethod` an array of one element containing the class object for `Color`.

Notice that the assignment does not use `getClass` to provide the class object for Color. The `getClass` method is useful for obtaining the class for an object reference, but when we know only the name of the class, we need another way. **Class literals** are Java's way to specify a class object statically. Syntactically, any class name followed by `.class` evaluates to a class object. In the example, George knows that `setObjectColor` always wants a method that takes one `Color` argument. He specifies this using `Color.class`.

`Class` has other methods for introspecting about methods. The signatures and return types for these methods are shown in table 1.1. As in the previous example, the queries use an array of `Class` to indicate the types of the parameters. In

Table 1.1 The methods defined by `Class` for method query

Method	Description
Method **getMethod**(String name, Class[] parameterTypes)	Returns a `Method` object that represents a public method (either declared or inherited) of the target `Class` object with the signature specified by the second parameters
Method[] **getMethods**()	Returns an array of `Method` objects that represent all of the public methods (either declared or inherited) supported by the target `Class` object
Method **getDeclaredMethod**(String name, Class[] parameterTypes)	Returns a `Method` object that represents a declared method of the target `Class` object with the signature specified by the second parameters
Method[] **getDeclaredMethods**()	Returns an array of `Method` objects that represent all of the methods declared by the target `Class` object

querying for a parameterless method, it is legal to supply null, which is treated the same as a zero-length array.

As their names indicate, getDeclaredMethod and getDeclaredMethods return method objects for methods explicitly declared by a class. The set of declared methods does not include methods that the class inherits. However, these two queries do return methods of all visibilities—public, protected, package, and private.

The queries getMethod and getMethods return method objects for a class's public methods. The set of methods covered by these two includes both methods declared by the class and those it inherits from superclasses. However, these queries return only a class's public methods.

A programmer querying a class using getDeclaredMethod might accidentally specify a method that the class does not declare. In this case, the query fails with a NoSuchMethodException. The same exception is thrown when getMethod fails to find a method among a class's public methods.

In the example, George needs to find a method, and he does so using one of the methods from table 1.1. Once retrieved, these method objects are used to access information about methods and even call them. We discuss method objects in detail later in this chapter, but first let's take a closer look at how class objects are used with the methods from table 1.1.

1.5 *Representing types with class objects*

The discussion of the methods from table 1.1 indicates that Java reflection uses instances of Class to represent types. For example, getMethod from listing 1.1 uses an array of Class to indicate the types of the parameters of the desired method. This seems fine for methods that take objects as parameters, but what about types not created by a class declaration?

Consider listing 1.2, which shows a fragment of java.util.Vector. One method has an interface type as a parameter, another an array, and the third a primitive. To program effectively with reflection, you must know how to introspect on classes such as Vector that have methods with such parameters.

> **Listing 1.2   A fragment of `java.util.Vector`**

```
public class Vector ... {
    public synchronized boolean     addAll( Collection c ) ...
    public synchronized void        copyInto( Object[] anArray ) ...
    public synchronized Object      get( int index ) ...

}
```

Table 1.2 Methods defined by `Class` that deal with type representation

Method	Description
String **getName**()	Returns the fully qualified name of the target `Class` object
Class **getComponentType**()	If the target object is a `Class` object for an array, returns the `Class` object representing the component type
boolean **isArray**()	Returns `true` if and only if the target `Class` object represents an array
boolean **isInterface**()	Returns `true` if and only if the target `Class` object represents an interface
boolean **isPrimitive**()	Returns `true` if and only if the target `Class` object represents a primitive type or `void`

Java represents primitive, array, and interface types by introducing class objects to represent them. These class objects cannot do everything that many other class objects can. For instance, you cannot create a new instance of a primitive or interface. However, such class objects are necessary for performing introspection. Table 1.2 shows the methods of `Class` that support type representation.

The rest of this section explains in greater detail how Java represents primitive, interface, and array types using class objects. By the end of this section, you should know how to use methods such as getMethod to introspect on `Vector.class` for the methods shown in listing 1.2.

1.5.1 *Representing primitive types*

Although primitives are not objects at all, Java uses class objects to represent all eight primitive types. These class objects can be indicated using a class literal when calling methods such as those in table 1.1. For example, to specify type int, use `int.class`. Querying the `Vector` class for its get method can be accomplished with

```
Method m = Vector.class.getMethod("get", new Class[] {int.class});
```

A class object that represents a primitive type can be identified using isPrimitive.

The keyword void is not a type in Java; it is used to indicate a method that does not return a value. However, Java does have a class object to represent void. The isPrimitive method returns true for void.class. In section 1.6, we cover introspection on methods. When introspecting for the return type of a method, void.class is used to indicate that a method returns no value.

1.5.2 *Representing interfaces*

Java also introduces a class object to represent each declared interface. These class objects can be used to indicate parameters of interface type. The addAll method of `Vector` takes an implementation of the `Collection` interface as an argument. Querying the `Vector` class for its `addAll` method can be written as

```
Method m = Vector.class.getMethod( "addAll",
                         new Class[] {Collection.class} );
```

A class object that represents an interface may be queried for the methods and constants supported by that interface. The `isInterface` method of `Class` can be used to identify class objects that represent interfaces.

1.5.3 Representing array types

Java arrays are objects, but their classes are created by the JVM at runtime. A new class is created for each element type and dimension. Java array classes implement both `Cloneable` and `java.io.Serializable`.

Class literals for arrays are specified like any other class literal. For instance, to specify a parameter of a single-dimension `Object` array, use the class literal `Object[].class`. A query of the `Vector` class for its `copyInto` method is written as

```
Method m = Vector.class.getMethod( "copyInto", new Class[]{Object[].class} );
```

Class objects that represent arrays can be identified using the `isArray` method of `Class`. The component type for an array class can be obtained using `getCompo-nentType`. Java treats multidimensional arrays like nested single-dimension arrays. Therefore, the line

```
int[][].class.getComponentType()
```

evaluates to `int[].class`. Note the distinction between component type and element type. For the array type `int[][]`, the component type is `int[]` while the element type is `int`.

Not all Java methods take non-interface, non-array object parameters like `set-Color` from our George example. In many cases, it is important to introspect for methods such as the `Vector` methods of listing 1.2. Now that you understand how to introspect for any Java method, let's examine what can be done once a method is retrieved.

1.6 Understanding method objects

Most of the examples over the last few sections have used the identifier `Method` but not explained it. `Method` is the type of the result of all of the method queries in table 1.1. George uses this class in listing 1.1 to invoke `setColor`. From this context, it should be no surprise that `java.lang.reflect.Method` is the class of the

Table 1.3   Methods defined by `Method`

Method	Description
Class **getDeclaringClass**()	Returns the `Class` object that declared the method represented by this `Method` object
Class[] **getExceptionTypes**()	Returns an array of `Class` objects representing the types of the exceptions declared to be thrown by the method represented by this `Method` object
int **getModifiers**()	Returns the modifiers for the method represented by this `Method` object encoded as an `int`
String **getName**()	Returns the name of the method represented by this `Method` object
Class[] **getParameterTypes**()	Returns an array of `Class` objects representing the formal parameters in the order in which they were declared
Class **getReturnType**()	Returns the `Class` object representing the type returned by the method represented by this `Method` object
Object **invoke**(Object obj, Object[] args)	Invokes the method represented by this `Method` object on the specified object with the arguments specified in the `Object` array

metaobjects that represent methods. Table 1.3 shows some of the methods supported by the metaobject class `Method`.

Each `Method` object provides information about a method including its name, parameter types, return type, and exceptions. A `Method` object also provides the ability to call the method that it represents. For our example, we are most interested in the ability to call methods, so the rest of this section focuses on the `invoke` method.

1.6.1   Using dynamic invocation

Dynamic invocation enables a program to call a method on an object at runtime without specifying which method at compile time. In section 1.2, George does not know which `setColor` method to call when he writes the program. His program relies upon introspection to examine the class of a parameter, `obj`, at runtime to find the right method. As a result of the introspection, the `Method` representing `setColor` is stored in the variable `method`.

Following the introspection in listing 1.1, `setColor` is invoked dynamically with this line:

```
method.invoke(obj, new Object[] {color});
```

where the variable `color` holds a value of type `Color`. This line uses the `invoke` method to call the `setColor` method found previously using introspection. The `setColor` method is invoked on `obj` and is passed the value of `color` as a parameter.

The first parameter to `invoke` is the target of the method call, or the `Object` on which to invoke the method. George passes in `obj` because he wants to call `set-Color` (the method represented by `method`) on `obj`. However, if `setColor` is declared `static` by the class of `obj`, the first parameter is ignored because static methods do not need invocation targets. For a static method, `null` can be supplied as the first argument to `invoke` without causing an exception.

The second parameter to `invoke`, `args`, is an `Object` array. The `invoke` method passes the elements of this array to the dynamically invoked method as actual parameters. For a method with no parameters, the second parameter may be either a zero-length array or `null`.

1.6.2 *Using primitives with dynamic invocation*

The second parameter to `invoke` is an array of `Object`, and the return value is also an `Object`. Of course, many methods in Java take primitive values as parameters and also return primitives. It is important to understand how to use primitives with the `invoke` method.

If the type of a parameter is a primitive, `invoke` expects the corresponding `args` array element to be a wrapper object containing the argument. For example, when invoking a method with an `int` parameter, wrap the `int` argument in a `java.lang.Integer` and pass it into the `args` array. The `invoke` method unwraps the argument before it passes it to the actual code for the method being invoked.

The `invoke` method handles primitive return types by wrapping them before they are returned. Thus, when invoking a method with an `int` return type, the program receives an object of type `Integer` in return. If the method being invoked is declared with a `void` return, `invoke` returns the value `null`.

So, primitives need to be wrapped when passed into a dynamic invocation and unwrapped when received as a return value. For clarity, consider the following dynamic call to `hashCode` method on our `obj` variable from the example.

```
Method method = obj.getClass().getMethod("hashCode", null);
int code = ((Integer) method.invoke(obj, null)).intValue();
```

The first line introspects for the method `hashCode` with no arguments. This query does not fail because that method is declared by `Object`. The `hashCode` method returns an `int`. The second line invokes `hashCode` dynamically and stores the return value in the variable `code`. Notice that the return value comes back wrapped

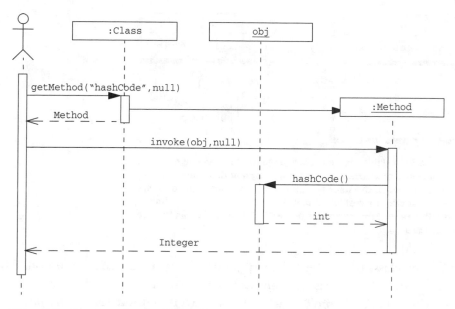

Figure 1.2 Sequence diagram illustrating the use of `getMethod` and `invoke`. The return arrows are labeled with the type of the value that is returned. Note that the call to `invoke` wraps the `int` return value in an `Integer` object.

in an `Integer`, and it is cast and unwrapped. The above snippet of code is illustrated in the sequence diagram in figure 1.2.

1.6.3 Avoiding invocation pitfalls

At one point, George thinks, "*If I have a `Method` representing `setColor`, why do I need to introspect for it every time? I'll just cache the first one that comes along and optimize out the rest of the queries.*" When he tries this, he gets an `IllegalArgumentException` from `invoke` on many of the subsequent calls. The exception message means that the *method was invoked on an object that is not an instance of the declaring class.*

George's optimization fails because it assumes that all methods with the same signature represent the same method. This is not the case. In Java, each method is identified by both its signature and its declaring class.

Let's take a closer look at this failure. Figure 1.3 shows the classes `Animal` and `Shape`, which both declare a `setColor` method with the same signature. These two `setColor` methods are not the same method in Java because they do not have the same declaring class.

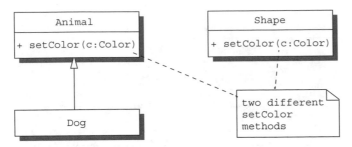

Figure 1.3 A Unified Modeling Language (UML) class diagram. `Dog` is a subclass of `Animal`. `Animal` and `Shape` both declare a `set-Color` method of the same signature. The Java language considers the two `setColor` methods shown to be different methods. However, the `setColor` method for `Dog` is the same method as the one for `Animal`.

Another class, `Dog`, extends `Animal` and inherits its `setColor` method. The `set-Color` method for `Dog` is the same as the `setColor` method for `Animal` because `Dog` inherits `setColor` from `Animal`. The `setColor` method for `Dog` is not the same method as the one for `Shape`. Therefore, when dealing with this situation, it is usually simplest to introspect for a `Method` each time instead of caching.

Several other exceptions can occur when calling `invoke`. If the class calling `invoke` does not have appropriate access privileges for the method, `invoke` throws an `IllegalAccessException`. For example, this exception can occur when attempting to invoke a private method from outside its declaring class.

`IllegalArgumentException` can be thrown by `invoke` under several circumstances. Supplying an invocation target whose class does not support the method being invoked causes an `IllegalArgumentException`. Supplying an `args` array of incorrect length or with entries of the wrong type also causes an `IllegalArgument-Exception`. If any exception is thrown by the method being invoked, that exception is wrapped in an `InvocationTargetException` and then thrown.

Dynamic invocation is a truly important feature in Java reflection. Without it, each method call must be hard-coded at compile time, denying programmers the flexibility of doing what George does in listing 1.1. In later chapters, we return to dynamic invocation for more advanced applications and expose other powerful ways to use information gained through introspection.

1.7 *Diagramming for reflection*

Throughout this book, we use the Unified Modeling Language (UML) for diagrams like figure 1.4. Those familiar with UML will probably notice that figure 1.4 combines UML class and object diagrams. Reflection represents all of the class diagram entities at runtime using metaobjects. Therefore, combining class and object diagrams is useful for clearly communicating reflective designs.

UML diagrams typically include only classes or only non-class objects. Modeling reflection calls for combining the two and using the `instanceOf` dependency to connect an object with its instantiating class. UML defines the `instanceOf` dependency with same meaning as the Java `instanceof` operator. However, this book uses the `instanceOf` dependency only to show that an object is a direct instance of a class. For clarity, we partition figure 1.4 into its base level and metalevel, although that partition is not standard UML. For more detail on UML, see appendix C.

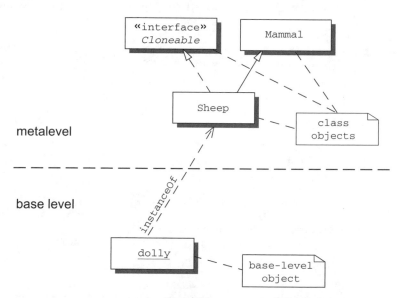

Figure 1.4 This is a Unified Modeling Language (UML) diagram describing Dolly the cloned sheep. The diagram shows an object, `dolly`, which is an instance of the class `Sheep`. It describes `Sheep` as a `Mammal` that implements `Cloneable`. The important thing to notice about this diagram is that it includes both objects and classes, as is necessary for describing reflective systems.

1.8 *Navigating the inheritance hierarchy*

After George's team has been using `setObjectColor` from listing 1.1 for a while, one of his team members, Martha, runs into a problem. Martha tells George that `setObjectColor` is not seeing a `setColor` method inherited by her component. After exploring the inheritance hierarchy, George and Martha discover that the inherited method is `protected`, and so it is not found by the line

```
Method method = cls.getMethod("setColor", new Class[] {Color.class});
```

George decides that he needs a method that introspects over methods of all visibilities, declared or inherited. Looking back at the methods from table 1.1, George notices that there is no method that does this, so he decides to write his own. Listing 1.3 shows the source code for `getSupportedMethod`, a method that George has written to accomplish that query. George has placed `getSupported-Method` in his own convenience facility called `Mopex`. This is one of many useful methods that George has put in `Mopex`, and throughout this book, we explain and make use of them.

Listing 1.3   Code for `Mopex.getSupportedMethod`

```
    public static Method getSupportedMethod( Class cls,
                                             String name,
                                             Class[] paramTypes)
        throws NoSuchMethodException
{
    if (cls == null) {
        throw new NoSuchMethodException();
    }
    try {
        return cls.getDeclaredMethod( name, paramTypes );
    }
    catch (NoSuchMethodException ex) {
      return getSupportedMethod( cls.getSuperclass(), name, paramTypes );
    }

}
```

The `getSupportedMethod` method is a recursive method that traverses the inheritance hierarchy looking for a method with the correct signature using `getDeclaredMethod`. It uses the line

```
    return getSupportedMethod( cls.getSuperclass(), name, paramTypes );
```

to accomplish this traversal. The getSuperclass method returns the class object representing the class that its target extends. If there is no extends clause, getSuperclass returns the class object for Object. If cls represents Object, getSuperclass returns null, and getSupportedMethod throws a NoSuchMethodException on the next call.

Now that George has implemented getSupportedMethod, which performs the introspection that he wants, he can change setObjectColor to use this new functionality. Listing 1.4 shows this update to setObjectColor.

Listing 1.4   setObjectColor updated to use getSupportedMethod

```
public static void setObjectColor( Object obj, Color color ) {
    Class cls = obj.getClass();
    try {
        Method method = Mopex.getSupportedMethod( cls,
                                        "setColor",
                                        new Class[]{Color.class}
                                        );
        method.invoke( obj, new Object[] {color} );
    }
    catch (NoSuchMethodException ex) {
        throw new IllegalArgumentException(
                            cls.getName() + " does not support"
                            + "method setColor(:Color)");
    }
    catch (IllegalAccessException ex) {
        throw new IllegalArgumentException(
                            "Insufficient access permissions to call"
                            + "setColor(:Color) in class "
                            + cls.getName());
    }
    catch (InvocationTargetException ex) {
        throw new RuntimeException(ex);
    }
}
```

This update allows setObjectColor to retrieve metaobjects for private, package, and protected methods that are not retrieved by getMethod. However, this update does not guarantee permission to invoke the method. If setObjectColor does not have access to Martha's inherited method, an IllegalAccessException is thrown instead of a NoSuchMethodException.

George has just observed one way that reflection can save him effort. Before the reflective enhancement, he and Martha needed to explore the inheritance hierarchy to diagnose Martha's problem. George's enhancement traverses the inheritance hierarchy and reports the problem, saving them the trouble. In chapter 2, we discuss bypassing visibility checks using reflection. For now, let's continue to discuss the tools that make George and Martha's enhancement possible.

1.8.1 *Introspecting the inheritance hierarchy*

As shown in the previous section, runtime access to information about the inheritance hierarchy can prevent extra work. Getting the superclass of a class is only one of the operations that Java reflection provides for working with the inheritance hierarchy. Table 1.4 shows the signatures and return types for the methods of Class for dealing with inheritance and interface implementation.

Table 1.4 Methods of Class that deal with inheritance

Method	Description
Class[] **getInterfaces**()	Returns an array of Class objects that represent the direct superinterfaces of the target Class object
Class **getSuperclass**()	Returns the Class object representing the direct superclass of the target Class object or null if the target represents Object, an interface, a primitive type, or void
boolean **isAssignableFrom**(Class cls)	Returns true if and only if the class or interface represented by the target Class object is either the same as or a superclass of or a superinterface of the specified Class parameter
boolean **isInstance**(Object obj)	Returns true if and only if the specified Object is assignment-compatible with the object represented by the target Class object

The getInterfaces method returns class objects that represent interfaces. When called on a class object that represents a class, getInterfaces returns class objects for interfaces specified in the implements clause of that class's declaration. When called on a class object that represents an interface, getInterfaces returns class objects specified in the extends clause of that interface's declaration.

Note the method names getInterfaces and getSuperclass are slightly inconsistent with terminology defined by the *Java Language Specification*. A **direct superclass** is the one named in the extends clause of a class declaration. A class X is a **superclass** of a class Y if there is a sequence of one or more direct superclass links from Y to X. There is a corresponding pair of definitions for **direct superinterface** and **superinterface**. Consequently, getSuperclass returns the direct superclass and getInterfaces returns the direct superinterfaces.

To get all of the methods of a class, a program must walk the inheritance hierarchy. Luckily, this walk is not necessary to query whether a class object represents a subtype of another class object. This query can be accomplished using the `isAssignableFrom` method. The name `isAssignableFrom` tends to be confusing. It helps to think of

```
X.isAssignableFrom(Y)
```

as "an `X` field *can be assigned* a value from a `Y` field." For example, the following lines evaluate to true:

```
Object.class.isAssignableFrom(String.class)

java.util.List.class.isAssignableFrom(java.util.Vector.class)

double.class.isAssignableFrom(double.class)
```

The line below, however, evaluates to false:

```
Object.class.isAssignableFrom(double.class)
```

The `isInstance` method is Java reflection's dynamic version of `instanceof`. If the target class object represents a class, `isInstance` returns `true` if its argument is an instance of that class or any subclass of that class. If the target class object represents an interface, `isInstance` returns `true` if its argument's class implements that interface or any subinterface of that interface.

1.8.2 *Exposing some surprises*

In the Java reflection API, there are some relationships that may be surprising upon first glance. Discussing these relationships now prepares us for encountering them later in the book and in reflective programming in general. Being prepared in this manner allows for better reflective programming.

The `isInstance` method can be used to show a very interesting fact about the arrangement of the classes in the Java reflection API. The line

```
Class.class.isInstance(Class.class)
```

evaluates to `true`. This means that the class object for `Class` is an instance of itself, yielding the circular `instanceOf` dependency of figure 1.5. `Class` is an example of a **metaclass**, which is a term used to describe classes whose instances are classes. `Class` is Java's only metaclass.

In Java, all objects have an instantiating class, and all classes are objects. Without the circular dependency, the system must support an infinite tower of class objects, each one an instance of the one above it. Instead, Java uses this circularity to solve this problem.

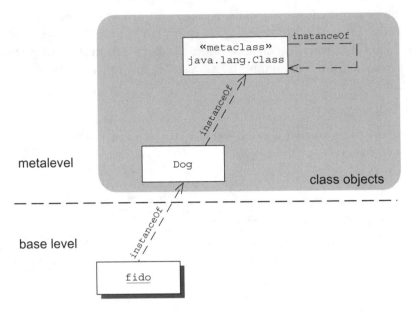

Figure 1.5 **The object** `fido` **is an instance of the** `Dog` **class.** `Dog` **is an instance of the class** `Class`. `Class` **is also an instance of** `Class`. `Class` **is a metaclass because it is a class whose instances are classes.**

The circularity presented in figure 1.5 makes people uncomfortable because we instinctively mistrust circular definitions. However, as programmers, we are familiar with other kinds of circular definitions. For example, consider recursion. A method that uses recursion is defined in terms of itself; that is, it has a circular definition. When used properly, recursion works just fine. Similarly, there are constraints on the definition of `java.lang.Class` that make this circularity work just fine.

For more information about this circularity, see *Putting Metaclasses to Work* [33]. *Putting Metaclasses to Work* is an advanced book on reflection and metaobject protocols written by one of the authors of this book. It is a good resource for readers who are interested in the theoretical and conceptual basis for reflection.

1.8.3 *Another reflective circularity*

Adding inheritance to our previous diagram yields the arrangement in figure 1.6. Inheritance adds more circularity to the picture. `Object` is an instance `Class`, which can be validated because the following line returns `true`:

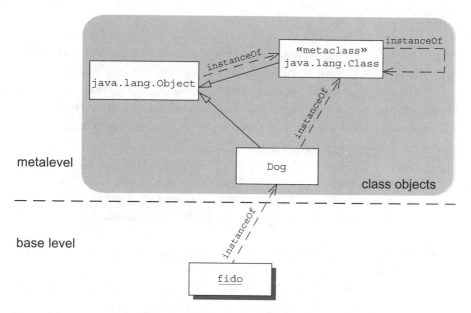

Figure 1.6 `Object` is the top of the Java inheritance hierarchy, so classes of metaobjects, including `Class`, are subclasses of `Object`. This means that the methods of `Object` are part of the reflection API. All Java classes are instances of its only metaclass, `Class`. These two conditions create a cycle in the diagram.

```
Class.class.isInstance(Object.class)
```

`Class` is also a subclass of `Object`, validated by

```
Object.class.isAssignableFrom(Class.class)
```

which also returns `true`. Conceptually, we already know these facts because in Java, each object has one instantiating class, and all classes are kinds of objects. However, it is comforting that the reflective model is consistent with our previous understanding of the language.

The new circularity implies additional constraints on the definitions of `Object` and `Class`. These constraints are satisfied when the Java Virtual Machine loads the `java.lang` package. Again, a full explanation of the constraints may be found in *Putting Metaclasses to Work* [33].

Figure 1.6 also illustrates why `Object` is considered part of the reflection API. All metaobjects extend `Object`, and so they inherit its methods. Therefore, each of those methods can be used in reflective programming.

1.9 Summary

Reflection allows programs to examine themselves and make changes to their structure and behavior at runtime. Even a simple use of reflection allows programmers to write code that does things that a programmer would normally do. These simple uses include getting the class of an object, examining the methods of a class, calling a method discovered at runtime, and exploring the inheritance hierarchy.

The metaobject classes `Class` and `Method` represent the classes and methods of running programs. Other metaobjects represent the other parts of the program such as fields, the call stack, and the loader. `Class` has additional methods to support these other metaobjects. Querying information from these metaobjects is called introspection.

Metaobjects also provide the ability to make changes to the structure and behavior of the program. Using dynamic invocation, a `Method` metaobject can be commanded to invoke the method that it represents. Reflection provides several other ways to affect the behavior and structure of a program such as reflective access, modification, construction, and dynamic loading.

There are several patterns for using reflection to solve problems. A reflective solution often starts with querying information about the running program from metaobjects. After gathering information using introspection, a reflective program uses that information to make changes in the behavior of the program.

Each new metaobject class allows us to grow our examples in scope and value. These examples reveal lessons that we have learned and techniques that we have applied. Each one follows the same basic pattern of gathering information with introspection and then using the information to change the program in some way.

Accessing fields reflectively

2

In this chapter

- Exploring the fields of a class
- Getting and setting field values
- Accessing nonpublic members

In chapter 1, we used reflection to call methods not known at compile time. Similar flexibility can be achieved with fields using reflection. Applications benefit from such flexibility in many ways. Here are just a few examples:

- **Memory leaks** in Java result from a program retaining references to unwanted objects. These references prevent the garbage collector from reclaiming memory. Memory leaks can cause either a gradual deterioration in performance or worse, a program failure. A reflective program can traverse those very same references and find unwanted objects using programmer-coded domain knowledge.

- **Serialization** is the conversion of an object into a contiguous text or binary representation. This representation can then be stored for later use. It can also be transmitted across a network to another program as a message or as a parameter or return value for a remote invocation. A general serialization system requires metadata in order to perform object conversion.

- **Property sheets** are visual editors that allow users to view and change the values of fields in an object. Such editors facilitate maintenance interfaces and configurators for many kinds of systems. They also assist in the visual development of user interfaces. Property sheets require metadata about the objects that can be edited.

These examples have one very important requirement in common: the need for metadata about the fields and their referents.

Fortunately, Java provides this metadata through its reflection API. Using reflection, a program can introspect on classes for their fields. Once a desired field is found, reflection can then be used to get and set its value. This chapter focuses on introspecting for fields and getting their values. Setting field values is left for chapter 3. Before exploring the details of these capabilities, let's join George and take a closer look at a serialization problem.

2.1 *Serializing objects*

Java has a built-in serialization facility. If the `Serializable` marker interface is implemented by a class, its instances can be serialized by the JVM. This serialization facility stores objects to and retrieves objects from a binary format. While this built-in facility is convenient, there are several advantages to using a custom serializer.

First, most people cannot read the binary format. Therefore, certain applications benefit from text serialization. For example, you might want to serialize objects for display in a web browser. Also, a person can use a text editor to modify the values in a text-serialized object. In addition, a text serializer might be useful as an alternative to binary during debugging.

Second, the built-in Java facility requires the implementation of the `Serializable` interface by the class of the object to be serialized. This requirement rules out the serializing objects from third-party libraries whose classes do not implement `Serializable`. A custom serializer need not require classes to implement `Serializable`.

Third, Java serialization is usable only within the Java platform. To send objects to other platforms, it is necessary to use a serialization format that is recognized by multiple platforms.

2.1.1 Serializing to XML

For the previous advantages, George's team has decided that they need a custom serializer and have chosen George to do the work. They have decided that their objects should be serialized to eXtensible Markup Language (XML). **XML** is a self-describing text format for encoding structured nested data. Using XML as a serialization format provides all of the advantages previously mentioned, plus widespread industry support for parsing, presentation, and Web services.

To structure data, XML uses tags that come in pairs where `<tag-name>` is an opening tag and `</tag-name>`, with a slash, is a closing tag. This pair together makes up an XML **element**. Other elements and text can be nested within the opening and closing tags of an element, for example:

```
<zoo>
    <animal>Panda</animal>
    <animal>Giraffe</animal>
</zoo>
```

An element that contains no other elements or text can also appear like this

```
<zoo />
```

with the opening tag ending with a slash before its closing angle bracket. In this case, no closing tag is necessary or appropriate. In addition, the opening tag of an element may contain name-value pairs called **attributes**. For example, an empty element with an attribute may look like this:

```
<tag-name attribute-name="attribute value" />
```

Each file, string, or stream of well-formed XML is called a **document**. An XML document has one element called its **root element** under which all other document content falls. There are several good Java libraries dealing with XML documents. This example uses JDOM (see www.jdom.org).

2.1.2 Choosing reflection

George considers several design alternatives and decides to use reflection. There are serious disadvantages to the other techniques on his list. He has seen many of them tried and failed. Here are some examples:

- *Mandate support of a* `toXML` *method by each serializable object*—This method returns the XML serialized version of the object. This technique requires editing of all existing classes to be serialized. Maintaining the serialization code becomes a nightmare because of its distribution. Third-party and JDK classes cannot be serialized in this way.

- *Use a third-party serialization library that uses preprocessors, generated code, or source-to-source translation to enable serialization*—These solutions have a steep associated learning curve and may be difficult to debug when problems arise. They also require developers to maintain extra code for each serializable class.

- *Use a third-party serialization library that requires maintenance of mapping files to enable serialization*—These files are bulky and require hand-editing. Mapping files must be modified each time a new serializable class is added and each time an existing one is changed. This alternative is difficult to scale and requires programmers to leave their programming language. (A serialization library that does not have such mapping files is using reflection.)

George chooses reflection because it enables a solution that does not invade existing classes. A reflective solution can work on in-house, third-party, and JDK classes simply by using the available metadata. Let's take a closer look at the necessary steps for a reflective serialization solution.

2.1.3 Designing serialization with reflection

George decides on a reflective alternative. He writes one method, `serialize-Object`, that takes as an argument one object to be serialized. This method should work well with all of his department's classes and third-party classes as they currently exist. To serialize objects in this way, `serializeObject` must accomplish several tasks:

1   Get from its argument, the object to be serialized, a list of its fields.

2   Find the declaring class and field name that uniquely identifies each field.

3   Get the value for each field.

4   If the field value is an object and it has not already been serialized, serialize that object.

5   If the field value is a primitive, store the value in a way that it can easily be retrieved.

George has a difficult problem to solve, but reflection provides the tools for the job.

    Reflection allows George's solution to scale well. It can examine and serialize any Java object. No additional coding is required for the class whose instances are serialized. The serialization code is the same for each class, so debugging happens in one central place. In addition, the choice of XML as an output format allows for human readability. George's solution is not without its complications, as we explain in chapter 3. However, it accurately showcases the strengths of using reflection to solve problems.

    The rest of this chapter explores the Java metaobjects for dealing with object data and reflective techniques for accessing that data. We show how these facilities can be leveraged to create a solution to George's serialization problem. Some parts of the serialization solution are also appropriate for the opposite process, deserialization. However, deserialization also requires dynamic loading and, therefore, is not addressed until chapter 3.

2.2 *Finding fields at runtime*

Serializing an object implies serializing the values of its fields. Therefore, the first task for `serializeObject` is to get a list of its argument's fields that need to be serialized. The class object for the argument, obtained using `getClass`, can be queried for a list of field objects.

    As we saw with method introspection, `Class` defines two kinds of introspection for accessing fields. The `getDeclaredField` and `getDeclaredFields` methods query from the set of fields declared by the class, irrespective of visibility. The `getField` and `getFields` methods query from the set of public fields declared and inherited by the class. The signatures and return values for these methods are shown in table 2.1.

    If parameters for either `getField` or `getDeclaredField` specify a field that does not exist, these methods throw a `NoSuchFieldException`. Querying for fields can be disabled in the Java security manager. If this feature is disabled, all of these methods throw a `SecurityException`.

Table 2.1   Methods of `Class` for field introspection

Method	Description
Field **getField**(String name)	Returns a `Field` object that represents the specified public member field of the class or interface represented by this `Class` object
Field[] **getFields**()	Returns an array of `Field` objects that represents all the accessible public fields of the class or interface represented by this `Class` object
Field **getDeclaredField**(String name)	Returns a `Field` object that represents the specified declared field of the class or interface represented by this `Class` object
Field[] **getDeclaredFields**()	Returns an array of `Field` objects that represents each field declared by the class or interface represented by this `Class` object

Unfortunately, neither `getFields` nor `getDeclaredFields` provides exactly the information necessary for serialization. To serialize an object, it is necessary to obtain the values of all of its fields, both declared and inherited. To accomplish this accumulation, George wrote the snippet shown in listing 2.1.

Listing 2.1   Snippet to obtain all the fields in an object

```
Class cls = obj.getClass();
List accum = new LinkedList();
while (cls != null) {
   Field[] f = cls.getDeclaredFields();
   for (int i=0; i<f.length; i++) {
     accum.add(f[i]);
   }
   cls = cls.getSuperclass();
}

Field[] allFields = (Field[]) accum.toArray(new Field[accum.size()]);
```

Listing 2.1 uses `getSuperclass` to traverse the inheritance hierarchy of the class. At each level, it uses `getDeclaredFields` to obtain all of the fields declared by that superclass. The `allFields` array contains all of the fields supported by the class. Having obtained this array, George's code has accomplished the task of getting the argument object's list of fields and can move on to the next task.

2.3 *Understanding field objects*

George's `serializeObject` method must associate the serialized value of a field with the identity of the field. The *Java Language Specification* defines a field as being identified by both the declaring class and field name. Both are necessary because Java allows a class to declare a field named the same as one declared by a superclass. The declaring class information disambiguates which field is bound to the name. Therefore, the second task for George's `serializeObject` method is to find both the declaring class and field name for each field.

In the previous section, George uses one or more applications of `get-DeclaredFields` to obtain the supported fields for a given class. The methods shown in table 2.1, including `getDeclaredFields`, return objects of type `java.lang.reflect.Field`. A `Field` metaobject represents a particular field of a class. Each `Field` metaobject provides metadata about the field's name, declaring class, and modifiers. `Field` also provides several methods for getting and setting values. Table 2.2 shows the signatures and return types for the methods defined by `Field`. Ellipses (...) below `getBoolean` and `setBoolean` indicate that a long list of similar methods exists, one method for each primitive type. For brevity, these methods are not included in the table.

Table 2.2   Methods defined by `Field`

Method	Description
Class **getType**()	Returns the `Class` object that represents the declared type for the field represented by this `Field` object
Class **getDeclaringClass**()	Returns the `Class` object that declared the field represented by this `Field` object
String **getName**()	Returns the name of the field represented by this `Field` object
int **getModifiers**()	Returns the modifiers for the field represented by this `Field` object encoded as an `int`
Object **get**(Object obj)	Returns the value in the specified object of the field represented by this `Field`
boolean **getBoolean**(Object obj) ...	Returns the value in the specified object of the boolean field represented by this `Field`

continued on next page

Table 2.2 **Methods defined by** `Field` *(continued)*

Method	Description
void **set**(Object obj, Object value)	Sets the field of the specified object represented by this `Field` object to the specified new value
void **setBoolean**(Object obj, boolean value) ...	Sets the field of the specified object represented by this `Field` object to the specified boolean value

If `field` refers to a field object, we can use the methods from table 2.2 to get the values necessary to identify it uniquely:

```
String fieldName = field.getName();
String fieldDeclClass = field.getDeclaringClass().getName();
```

This string information is stored in the serialized form along with the value of the field. The deserializer (in chapter 3) can use this information to and obtain the corresponding field object in preparation for setting its value. With the corresponding class object for `fieldDeclClass` and the field name, the deserializer can obtain the field object corresponding to `field`. At deserialization time, the class specified in `fieldDeclClass` may need to be loaded, which is why deserialization is explored in chapter 3 under the dynamic loading discussion. Having identified the argument's fields uniquely, George's `serializeObject` method can move on to its next task.

2.4 *Getting and setting field values*

To successfully serialize an object, the values of its fields must be stored. George's `serializeObject` method must first obtain those values. If any of those values are object references, each referenced object must also be serialized.

The argument to `serializeObject` is typed `Object`. Without knowing more about the type of the argument, getting its field values is difficult because you cannot access those fields directly or call accessor methods. You could cast to discover the type, allowing you direct access. However, this casting would limit the applicability of the serializer to only those types known when it is compiled, which is not a very flexible solution.

Reflection enables manipulation of fields through *reflective access and modification*. Table 2.2 contains a number of methods that begin with `get` and `set`. These methods are reflective accessors and modifiers that allow a program to use a field object to get and set field values on an object that supports that field.

If `field` refers to a field object appropriate for class of the object `obj`, we can access the value with:

```
Object value = field.get(obj);
```

If the field type is primitive, Java wraps the value in an appropriate wrapper object. Alternatively, knowing the type of primitive, the code can access the value directly using one of the primitive access methods (`getBoolean` and so on).

The following line sets the value of the field back to the value just extracted.

```
field.set(obj, value);
```

If the type of field is primitive, wrapping the value in the appropriate wrapper class allows successful use of the `set` method. There is also a corresponding group of methods for each primitive, which do not require wrapping. The `set` method is useful later for deserialization.

If the field is not defined or inherited by the object in the first argument to `get` or the first argument to `set`, these methods throw an `IllegalArgumentException`. If a `set` method is called with a value argument that is not assignable to the field, an `IllegalArgumentException` is thrown. An `IllegalArgumentException` is also thrown if a primitive `get` method is called and the value of the field cannot be converted into that primitive. If the class calling `get` or `set` does not have visibility into the field, it throws an `IllegalAccessException`. These access checks can be suppressed as explained in section 2.6.

2.5 *Examining modifiers*

Thus far, we have progressed through the steps for serialization, explaining how to make them happen reflectively. However, now that we have examined `Field` in more detail, we need to backtrack to step one for a moment. Step one is to *get a list of fields that need to be serialized.* By examining the snippet in listing 2.1 we can see that it does not do exactly what is needed.

Static fields should not be serialized. However, listing 2.1, accumulates both static and nonstatic fields. George wants `serializeObject` to serialize only **instance variables**, which are nonstatic fields. Therefore, it is important to be able to differentiate between fields by their modifiers, such as `static`.

2.5.1 *Introducing Member*

Both `Method` and `Field` implement the interface `java.lang.reflect.Member`, whose methods are shown in table 2.3. We have already explored `getName` and `getDeclaringClass`. The `getModifiers` method returns an `int`, which serves as a bit vector. The bit vector returned by `getModifiers` identifies the modifiers present in the `Member`. It is interesting to note that all of the methods of `Member` are supported by `Class`, as well. However, `Class` does not implement `Member`.

Table 2.3 Methods declared by the interface `Member`

Method	Description
Class **getDeclaringClass**()	Returns the `Class` object that declared the member
String **getName**()	Returns the name of the member
int **getModifiers**()	Returns the modifiers for the member encoded as an `int`

Syntactically, there are eleven modifiers in Java:

public	static	native
volatile	protected	abstract
synchronized	strictfp	private
final	transient	

Each of these modifiers is assigned a bit in the `int` returned by `getModifiers`. The Java reflection API introduces the `Modifier` convenience class to decode the return value of `getModifiers`. Table 2.4 shows the signatures and return values for methods defined by the `Modifier` convenience class.

Table 2.4 Methods defined by `Modifier`

Method	Description
static boolean **isPublic**(int mod)	Returns `true` if and only if the `public` modifier is present in the set of modifiers represented by the `int` argument
static boolean **isPrivate**(int mod)	Returns `true` if and only if the `private` modifier is present in the set of modifiers represented by the `int` argument
static boolean **isProtected**(int mod)	Returns `true` if and only if the `protected` modifier is present in the set of modifiers represented by the `int` argument
static boolean **isStatic**(int mod)	Returns `true` if and only if the `static` modifier is present in the set of modifiers represented by the `int` argument

continued on next page

Table 2.4 Methods defined by `Modifier` *(continued)*

Method	Description
static boolean **isFinal**(int mod)	Returns `true` if and only if the `final` modifier is present in the set of modifiers represented by the `int` argument
static boolean **isSynchronized**(int mod)	Returns `true` if and only if the `synchronized` modifier is present in the set of modifiers represented by the `int` argument
static boolean **isVolatile**(int mod)	Returns `true` if and only if the `volatile` modifier is present in the set of modifiers represented by the int argument
static boolean **isNative**(int mod)	Returns `true` if and only if the `native` modifier is present in the set of modifiers represented by the `int` argument
static boolean **isInterface**(int mod)	Returns `true` if and only if the `int` argument comes from an interface rather than a class
static boolean **isTransient**(int mod)	Returns `true` if and only if the `transient` modifier is present in the set of modifiers represented by the int argument
static boolean **isAbstract**(int mod)	Returns `true` if and only if the `abstract` modifier is present in the set of modifiers represented by the `int` argument
static boolean **isStrict**(int mod)	Returns `true` if and only if the `strictfp` modifier is present in the set of modifiers represented by the `int` argument

2.5.2 *Interface introspection pitfall*

The `Modifier` class also has a `toString` static method that supplies a `String` value that contains the identifier for each of the modifiers in a bit vector. Here is a little exercise: What does the following fragment print?

```
System.out.print( Modifier.toString( Member.class.getModifiers() ) );
```

Due to the oddities of the definition of the `Modifier` class (as opposed to what the Java syntax defines to be a modifier), this code fragment prints the string `"public abstract interface"`. This result may be surprising, but it is consistent with the Interface Modifiers section of the *Java Language Specification*, which states, "Every interface is implicitly `abstract`. This modifier is obsolete and should not be used in new programs." Both the result and the excerpt from the *Java Language Specification* are consistent with the view of a Java interface as an abstract class with no implied implementation that can be multiply inherited.

2.5.3 *Introspecting for instance variables*

`Modifier` enables serialization code to query a field to see if it is static. For example, given `field`, a `Field` reference,

```
Modifier.isStatic( field.getModifiers() );
```

returns `true` if and only if `field` represents a static field. We can combine the use of `Modifier` with the code from listing 2.1 to get the `Mopex.getInstanceVariables` method in listing 2.2.

> **Listing 2.2   `getInstanceVariables`, a method of `Mopex`**

```
public static Field[] getInstanceVariables(Class cls) {
    List accum = new LinkedList();
    while (cls != null) {
        Field[] fields = cls.getDeclaredFields();
        for (int i=0; i<fields.length; i++) {
            if (!Modifier.isStatic(fields[i].getModifiers())) {
                accum.add(fields[i]);
            }
        }
        cls = cls.getSuperclass();
    }
    Field[] retvalue = new Field[accum.size()];
    return (Field[]) accum.toArray(retvalue);
}
```

The `getInstanceVariables` method traverses up the inheritance hierarchy, accumulating declared fields on the way up. However, this time it uses `getModifiers` and `Modifier.isStatic` to filter out static fields. In the end, the returned array has the entire set of nonstatic fields for the class.

In `serializeObject`, George uses `getInstanceVariables` from listing 2.2 instead of the snippet from listing 2.1. This change allows `serializeObject` to really accomplish the first step of finding fields that need to be serialized.

2.6 *Accessing nonpublic members*

Earlier, we mentioned that Java access checks could be suppressed. This suppression allows reflective code to access protected, package, and private data that would otherwise be unreachable. Without this access, a serialization solution cannot be successful.

The class `java.lang.reflect.AccessibleObject` is the parent class of both `Field` and `Method`. `AccessibleObject` introduces a method called `setAccessible` that suppresses or enables runtime access checking. For `field` of type `Field`,

```
field.setAccessible(true);
```

disables all runtime access checks on uses of the metaobject referred to by `field`. This allows reflective access to its value from outside the scope of its visibility. A parameter of `false` reenables the runtime access checks. Put together with what we have learned about modifiers, the lines

```
if (!Modifier.isPublic(field.getModifiers())) {
    field.setAccessible(true);
}
Object value = field.get();
```

perform the necessary access for reflective serialization. The `setAccessible` method works for all of the `get` and `set` methods of `Field` and also for the `invoke` method of `Method`. The method signatures and return types for `AccessibleObject` are shown in table 2.5.

Table 2.5   Methods defined by `AccessibleObject`

Method	Description
void **setAccessible**(boolean flag)	Sets the accessible flag of the target object to the value of the argument
boolean **isAccessible**()	Returns `true` if and only if the value of the accessible flag of the target object is true

static
void **setAccessible**(
            AccessibleObject[] array,
            boolean flag)
	Sets the accessible flags for each element of an array of accessible objects

`AccessibleObject` also provides the `isAccessible` method to see whether or not an `AccessibleObject` has been set accessible. The static `setAccessible` method is supplied as a convenience for performing that operation on many `Accessible-Objects` at once.

Setting objects as accessible can be disabled in the security manager. If this feature has been disabled, the `setAccessible` methods each throw a `SecurityException`. The default security manager permits the use of `setAccessible` on members of classes loaded by the same class loader as the caller. Supplying a custom security manager can change this policy. For details on security managers, consult the Java documentation.

The use of `setAccessible` should never be taken lightly, because the encapsulating class is responsible for the internal consistency of an object. In the case of serialization, the use of `setAccessible` is necessary because of the need to serialize objects with private fields. Without this ability the utility of the serializer is greatly reduced. Furthermore, reflection allows the serializer to be centralized for maintenance purposes.

George's `serializeObject` method can use the previous lines to access the value of any field. Given this access, we are very close to a full serialization solution.

2.7 *Working with arrays*

There is one more issue to address before putting all of the tasks of `serialize-Object` together. Recall that evaluating `isArray` for an object's class tells you whether the object is an array. On his first serialization attempt, George tried casting arrays to `Object[]`. This program threw a `ClassCastException` when serializing many objects because of attempts to cast primitive arrays.

Primitive arrays cannot be cast to `Object[]`. George needs an alternative that allows him to work with arrays of objects and primitives uniformly. Java provides `java.lang.reflect.Array` as a convenience facility for performing reflective operations on all array objects.

The length of an array must be determined in order to serialize it. If `obj` refers to an array, the assignment statement

```
int length = Array.getLength(obj);
```

uses `Array` to introspect on `obj` for its `length`. Serialization also requires access to the components of an array. The line

```
Array.get(obj, i)
```

performs reflective access on the `i`th element of the array. If the component type of the array is primitive, `get` wraps the accessed value in its corresponding wrapper.

Table 2.6 shows signatures and return types for the methods of `Array`. There are `get` and `set` methods for each primitive type. The ones that are not shown are similar to the `get` and `set` methods for `boolean`.

Table 2.6 Methods defined by `Array` for component access and construction

Method	Description
Object **newInstance**(Class componentType, int length)	Creates a new array that has the specified component type and length.
Object **newInstance**(Class elementType, int[] dimensions)	Creates a new array that has the specified element type and `dimensions.length` dimensions.
int **getLength**(Object array)	Returns the number of components of the specified array.
Object **get**(Object array, int index)	Returns the component value at index. Wraps primitives if necessary.

continued on next page

Table 2.6 Methods defined by `Array` for component access and construction *(continued)*

Method	Description
boolean **getBoolean**(Object array, int index) ...	If the component type of the specified array is `bool-ean`, the component value at `index` is returned.
void **set**(Object array, int index, Object value)	Sets the component at `index` to the specified value. Unwraps primitives, if necessary.
void **setBoolean**(Object array, int index, boolean value) ...	If the component type of the specified array is `bool-ean`, the component at `index` is set to the specified value.

The `set` and `newInstance` methods are valuable for deserialization. We discuss them further in chapter 3. We now have all of the reflective tools necessary for the serialization solution. Let's turn our attention to the big picture of the serialization library.

2.8 Serialization: putting it all together

In analyzing the problem of serialization, we identified five tasks for George's code to perform. In examining the `Field` metaobject, we have established that reflection provides all of the information necessary to perform those tasks. Let's now examine the full reflective serialization solution. Listing 2.3 shows the `serializeObject` method and a helper method that implements much of the main functionality.

Listing 2.3 George's reflective serialization solution

```
public static Document serializeObject( Object source )
    throws Exception
{
    return serializeHelper( source,
                            new Document( new Element("serialized") ),
                            new IdentityHashMap () );
}

private static Document serializeHelper( Object source,
                                         Document target,
                                         Map table )
    throws Exception
{
    String id = Integer.toString( table.size() );
    table.put( source, id );
    Class sourceclass = source.getClass();
```

❶ Creates a unique identifier for object to be serialized

```
    Element oElt = new Element("object");                    2  Creates an XML
  oElt.setAttribute( "class", sourceclass.getName() );          element for object
  oElt.setAttribute( "id", id );
  target.getRootElement().addContent(oElt);
                                                      3  Handles arrays
                                                         differently from scalars
  if ( !sourceclass.isArray() ) {       ◄─────────┘
      Field[] fields = Mopex.getInstanceVariables(sourceclass);
      for (int i=0; i<fields.length; i++) {        Obtains nonstatic fields  4

          if ( !Modifier.isPublic(fields[i].getModifiers()) )
              fields[i].setAccessible(true);          Permits access,   5
                                                       if necessary
          Element fElt = new Element("field");
          fElt.setAttribute( "name", fields[i].getName() );
          Class declClass = fields[i].getDeclaringClass();
          fElt.setAttribute( "declaringclass",
                             declClass.getName() );        Creates   6
                                                           new XML
          Class fieldtype = fields[i].getType();           elements
          Object child = fields[i].get(source);

          if ( Modifier.isTransient(fields[i].getModifiers()) ){
              child = null;
          }
          fElt.addContent( serializeVariable( fieldtype, child,
                                              target, table));

          oElt.addContent(fElt);
      }
  }
  else {                                              Adds components  7
                                                        of the array
      Class componentType = sourceclass.getComponentType();

      int length = Array.getLength(source);
      oElt.setAttribute( "length", Integer.toString(length) );
      for (int i=0; i<length; i++) {
          oElt.addContent( serializeVariable( componentType,
                                              Array.get(source,i),
                                              target,
                                              table ) );
      }
  }
  return target;

}
```

The serializeObject method is the user's public method to access the facility. That method creates the XML document and a table that stores references to all of the component objects to the argument. This table is used to ensure that each component object is serialized only once no matter how many times it is referenced. That guarantee allows serializeObject to serialize objects with containment cycles and multiple references to the same object. The details are discussed next.

2.8.1 *Serializing each component*

The serializeHelper method is called recursively on each component object to be serialized. It creates the necessary XML structures, populates the reference table, and populates the XML with the contents of an array or non-array object. Here is a detailed discussion:

❶ A unique identifier is created for the object to be serialized. The object and identifier are stored in the reference table using the object as the key. If the object is encountered again during the serialization process, the identifier is easily found. While the serialized form of the object is stored in the XML document, references to it are replaced by its identifier so that only one copy appears.

❷ An XML element for the object is created and its class name and identifier are stored as attributes. Eventually, through the recursive use of serializeHelper, each component object of the original parameter to serializeObject has an XML element created here.

❸ Arrays are handled differently from scalars. This test make the separation.

❹ Mopex.getInstanceVariables obtains all of the nonstatic fields supported by the class of the object being serialized. For each instance variable, the following two steps are performed.

❺ If the field is not accessible to serializeHelper, setAccessible is used to permit access.

❻ An new XML element is created for each field in which the value and relevant metadata are stored using the method serializeVariable. If the field is transient, serializeVariable is passed null as the value of the field.

❼ For the array field, serializeHelper simply adds the components of the array.

2.8.2 *Serializing instance variables*

Both object and array serialization use the serializeVariable method to serialize the value of each instance variable or array element. Listing 2.4 shows the implementation of serializeVariable.

Listing 2.4 `serializeVariable`

```
private static Element serializeVariable( Class fieldtype,
                                          Object child,
                                          Document target,
                                          Map table)
    throws Exception
{
    if (child == null) {
        return new Element("null");
    }
    else if (!fieldtype.isPrimitive()) {
        Element reference = new Element("reference");
        if (table.containsKey(child)) {
            reference.setText(table.get(child).toString());
        }
        else {
            reference.setText( Integer.toString(table.size()) );
            serializeHelper(child, target, table);
        }
        return reference;
    }
    else {
        Element value = new Element("value");
        value.setText(child.toString());
        return value;
    }
}
```

The `serializeVariable` method examines the contents of a variable and decides how to store it. If primitive, `serializeVariable` creates a value element containing the `String` version of the primitive.

If the value is an object, that object may have already been serialized. The `table` passed into `serializeVariable` is a map of serialized objects to their assigned identifiers. The `serializeVariable` method queries the table for the identifier of the object. If the table does not contain the object, it is serialized by calling `serializeHelper`. Using this table, `serializeVariable` avoids duplicate serialization of multiply referenced objects and avoids looping endlessly for a set of objects that have a cycle of references. After obtaining the identifier for the object, `serializeVariable` stores the identifier in the field element as a reference to the serialized object.

2.9 *Using reflective serialization*

To better understand the functionality provided by the serializer, let's examine one of George's test cases. Figure 2.1 shows a class diagram that models the animal inventory of a small zoo. This is a good, simple test case because while each class has fields that hold attributes of the instances, there is also a bit of complex nesting because each Zoo contains many instances of Animal.

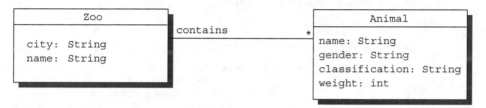

Figure 2.1   Class diagram for a small zoo inventory application. This is one of George's test cases for reflective serialization.

The data for the test case is depicted in the object diagram in figure 2.2. It represents a small subset of the animals in the National Zoological Park in Washington, D.C. The animals represented are a pair of pandas, Tian Tian and Mei Xiang.

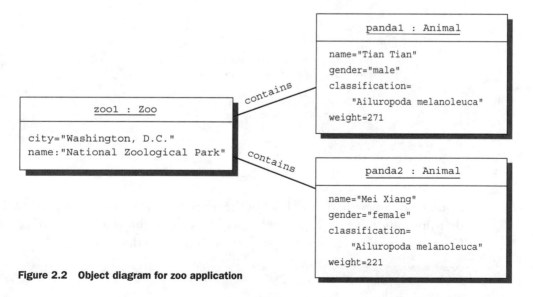

Figure 2.2   Object diagram for zoo application

The ZooTest program in listing 2.5 first creates two instances of Animal and a containing instance of Zoo. After populating the Zoo, ZooTest serializes it with the call to serializeObject. Following the serialization in ZooTest, the XML is printed to standard out using a JDOM facility.

Listing 2.5   ZooTest program

```
import org.jdom.Document;
import org.jdom.output.XMLOutputter;

public class ZooTest {

    public static void main( String[] args ) {

        Animal panda1 = new Animal( "Tian Tian",
                                    "male",
                                    "Ailuropoda melanoleuca",
                                    271 );
        Animal panda2 = new Animal( "Mei Xiang",
                                    "female",
                                    "Ailuropoda melanoleuca",
                                    221 );
        Zoo national = new Zoo( "National Zoological Park",
                                "Washington, D.C." );

        national.add( panda1 );
        national.add( panda2 );

        try {
            XMLOutputter out = new XMLOutputter("\t",true);

            Document d = Driver.serializeObject( national );
            out.output(d, System.out);
        }
        catch (Exception ex) {
            ex.printStackTrace();
        }
    }
}
```

Listing 2.6 shows the first 40 lines of the output of the serialization process. Notice that the values of the private fields are shown and the references are preserved. George's serializer is a success because of its use of reflection.

Listing 2.6   ZooTest output

```
<?xml version="1.0" encoding="UTF-8"?>
<serialized>
        <object class="Zoo" id="0">
```

```
                    <field name="name" declaringclass="Zoo">
                            <reference>1</reference>
                    </field>
                    <field name="city" declaringclass="Zoo">
                            <reference>3</reference>
                    </field>
                    <field name="contains" declaringclass="Zoo">
                            <reference>5</reference>
                    </field>
            </object>
            <object class="java.lang.String" id="1">
                    <field name="value" declaringclass="java.lang.String">
                            <reference>2</reference>
                    </field>
                    <field name="offset" declaringclass="java.lang.String">
                            <value>0</value>
                    </field>
                    <field name="count" declaringclass="java.lang.String">
                            <value>24</value>
                    </field>
                    <field name="hash" declaringclass="java.lang.String">
                            <value>0</value>
                    </field>
            </object>
            <object class="[C" id="2" length="24">
                    <value>N</value>
                    <value>a</value>
                    <value>t</value>
                    <value>i</value>
                    <value>o</value>
                    <value>n</value>
                    <value>a</value>
                    <value>l</value>
                    <value />
                    <value>Z</value>
                    <value>o</value>
                    <value>o</value>
```

Let's briefly examine the XML in listing 2.6. The instance of Zoo looks as expected from figure 2.1 and figure 2.2. The second object is an instance of String, and the offset, count, and hash fields are shown with their values. The value field is shown with a reference to the char array ("[C" means char array, as will be explained in the next chapter). The partial listing ends in the middle of this array.

It might be tempting to make String a special case that is stored by value instead of by reference. This change improves the readability and the compactness of the XML. Doing so is risky, however, because some applications rely on referential equality (`==`) rather than equivalence (`equals`). While for known `String` variables, best practices dictate the use of `equals`, the type of an object is not always known. After weighing the trade-offs, George decided to represent strings like any other object.

By using reflection, George has implemented a solution that works with any object in his department's application. None of his department's previous code needs to be changed to work with his serialization code. This generality is achieved by introspecting on the information stored in Java's metaobjects and using reflective techniques for accessing the data. Similar generality can be achieved in deserialization by using dynamic loading and reflective construction, which are the topics of the next chapter.

2.10 *Summary*

Using field metadata allows a program to handle objects of classes that its writer has never seen, including classes developed after the program was written. This flexibility is important for applications such as memory leak checking, serialization, and property sheets, where any object in the system is a possible candidate for processing.

Java reflection provides access to metadata about fields through metaobjects that are instances of `Field`. Field objects expose the attributes of a field, such as its name and its modifiers. They also allow access and modification of field values. The convenience facility `Array` is provided to allow similar functionality for arrays.

Java reflection also allows the ability to access nonpublic members of a class. This ability provides a great deal of benefit to developers seeking to centralize functionality for maintenance purposes. Although encapsulation should normally be preserved, accessibility can be used in a sufficiently general way that does not violate object-oriented principles.

The ability to use metadata about fields gives us concrete benefits. It allows applications like the ones in this chapter to be used on previously developed classes without modification. This ability increases the cohesion of those implementations and broadens their applicability to classes not developed in-house. It also reduces or eliminates the maintenance for applying these implementations to unforeseen future code.

3

Dynamic loading
and reflective construction

In this chapter

- Loading classes at runtime
- Instantiating objects using reflection
- Enhancing delegation with reflection

The previous chapters have explained how to use reflection in the context of objects and classes known at compile time. However, requirements always change over the lifecycle of an application. In order to satisfy these changing requirements, we need to be able to load new code into previously written applications.

Web servers are a good example of such an application. All web servers support frameworks for extension. One such web server is Apache Tomcat. Written in Java, Tomcat is the reference implementation for the Java Servlet framework. **Servlets** are classes that define behavior extensions for how web servers handle HTTP requests.

The idea of servlets is simple. Any Java developer with a new requirement for Tomcat can define the behavior by implementing the requirement in a servlet. The developer then installs the servlet properly, and Tomcat uses the servlet code to respond to web requests. This extension happens while the web server is running.

It is easy to see that loading and executing new code are essential for Tomcat to do its job. Java applications such as Tomcat make this happen using reflection. Java reflection includes mechanisms for loading new classes into a running program and creating new instances of those classes.

Outside of Java, this kind of flexibility is partially achieved using dynamically linked libraries. However, because dynamically linked libraries are an operating system primitive, they force you to work outside your programming language. This produces applications that are platform dependent. In addition, as the name implies, a dynamically linked library has the granularity of a library rather than an individual class.

Reflection allows Java programs to load new classes individually, achieving a higher degree of flexibility. Because this operation happens fully within Java, it also preserves portability. This chapter explores the reflective mechanisms for loading and instantiating new classes. We begin our exploration, as usual, with our friend and colleague, George, and an example of small scope. Later in the chapter, we show how these mechanisms contribute to deserializing objects serialized in the previous chapter.

3.1 George's deployment problem

George, our developer from Wildlife Components, Inc. (WCI), has been tasked with a new problem. Although WCI specializes in selling animal class libraries, an important client, Noah's Pets, Ltd., has asked WCI to build an e-commerce portal using the WCI libraries. For fear of losing his commission, the WCI sales representative has agreed that WCI will provide the application. This application has fallen to George to develop.[1]

For the purposes of this chapter, we need only focus on one important facet of George's design problem rather than the whole application. Noah's Pets has an existing customer database that the application must query for information. They have provided a schema, but there is neither budget to replicate the client's environment nor budget to allow George to travel until deployment. In addition, George's manager has instructed him to generalize this application for potential sales to other clients. Consequently, several deployment versions are possible.

3.1.1 Designing with patterns

To ensure that his application can be productized, George must separate customer-specific database access code from the rest of the application. He must also allow different versions of the database access code to be used during implementation, testing, and deployment.

George uses patterns and delegation to achieve more flexibility. **Delegation** is an arrangement where one object depends upon another object for implementation of a certain behavior. George applies the following patterns which use delegation to his design:

- The **Facade** pattern provides "a unified interface to a set of interfaces in a subsystem" [38]. George sets up an interface that represents all of the services provided by the database of Noah's Pets. His application uses implementations of this interface for all database queries. The choice of which database to query can vary independently from the rest of the application using this design.

- The **Factory Method** pattern provides a method for creating objects without specifying their concrete classes. George's application calls this method to construct the implementation of his facade. This design allows George to change which facade gets created without changing the rest of the application.

Figure 3.1 shows the UML class diagram for this part of George's design. The facade interface, `CustomerDatabase`, is implemented by a stub for programming the application, a file system database for testing the application, and the final deployment implementation. If the application is productized, there will be many

---

[1] This scenario is an abstraction of a problem that actually befell one of the authors in 2001.

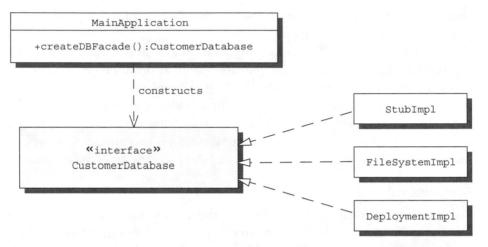

Figure 3.1   UML class diagram for the separating the application from the database. A factory method, `createDBFacade`, decides which implementation of `CustomerDatabase` to construct at runtime. Implementations of the `CustomerDatabase` facade interface are shown here for implementation, testing, and deployment to Noah's Pets. Several implementations for each WCI deployment may eventually exist.

such deployment implementations. The factory method, `createDBFacade`, constructs the desired implementations of `CustomerDatabase` for the rest of the application to use.

This design builds a great deal of flexibility into George's application. However, due to George's travel and budget constraints, he cannot develop the entire application before it is deployed. Therefore, he also needs to use reflection to build in the ability to bring new code into the application after its deployment.

3.1.2 *Programming a reflective solution*

The key to building the desired solution is in the implementation of the factory method. Listing 3.1 shows the factory method in George's application. The application has an instance variable, `props`, referencing an instance of `java.util.Properties`, that is used to load configuration strings into the system. One of the configuration entries stored in `props` is the key `db.class` and its value. The value of `db.class` is a fully qualified class name that is used to identify the class of the correct database facade for the system to use. Anyone with access to the properties file can change this property to determine what database facade the application uses.

Listing 3.1   Reading the configuration and loading the façade

```java
public class MainApplication {
    //...
    private Properties props;
    private CustomerDatabase custDB;
    //...
    public synchronized CustomerDatabase createDBFacade() {
        if ( custDB == null ) {
            try {
                String dbClassName
                    = props.getProperty( "db.class",
                                        "com.wci.app.StubCustomerDB");
                Class cls = Class.forName(dbClassName);
                custDB = (CustomerDatabase) cls.newInstance();
            }
            catch (ClassNotFoundException ex) {
                // ...
            }
            catch (InstantiationException ex) {
                // ...
            }
            catch (IllegalAccessException ex) {
                // ...
            }
        }
        return custDB;
    }
}
```

The factory method uses dynamic loading to retrieve a class object for the class named with the property key db.class. Dynamic loading is the process by which the Java virtual machine creates classes from bytecodes at runtime. The line

```java
Class cls = Class.forName(dbClassName);
```

uses forName, a static convenience method introduced by Class, to obtain the class object for the name referenced by dbClassName. Typically, the class being sought by forName is retrieved from the class path, but, as you will learn in chapter 6, this is not always the case.

George's code must create an instance of the newly obtained class for the application to put into use. This instantiation is accomplished using reflective construction in the following line:

```java
custDB = (CustomerDatabase) cls.newInstance();
```

The line uses the newly obtained class object to create a new instance of the class. The new instance is cast to a `CustomerDatabase` and assigned to `custDB` where it can be accessed by the rest of the application.

3.1.3 *Enhancing the factory method with reflection*

Dynamic loading and reflective construction in the factory method relieve George of the problem having to patch or rebuild when he wants to change the application's database facade. Instead, he changes the behavior of the system by putting a class file in the classpath and changing the text in a property file. Installing a new facade is this easy even if the system has already been deployed when the facade implementation is written and compiled.

This factory method still necessitates a shutdown of the application to change its database facade. However, if all components reference the facade through the factory method, the application can easily replace the facade. This change is made simply by changing what the factory method returns. Factory Method is not the only pattern that benefits from reflection. Let's examine some others.

3.1.4 *Combining benefits of delegation and reflection*

Reflection combines with effective object-oriented design to allow programs to be more flexible. Delegation is useful because it allows an object to change behavior at runtime. This change in behavior happens when one delegate that provides one behavior is replaced with another delegate that provides a different behavior. The number of different delegates available defines the amount that this behavior can vary.

Without reflective mechanisms, the number of delegates is limited to only the set of classes that are included in the system at compile time. Reflection increases this range of variation by allowing the system to use classes that are written later. There are several noteworthy aspects of this relationship:

- George dynamically loads new facades into his application to extend its behavior. New commands, strategies, states, and visitors can similarly be loaded dynamically into an application to extend its behavior.

- George uses dynamic loading and reflective construction to generalize a factory method. Dynamic loading and reflective construction can also be used to generalize the implementation of several of the other creational patterns (see *Design Patterns* [38]) such as Builder and Abstract Factory.)

- Dynamic loading and reflective construction is not the only technique for dynamically introducing new behavior. Chapter 4 explains proxy generation with `java.lang.reflect.Proxy`. Chapters 7 and 8 explain reflective code generation for transforming the behavior of existing classes. Both of these techniques can be used in cooperation with delegation relationships to get similar results.

George achieves a solution that balances his difficult development conditions with the goals of working properly with his customer's database and eventual productization. Good software design and implementation allow these changes to occur without significant refactoring. However, it is reflection that specifically facilitates the integration of new functionality. We now take a closer look at the reflective elements of George's solution.

3.2 Loading classes dynamically

The convenience method `Class.forName` returns a class object given a fully qualified class name. Remember the functionality of this method by thinking of it as *get class for name*. We call `forName` a convenience method because it is a static method for programming convenience, in this case, streamlining the use of the class loader.

3.2.1 Basics of forName

The big difference between using `forName` and a class literal is that `forName` does not require the name of the class at compile time. This difference leads to the main benefit of listing 3.1. The line

```
Class cls = Class.forName( dbClassName );
```

allows the class used for the customer database facade to be changed without rewriting or rebuilding the application's source code.

`Class.forName` ensures that the class is loaded and returns a reference to the class object. This is accomplished by using a class loader, typically the one associated with the class of the object that called `forName` (chapter 6 explains this in much greater detail). The class loader may have already loaded the class. If so, the class loader merely returns the class object that was loaded earlier.

If the class has not already been loaded, the system class loader typically searches the classpath for the appropriate `.class` file. If a file is found, the bytecodes are read and the loader constructs a class object. If the file is not found, the loader throws a `ClassNotFoundException`. The behavior described here is the behavior for the system class loader. Again, more details about class loaders can be found in chapter 6.

3.2.2 *Getting array classes*

Although there are no class files for arrays, forName can still be used to obtain their class objects. During his experience with the Noah's Pets application, George decides to try dynamic loading with array classes. He is surprised when the line

```
Class cls = Class.forName("java.lang.String[]");
```

produces a ClassNotFoundException.

However, this result is not that surprising when you consider the naming of these array classes. Most class objects respond to getName with a compilable Java class name. Generated array classes do not.

The names of array classes look strange. For example, the name of the class object for a one-dimensional int array is [I. However, these names are generated using a straightforward process. For each dimension of the array, the name begins with a left bracket. The brackets are succeeded by one of the codes in table 3.1 for the element type.

When George runs the following line

Table 3.1   Codes used to name Java array classes

Encoding	Element type
B	byte
C	char
D	double
F	float
I	int
J	long
L<element-type>;	reference type
S	short
Z	boolean

```
System.out.println(String[].class.getName());
```

Java prints [Ljava.lang.String; as a result. The previous ClassCastException occurs because the name of the desired class does not match the compilable Java code that identifies it. When George changes the line to

```
Class cls = Class.forName("[Ljava.lang.String;");
```

it produces the desired class object for a string array.

3.2.3 *Primitives and forName*

Class objects for primitives cannot be retrieved using forName. The line

```
Class.forName(char.class.getName());
```

produces a ClassNotFoundException. It is unclear why forName was implemented this way. However, from the many postings on the newsgroups, this seems to be very frustrating for developers. When you need forName to handle primitive classes as well, our suggestion is to write a convenience method that calls forName but checks for primitive types when catching a ClassNotFoundException.

3.3 *Constructing objects reflectively*

Once a class is loaded, its static members can be used. However, most of a class's utility comes from its instances. Therefore, constructing instances of a class is highly important. There are many ways to construct objects reflectively. Let's take a closer look.

3.3.1 *Reflective construction basics*

The `newInstance` method of `Class` creates a new instance of the class represented by the class object. Calling this method is equivalent to calling the class's constructor with no arguments. That is, `X.class.newInstance()` is the same as `new X()`.

Again the big difference is that `newInstance` may be used to instantiate a class object returned by `forName`, whose name need not be known at compile time. This difference also contributes to the effectiveness of listing 3.1. The line

```
custDB = (CustomerDatabase) cls.newInstance();
```

constructs a new instance of the database facade class loaded by the previous line.

The cast illustrates why *Design Patterns* [38] prescribes that you should program to interface instead of implementation. The `CustomerDatabase` interface defines a service required by the application. Any class that provides this service, regardless of implementation, or in our case, creation date, can do the job.

In our example, any class can be specified in the property file. This means that the line above can throw a `ClassCastException`, which should be handled by the surrounding code. If a failure occurs inside the constructor, `newInstance` throws an `InstantiationException`. If the visibility of the no-argument constructor makes it inaccessible from the calling context, `newInstance` throws an `IllegalAccessException`.

3.3.2 *Using constructor objects*

The `newInstance` method is not the only way to instantiate a class reflectively. The Java Reflection API has a class of metaobjects, `java.lang.reflect.Constructor`, for representing constructors. Table 3.2 shows the methods of `Class` that allow constructor introspection.

The `getConstructor` method allows code to query for a public constructor that takes specific parameter types. For example, the command

```
cls.getConstructor( new Class[] {String.class, String.class} )
```

introspects for a constructor that takes two `String` parameters. Note that class objects returned by `forName` may be used in the specification of a parameter

Table 3.2 Methods of Class for constructor introspection

Method	Description
Constructor **getConstructor**(Class[ ] parameterTypes)	Returns the public constructor with specified argument types if one is supported by the target class
Constructor **getDeclaredConstructor**(Class[ ] parameterTypes)	Returns the constructor with specified argument types if one is supported by the target class
Constructor[] **getConstructors**()	Returns an array containing all of the public constructors supported by the target class
Constructor[] **getDeclaredConstructors**()	Returns an array containing all of the constructors supported by the target class

list. The getConstructors method can be used to get all of the public constructors declared by a class. There are corresponding getDeclaredConstructor and getDeclaredConstructors methods for finding constructors whether or not they are public.

If there is no constructor declared for the parameter list specified, getConstructor and getDeclaredConstructor throw the NoSuchMethodException. Although you might expect a NoSuchConstructorException, this exception does not exist in Java. If this kind of introspection has been disabled in the security manager, both methods throw a SecurityException.

Constructor is the class of metaobjects that represents Java constructors. The interface to Constructor is very much like the interface to Method, except it supports a newInstance method instead of invoke. Table 3.3 shows the reflective methods of Constructor.

Table 3.3 Reflective methods of Constructor

Method	Constructor
Class **getDeclaringClass**()	Returns the class object that declares the constructor represented by this Constructor
Class[ ] **getExceptionTypes**()	Returns a Class array representing the types of exceptions that can be thrown from the body of this Constructor
int **getModifiers**()	Returns a bit vector encoding the modifiers present and absent for this member
String **getName**()	Returns the name of the constructor

continued on next page

Table 3.3   Reflective methods of `Constructor`   *(continued)*

Method	Constructor
Class[ ] **getParameterTypes**()	Returns a `Class` array representing the parameter types that are accepted by this constructor in order
Object **newInstance**(Object[ ] initargs)	Invokes the constructor with the specified parameters and returns the newly constructed instance

The `newInstance` method of `Constructor` responds the same way as the `newInstance` method of `Class`. It constructs a new instance of its declaring class, invoking the represented constructor with the arguments supplied in `initargs`, which must conform to the types of the constructor's parameter list.

`Constructor` implements the `Member` interface similarly to both `Method` and `Field`. `Constructor` is also a subclass of `AccessibleObject`. Although a call to `newInstance` is subject to throwing `IllegalAccessException`, `setAccessible` can be used to disable those checks. At this point, all of the metaobject classes implementing `Member` have been covered. Figure 3.2 presents a class diagram for the classes implementing `Member`.

3.3.3 Constructing arrays reflectively

As mentioned in section 2.7, arrays can also be constructed reflectively. The convenience facility `Array` introduces two `newInstance` methods. These methods respond similarly to their counterparts in `Class` and `Constructor`.

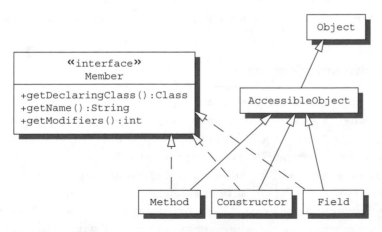

Figure 3.2   Class diagram for classes implementing `java.lang.reflect.Member`

One version of `Array.newInstance` allows you to specify a component type and a length in one dimension. The line

```
Array.newInstance(String.class, 5);
```

returns a `String` array of length 5 with all elements initialized to `null`. If the component type is a scalar, as shown here, the call results in a one-dimensional array. If the component type is an array class, the call results in an array with one more dimension than the component type. For example,

```
Array.newInstance(String[].class, 5);
```

constructs an array of `String` arrays of length 5.

The other version of `Array.newInstance` takes an `int` array parameter that specifies length in several dimensions. The line

```
Array.newInstance(String.class, new int[] {2, 3});
```

constructs a two-dimensional `String` array. The top-level array is a length-two array of `String` arrays with each component initialized to an array of `String` of length 3. Each second-level array has its elements initialized to `null`. As with the other `newInstance`, if the component type is an array class, then the new dimensions are added on top. Thus,

```
Array.newInstance(String[].class, new int[] {2, 3});
```

creates a three-dimensional array of `String` with the top two dimensions initialized and the third set to `null`.

We now have a full set of tools for constructing objects reflectively, so we can move on to examine how dynamic loading and reflective construction interact in a design.

3.4 Designing for dynamic loading

A subtle design issue involving a choice of constructors arises in writing classes to be dynamically loaded. A good design technique is to implement only the default constructor and use instance methods for object initialization. This design recommendation, which our experience bears out, is justified as follows.

In the context of a dynamically loaded class, there is an interface that has a number of implementations. For the sake of concreteness, let's call the interface `Parrot` and its implementations `ParrotImpl1`, `ParrotImpl2`, and so on. Note that not all of these implementations initially exist, nor are they all written by the same

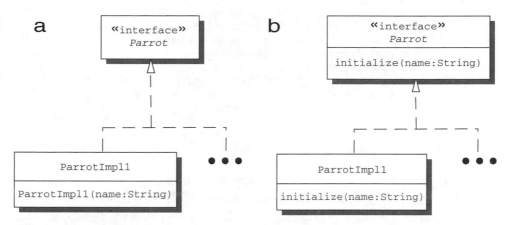

Figure 3.3 a) The left side shows implementations of `Parrot` using constructors with arguments to initialize themselves. b) The right side shows `Parrot` implementations using a method introduced by `Parrot` to initialize themselves.

programmer. Figure 3.3 shows the two basic design alternatives for such a class with respect to constructors and initialization of instances.

The first alternative, shown in figure 3.3a, has an interface implemented with a class containing a constructor with parameters. Java solutions typically use this structure. The advantage of this implementation is that instances are properly initialized when created. When you load classes dynamically, this design alternative introduces several disadvantages.

3.4.1 *Disadvantages of reflective construction with arguments*

The first alternative makes dynamic loading more complicated. Listing 3.2 contains the minimum code necessary to load and use this first alternative. The user of `Parrot` must query for the proper constructor and call it.

Using this query, the loading and construction are done with three statements, and there are five exceptions to handle. The two statements to get the constructor and create a new object are especially complex to write. In addition, there must be an implicit agreement among the programmers about which constructor to call.

Listing 3.2 Minimal user code for the first alternative design for `Parrot`

```
import java.lang.reflect.*;
public class ParrotUser {
    static public void main( String[] args )
            throws ClassNotFoundException,
                InstantiationException,
```

```
                    IllegalAccessException,
                    NoSuchMethodException,
                    InvocationTargetException {
        Class parrotClass = Class.forName( "ParrotImpl1" );
        Constructor pc
            = parrotClass.getConstructor( new Class[]{ String.class } );
        Parrot polly = (Parrot)pc.newInstance( new String[]{ "Polly" } );
        // Parrot object may now be used
    }
}
```

This first alternative also introduces complexity into `Parrot` implementations. The implicit agreement about the constructors is not constrained within the Java language. This lack of constraint may lead to unnecessary development mistakes.

Also, subclasses of `Parrot` implementations do not automatically inherit constructors. Subclassers must necessarily write the agreed-upon constructor and make a `super` call. This leads to bulkier subclasses.

If a required constructor is not present, the subclass does not work properly. Because the construction is reflective, there is no compile time error to flag the mistake. Instead, the mistake is not uncovered until the first time the application attempts to load and construct the subclass. These disadvantages make the second alternative worth examining.

3.4.2 *Initializing through an interface*

The second design alternative, shown in figure 3.3b, removes several burdens from both the implementor and the user of `Parrot`. First let's consider the user's perspective. Listing 3.3 shows the minimal code needed to load and use the second alternative.

Listing 3.3   Minimal user code for the second alternative design for `Parrot`

```
public class ParrotUser {
    static public void main( String[] args )
            throws ClassNotFoundException,
                    InstantiationException,
                    IllegalAccessException{
        Class parrotClass = Class.forName( "ParrotImpl1" );
        Parrot polly = (Parrot)parrotClass.newInstance();
        polly.initialize( "Polly" );
        // Parrot object may now be used
    }
}
```

The user can use the `newInstance` method of `Class` instead of querying for a constructor. This convenience eliminates the more complex statements from listing 3.2 and two of the five original exceptions. The user code becomes dramatically simpler.

The second alternative also eliminates complexity for implementors:

- Defining `initialize` with the correct signature is enforced by the Java language. This enforcement eliminates some programming mistakes about constructor signatures allowed by the first alternative.

- Subclasses of `Parrot` implementations inherit `initialize`. No override to `initialize` is necessary except where additional initialization is needed.

- Subclasses of `Parrot` implementations automatically have a default constructor. No additional constructor code is necessary.

Using this technique does not come without cost. Constructors with parameters can ensure that instances are properly initialized. The second alternative allows construction of objects that are not ready for use. The implementor may need to write additional code to guard against the use of uninitialized objects. However, experience shows that in most cases, the second alternative reduces overall complexity for dynamically loaded classes.

You now have a basic understanding of the tools needed to complete the example from chapter 2. We continue our discussion of dynamic loading and reflective construction by implementing a general deserialization facility.

3.5 *Implementing deserialization*

In the previous chapter, we serialized objects to XML. We have delayed the discussion of restoring the XML to objects because we previously hadn't explained how to load a class dynamically and reflectively construct instances. Now that you understand `forName` and `newInstance`, our discussion can proceed.

Deserialization is the inverse process of serialization: the conversion of streams into object structures. In our case, we restore objects from XML as serialized in chapter 2. Dynamic loading and reflective construction play essential roles in our solution because not all of the classes of the deserialized objects were compiled with the deserialization library.

In chapter 1, we said that every object is an instance of a class. This implies that before we deserialize a stream into an object, we must establish the object's class.[1]

---

[1] In some languages, such as Perl, objects can be constructed and later associated with a class.

In chapter 2, we prepared for establishing the object's class by storing a fully qualified class name with each serialized object. Thus, for the first object in listing 2.6, the line

```
<object class="Zoo" id="0"> ...
```

indicates that the element represents an object of class `Zoo` in the default package. Given that information, we can use `Class.forName` to obtain a reference to the class of this object.

Next, we must create an instance of the object's class to serve as the deserialized object. We can do this by calling `newInstance` on our newly obtained class object. However, this gives us an instance without the properly initialized fields, so the task is not complete.

After constructing our new instance, we must populate its instance variables. We can populate primitive typed instance variables easily by reading their values directly from the stream. However, for instance variables that refer to objects, the previous two steps must first be accomplished for the values that they reference. Once the values of object typed instance variables have object representations, we can populate all instance variables using the fields of the class object.

To review, here are the steps of our deserialization solution:

1   For each object stored in the XML file, load its class and construct an instance. Use Class.forName for dynamic loading and `newInstance` for reflective construction.

2   For each instance variable in each deserialized object, populate it with its value. Examine the class object for a field using `getDeclaredField`, and then call one of the `set` methods, and possibly `setAccessible`, to populate it.

Now that we have organized the tools and concepts to accomplish the task, let's look at the details of a solution.

3.5.1   *Initiating deserialization*

George's solution for deserialization starts with the `deserializeObject` method in listing 3.4. It first obtains the list of children in the XML document. Remember that each element of the document represents some object. This list shows which objects to construct for the first step of our solution.

Next, `deserializeObject` creates a `HashMap` that is used to map identifiers to deserialized objects. During the serialization process in chapter 2, each object is assigned a unique identifier. This identifier is the key to reassembling the object structure in the second step of our solution because the identifier plays the role of an object reference. With initialization complete, deserializeObject can execute the steps of deserialization.

Listing 3.4   The deserializeObject method

```
public static Object deserializeObject( Document source )
    throws Exception
{
    List objList = source.getRootElement().getChildren();

    Map table = new HashMap();

    createInstances( table, objList );

    assignFieldValues( table, objList );

    return table.get("0");
}
```

The deserializeObject method executes the first step of our solution by calling the createInstances method, which loads classes, constructs instances, and maps them to their identifiers. Next, deserializeObject calls assignFieldValues to execute the second step of our solution by assigning values to instance variables. Finally, after running the entire process, the deserialized object is returned to the caller.

3.5.2 Constructing the instances

The createInstances method executes our first deserialization step by iterating over the list of serialized objects in the XML document. During this iteration, it dynamically loads the class for each object and constructs an instance using reflective construction. Listing 3.5 shows the source code for createInstances.

Listing 3.5   The createInstances method

```
private static void createInstances( Map table, List objList )
    throws Exception
{
    for (int i = 0; i < objList.size(); i++) {
        Element oElt = (Element) objList.get(i);
        Class cls = Class.forName(oElt.getAttributeValue("class"));
        Object instance = null;
        if (!cls.isArray()) {
            Constructor c = cls.getDeclaredConstructor(null);
            if (!Modifier.isPublic(c.getModifiers())) {
                c.setAccessible(true);
```

```
            }
            instance = c.newInstance(null);
        }
        else {
            instance =
                Array.newInstance(
                    cls.getComponentType(),
                    Integer.parseInt(oElt.getAttributeValue("length")));
        }
        table.put(oElt.getAttributeValue("id"), instance);
    }
}
```

The line

```
Class cls = Class.forName( oElt.getAttributeValue("class") );
```

queries the document for the name of the class of a serialized object and loads
that class. Next, the method constructs an instance of the loaded class. If the class
is not an array class, the following lines are used:

```
Constructor c = cls.getDeclaredConstructor(null);
if (!Modifier.isPublic(c.getModifiers())) {
    c.setAccessible(true);
}
instance = c.newInstance(null);
```

The no-argument constructor is set accessible, if necessary, and then called to
instantiate an object. This assumption, of course, limits what can be deserialized.
This and other limitations of this solution are discussed in section 3.6.

If the class is an array class, the Array convenience facility is used to create a
new array of the correct component type and length as specified in the XML document. Finally, the new object is stored in the map, using the object's identifier as
the key. With instances constructed and the map populated, we can move on to
step 2 in our process.

3.5.3 Restoring the object structure

The assignFieldValues method in listing 3.6 iterates back over the newly constructed objects to initialize each instance variable. For each instance variable,
there are two cases to cover, depending on whether or not the contained object
is an array. If the object is an array, assignFieldValues loops over the array components in the XML document to fill in the array. Otherwise, assignFieldValues
initializes each instance variable with the value stored in the XML document. In

both cases, the deserializeValue method in listing 3.7 is called to accomplish the setting of the instance variable or the elements of the array.

Listing 3.6   The assignFieldValues method

```
private static void assignFieldValues( Map table, List objList )
    throws Exception
{
    for (int i = 0; i < objList.size(); i++) {
        Element oElt = (Element) objList.get(i);
        Object instance = table.get( oElt.getAttributeValue("id") );
        List fElts = oElt.getChildren();
        if (!instance.getClass().isArray()) {
            for (int j=0; j<fElts.size(); j++) {
                Element fElt = (Element) fElts.get(j);
                String className
                    = fElt.getAttributeValue("declaringclass");
                Class fieldDC = Class.forName(className);
                String fieldName = fElt.getAttributeValue("name");
                Field f = fieldDC.getDeclaredField(fieldName);
                if (!Modifier.isPublic(f.getModifiers())) {
                    f.setAccessible(true);
                }

                Element vElt = (Element) fElt.getChildren().get(0);
                f.set( instance,
                        deserializeValue( vElt, f.getType(), table ) );
            }
        }
        else {
            Class comptype =
                instance.getClass().getComponentType();
            for ( int j = 0; j < fElts.size(); j++) {
                Array.set( instance, j,
                            deserializeValue( (Element)fElts.get(j),
                                            comptype, table ));
            }
        }
    }
}
```

The deserializeValue method in listing 3.7 examines an XML element for an instance variable or array element and returns an object. There are several cases to be considered. If the value of the XML element is null, deserializeValue simply returns null. If the value is an object, deserializeValue finds the object using the map and returns it. Primitive values are parsed, wrapped, and returned.

Listing 3.7 The deserializeValue method

```java
private static Object deserializeValue( Element vElt,
                                        Class fieldType,
                                        Map table )

    throws ClassNotFoundException
{
    String valtype = vElt.getName();
    if (valtype.equals("null")) {
        return null;
    }
    else if (valtype.equals("reference")) {
        return table.get(vElt.getText());
    }
    else {
        if (fieldType.equals(boolean.class)) {
            if (vElt.getText().equals("true")) {
                return Boolean.TRUE;
            }
            else {
                return Boolean.FALSE;
            }
        }
        else if (fieldType.equals(byte.class)) {
            return Byte.valueOf(vElt.getText());
        }
        else if (fieldType.equals(short.class)) {
            return Short.valueOf(vElt.getText());
        }
        else if (fieldType.equals(int.class)) {
            return Integer.valueOf(vElt.getText());
        }
        else if (fieldType.equals(long.class)) {
            return Long.valueOf(vElt.getText());
        }
        else if (fieldType.equals(float.class)) {
            return Float.valueOf(vElt.getText());
        }
        else if (fieldType.equals(double.class)) {
            return Double.valueOf(vElt.getText());
        }
        else if (fieldType.equals(char.class)) {
            return new Character(vElt.getText().charAt(0));
        }
        else {
            return vElt.getText();
        }
    }
}
```

George's deserialization code mirrors the flexibility of his serialization code. Because of the use of dynamic loading, reflective construction, and reflective access to fields, George's code adapts as applications add new classes or new instance variables. Although a very general solution, it has limitations. Let's take a closer look at these limitations.

3.6 George's serialization: limitations

The serialization example in the previous two chapters illustrates many features of Java reflection, but the example is not a complete facility. Including such details would obscure the explanation of the reflective facilities. Because our goal is to explore reflection, we have made limiting assumptions to allow us to more easily illustrate the reflective concepts. In many cases, you can overcome these limiting assumptions by simply adding code or changing the design. This section discusses those limiting assumptions to more fully illustrate the demands of production serialization.

3.6.1 No interaction with readObject or writeObject

Standard serialization in Java interacts with two methods, readObject and writeObject, that provide hooks for trapping serialization and deserialization. These methods can be used for pre- and post-processing transient fields. These methods are passed the actual streams for serialization and deserialization to allow control over what is written and read. George's solution does not interact with these methods.

The entries in a java.util.HashMap are transient, and their serialization and deserialization are handled by readObject and writeObject. The writeObject method writes each key and each value to the stream as objects, one after the other. The readObject method reverses the process and puts them into the map. This arrangement means that George's code, in its current implementation, will not do an effective job of serializing a HashMap.

To handle classes that override readObject and writeObject, George's solution must be augmented to interact with readObject and writeObject. Here is one possible augmentation. The XML serialization could be made to send the output of each existing writeObject to a file and include a link to each file in the XML. With that link, the XML deserialization would open the file, read it into a stream, and pass that stream to readObject. In an alternative augmentation, the output of writeObject could be encoded as text and included in the XML.

3.6.2 *No handling of final instance variables*

Classes that declare or inherit final instance variables can cause problems for this solution. The value of a final instance variable is permanently set during object construction. In the example, this happens in `createInstances`. However, `assignFieldValues` also makes an attempt to assign the value stored in the XML document. This second attempt leads to an exception. Consequently, serialized objects that have final instance variables cannot be deserialized by our example code, because the code as written does not check for final instance variables.

Seemingly, you could just change `assignFieldValues` to not attempt to set final instance variables, trusting the value to be properly set during object construction. This, however, can lead to incorrect behavior. Consider a program that sets the original value of a final instance variable based upon the current program state. That value is the one written in the XML document when the object is serialized. Upon deserialization, the program may be in a state where the final instance variable is initialized differently. Whether or not this new value is appropriate is problematic.

3.6.3 *Only no-argument constructors*

This example requires that constructors with no arguments be available for deserialization. Section 3.4 (on page 60) makes an argument for designing classes for dynamic loading to have constructors with no arguments. The `createInstances` method throws an exception if it encounters an object whose class does not support a no-argument constructor.

There are several ways to extend the example such that it handles other construction options. One technique is to create mapping files that describe which instance variables can be fed as arguments into which constructors. A deserializer can then use the mapping to choose which constructor to use and decide which arguments to supply it. Several custom serialization libraries such as Castor use this technique.

Another technique is to apply custom serialization XML schemas to certain kinds of objects. Notice that arrays are handled differently than other objects in George's code. He uses a special schema that better fits the structure of an array. He also uses special code to introspect on the contents of the array. Similar techniques can be used for primitive wrapper classes, container classes, and so on.

3.6.4 *No handling of illegal XML characters*

Not all Unicode characters are legal in XML. The XML specification defines escapes that can be used for these characters. Some XML APIs handle this escaping for you, while others do not. Though the version of JDOM used for developing these examples did not handle all escapes properly, this issue has been left untreated for the sake of simplicity. For details on the legal XML character set, see the XML specification at www.w3c.org.

3.6.5 *Performance*

There are many ways to improve the performance of George's deserializer. One possible optimization sets the value of instance variables inside `deserializeValue` instead of having it return the value. This change would allow `deserializeValue` to use the primitive set methods for primitive values instead of wrapping them and returning them. However, for simplicity, we do not present that solution.

3.7 *Summary*

True flexibility demands that applications be able to incorporate new code. Without this capability, requirements eventually diverge from an application's implementation, leaving it obsolete. Dynamic loading allows a Java application to find and use classes not available when the application was written. When combined with a good object-oriented design, this increases the flexibility of Java applications, increasing the likelihood of keeping pace with changes in requirements.

Dynamic loading produces class objects. Therefore, instantiating those class objects becomes essential. Java supplies two options for creating instances from class objects: one using the class object itself and another using metaobjects representing the class's constructors. When an array is desired, the `Array` convenience facility can be used to construct an array reflectively.

Dynamic loading and reflective construction work to enhance delegation. Delegation permits different parts of a program to vary independently from each other. Reflection broadens the range of variation in a delegation relationship by making more kinds of objects available. The use of reflection also enhances creational patterns in similar ways.

When designing classes for dynamic loading, consider using the no-argument constructor. Dynamic loading and reflective construction are much simpler to implement when querying for a constructor object is not needed. Also, no-argument constructors and initialization methods can be inherited by subclasses with no extra programming, whereas constructors with arguments cannot.

Using Java's dynamic proxy

In this chapter

- How to use `java.lang.reflect.Proxy`
- Using proxy to implement decorators
- Chaining proxies
- Pitfalls of using `Proxy`

The dictionary [68] tells us that a proxy is an "agency, function, or office of a deputy who acts as a substitute for another." When this idea is applied to object-oriented programming, the result is an object, a *proxy*, that supports the interface of another object, its *target*, so that the proxy can substitute for the target for all practical purposes.

The keys to this arrangement are implementation and delegation. The proxy implements the same interface as the target so that it can be used in exactly the same way. The proxy delegates some or all of the calls that it receives to its target and thus acts as either an intermediary or a substitute. In its role as an intermediary, the proxy may add functionality either before or after the method is forwarded to the target. This gives the reflective programmer the capability to add behavior to objects. This chapter discusses this and other uses of proxies.

4.1 Working with proxies

The sequence diagram in figure 4.1 depicts the most common situation where the proxy instance receives a method call and forwards it to the target. Even this arrangement has a use; it hides the location of the target from the client. If you have used remote method invocation, you are familiar with proxies that are local substitutes for remote objects.

The Java reflection API contains a dynamic proxy-creation facility, `java.lang.reflect.Proxy`. This class is part of Java reflection because `Proxy` is Java's only way of approximating method invocation intercession. Let's dissect the previous phrase. **Intercession** is any reflective ability that modifies the behavior of a program by directly taking control of that behavior. Method invocation intercession is the ability to intercept method calls. The intercepting code can determine the behavior that results from the method call.

We say *approximating* because Java does not support reflective facilities for interceding on method calls. Therefore, we must use proxies as an approximation. Referring to figure 4.1, we see that proxies also allow the ability to pre- and post-process method calls. Let's examine the benefits achieved from doing this.

Programmers commonly discuss properties of classes. For example, a class that records its method calls is often referred to as a *tracing* class. A class that ensures that a failed operation does not leave an object in an intermediate state is often referred to as an *atomic* class.

The code that implements such properties is usually spread among the definitions of each of the methods of the class, almost always at the beginning and at the return points. The ability to intercede on method invocation permits the

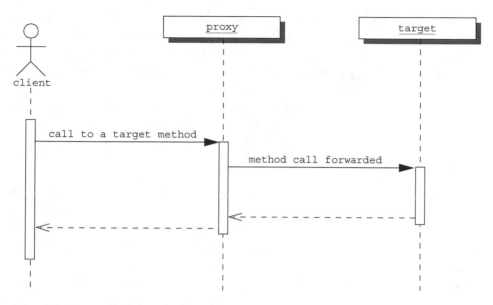

Figure 4.1 Sequence diagram for the typical use of a proxy. The proxy forwards received method calls to its target. The proxy may or may not do some pre- and post-processing.

programmer to gather this property-implementing code together in one place. This property can later combine with classes, yielding the desired effect.

The case for this combination of classes and properties is more real for software projects than you would think. A colleague once observed that when an object-oriented database is first brought into a programming shop, the number of classes doubles. The shop has added one property, *persistence*, to their application. Each class now requires a persistent and a nonpersistent version [18].

Developers get many key benefits from separating property-implementing code. One benefit of this separation is low maintenance cost for applications. Each such property can be modified by making a change in only one place in the code base. Another benefit of separating properties is improved reusability. The separated property can be used in many places in many applications.

There is also a compelling argument to present to management for such separation. Consider George's employer, Wildlife Components, which sells a class library of n classes. There are p properties that they wish their classes to have in all combinations. Both the number of classes and the number of properties grow as the company evolves to meet the increasing business demands. WCI faces the possibility of having to support a class library of at least $n2^p$ classes if they must write new classes to implement and combine properties in their original classes.

This additional maintenance is a serious enough concern to win management over. Isolating properties into reusable components and composing them later, as can be done with `Proxy`, yields a much smaller library of size $n+p$. This represents an enormous savings to WCI or any other company. This effect may not be as pronounced in other organizations, but it does exist.

Now that we have discussed the abstract benefits of `Proxy`, let's pay a visit to George and look at a simple example.

4.2 George's tracing problem

George has been assigned the task of creating tracing versions of several of the classes that he maintains. In a tracing class, each method records information about its entry and, after method execution, records information about its return. George's employer, WCI, wants tracing available for their classes because tracing helps with problem determination in deployed software.

Consider the following scenario. A customer calls WCI technical support with a defect report. Tech support asks the customer to turn tracing on in their software and follow the steps to reproduce the defect. Because tracing is turned on, the customer can then send WCI a file containing the path through the WCI source code.

This information solves many problems for the WCI technical team. It tells them a great deal about the state of the program during the failure. It also may prevent them from having to replicate their customer's environment and data.

While tracing is a useful feature, it is also very I/O intensive. Therefore, classes should be able to turn tracing on and off. However, including tracing code and guards to turn it on and off in each class bloats the classes and makes them slower because of the execution of the `if` statements. Due to these constraints, George decides to make tracing and nontracing versions of his classes.

One option George considers is subclassing each nontraced class and overriding each method with traces and `super` calls. He can then set up a process for either instantiating the traced or nontraced version depending upon some command-line argument. George quickly realizes that this option has the following shortcomings:

- *Tedium*—Executing this option is boring and mechanical. In fact, a computer program can be written to do this job.

- *Error-proneness*—George can easily misdeclare an override, misspelling the method name or including the wrong parameter list. He could also forget or overlook a method. At best, he may have a compile error to warn him that his process broke. Otherwise, the class may not behave as expected.

- *Fragility*—If anyone in George's department adds, deletes, or changes the signature on a method in the superclass, the traced subclass breaks either by not building or by not tracing as expected.

Clearly, George is in need of a better solution. George needs to separate the concern of tracing from the rest of the source code and implement it in a separate module. George reasons that this can be done with a proxy, where the proxy traces the call before and after delegating the method invocation to the target. Although there will be one proxy object for every target, with the use of reflection, all of the proxies can be instances of one proxy class, which addresses the shortcomings raised previously. Before presenting George's solution, let's examine `java.lang.reflect.Proxy`.

4.3 Exploring Proxy

As stated previously, the two important tasks for any proxy are interface implementation and delegation. The Java `Proxy` class accomplishes implementation of interfaces by dynamically creating a class that implements a set of given interfaces. This dynamic class creation is accomplished with the static `getProxyClass` and `newProxyInstance` factory methods, shown in listing 4.1.

Listing 4.1 Partial declaration for `java.lang.reflect.Proxy`

```
public class Proxy implements java.io.Serializable {
   ...
   public static Class getProxyClass( ClassLoader loader,
                                 Class[] interfaces )
                    throws IllegalArgumentException ...

   public static Object newProxyInstance( ClassLoader loader,
                                 Class[] interfaces,
                                 InvocationHandler h )
                    throws IllegalArgumentException ...

   public static boolean isProxyClass( Class cl ) ...

   public static InvocationHandler getInvocationHandler( Object proxy )
                    throws IllegalArgumentException ...
}
```

Each class constructed by these factory methods is a public final subclass of `Proxy`, referred to as a **proxy class**. We refer to an instance of one of these dynamically constructed proxies as a **proxy instance**. We call the interfaces that the proxy class implements in this way **proxied interfaces**. A proxy instance is assignment-compatible with all of its proxied interfaces.

The `getProxyClass` method retrieves the proxy class specified by a class loader and an array of interfaces. If such a proxy class does not exist, it is dynamically constructed. Because each Java class object is associated with a class loader, in order to dynamically create a proxy class, `getProxyClass` must have a class loader parameter (the reason for this requirement is explained in chapter 6). The name of each proxy class begins with `$Proxy` followed by a number, which is the value of an index that is increased each time a proxy class is created.

All proxy classes have a constructor that takes an `InvocationHandler` parameter. `InvocationHandler` is an interface for objects that handle methods received by proxy instances through their proxied interfaces. We discuss invocation handlers further after we finish with the methods of `Proxy`. A combination of `getConstructor` and `newInstance` may be used to construct proxy instances, as in the following lines

```
Proxy cl = getProxyClass( SomeInterface.getClassLoader(),
                          Class[]{SomeInterface.class} );
Constructor cons = cl.getConstructor( new Class[]{InvocationHandler.class} );
Object proxy = cons.newInstance( new Object[] { new SomeIH( obj ) } );
```

where `SomeIH` is a class that implements `InvocationHandler`. Alternatively, this sequence can be accomplished with a single call to `newProxyInstance`:

```
Object proxy = Proxy.newProxyInstance( SomeInterface.getClassLoader(),
                                       Class[]{SomeInterface.class},
                                       new SomeIH( obj ) );
```

This call implicitly creates the proxy class, which can be retrieved with `getProxyClass`.

The static method `isProxyClass` is used to determine if a class object represents a proxy class. The line

```
Proxy.isProxyClass(obj.getClass())
```

may be use to determine if `obj` refers to a proxy instance. If `p` refers to a proxy instance,

```
Proxy.getInvocationHandler(p)
```

returns the `InvocationHandler` that was used to construct `p`.

4.3.1 *Understanding invocation handlers*

`Proxy` allows programmers to accomplish the delegation task by providing the `InvocationHandler` interface. Instances of `InvocationHandler`, also referred to as **invocation handlers**, are objects that handle each method call for a proxy instance. Invocation handlers are also responsible for holding any references to targets of the proxy instance. Listing 4.2 shows the `InvocationHandler` interface.

Listing 4.2   The `InvocationHandler` interface

```
public interface InvocationHandler {

    public Object invoke( Object proxy, Method method, Object[] args )
                               throws Throwable;

}
```

A proxy instance forwards method calls to its invocation handler by calling `invoke`. The original arguments for the method call are passed to `invoke` as an object array. In addition, the proxy instance provides a reference to itself and to a `Method` object representing the invoked method.

Notice that the parameters passed to `invoke` are exactly the objects needed to forward a method call to another object reflectively. If `target` refers to the object being proxied, the lines

```
public Object invoke( Object proxy, Method method, Object[] args)
    throws Throwable
{
    return method.invoke(target, args);
}
```

implement an `invoke` method that passes every call transparently. More complex `invoke` methods may perform pre- and post-processing on the arguments. Note that invocation handlers may also forward to many targets or none at all.

Figure 4.1 depicts an abstraction of forwarding a method through a proxy. Figure 4.2 depicts that actual sequence of calls when the invocation handler is implemented as shown previously. For clarity, UML is often used to present the minimal relevant detail to convey understanding. With this idea in mind, our subsequent diagrams for proxy present the abstraction rather than the implementation detail.

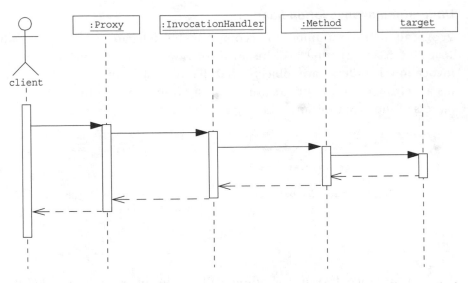

Figure 4.2   Sequence diagram illustrating the actual objects involved in forwarding a method when the invocation handler of the proxy uses the `invoke` method of `Method`.

4.3.2 *Handling the methods of Object*

A proxy instance is an object, and so it responds to the methods declared by `java.lang.Object`. This raises the issue of whether or not these methods should be handled by `invoke`. The issue is resolved as follows:

- `hashCode`, `equals`, and `toString` are dispatched to the invoke method in the same manner as any other proxied method.

- If a proxied interface extends `Cloneable`, then the invocation handler does intercede on the invocations to `clone`. However, unless the proxied interface makes `clone` public, it remains a protected method.

- If any proxied interface declares an override to `finalize`, then invocation handlers do intercede on calls to `finalize`.

- Method intercession does not take place for the other methods declared by `java.lang.Object`. Consequently, these methods behave as expected for any instance of `java.lang.Object`. In other words, a call to `wait` on a proxy instance waits on the proxy instance's lock, rather than being forwarded to an invocation handler.

The information in the last bullet is welcome because it means that an invocation handler cannot make a proxy instance lie about its class or interfere with multithreaded locking. Now that you understand the basics of Proxy, let's return to George's tracing problem.

4.4 Implementing a tracing proxy

George solves his tracing problem using Proxy. From his exploration of Proxy, George readily understands that his solution must have an invocation handler in which the invoke method forwards all method calls to the target. This forwarding is readily accomplished with the invoke method of Method. The next design decision involves the creation of the proxy and the invocation handler. George decides that all of his creation code can be located in the class written for the invocation handler. This is accomplished with a static method, createProxy. This static method is passed the target, which is examined introspectively to create an appropriate proxy and invocation handler. Listing 4.3 shows the invocation handler that George created. With this invocation handler, George can add tracing of any interface to an individual object. Let's examine the solution in detail.

Listing 4.3 An invocation handler for a proxy that traces calls

```
import java.lang.reflect.*;
import java.io.PrintWriter;

public class TracingIH implements InvocationHandler {

    public static Object createProxy( Object obj, PrintWriter out ) {
        return Proxy.newProxyInstance( obj.getClass().getClassLoader(),
                                       obj.getClass().getInterfaces(),
                                       new TracingIH( obj, out ) );
    }

    private Object target;
    private PrintWriter out;

    private TracingIH( Object obj, PrintWriter out ) {
        target = obj;
        this.out = out;
    }

    public Object invoke( Object proxy, Method method, Object[] args )
        throws Throwable
    {
        Object result = null;
        try {
            out.println( method.getName() + "(...) called" );
            result = method.invoke( target, args );
        } catch (InvocationTargetException e) {
            out.println( method.getName() + " throws " + e.getCause() );
            throw e.getCause();
```

```
        }
        out.println( method.getName() + " returns" );
        return result;
    }
}
```

The implementation part of George's solution happens in the `createProxy` method. The static factory method `createProxy` wraps its argument in a proxy that performs tracing. First, `createProxy` examines its argument object for the direct interfaces that its class implements. It sends that array of interfaces to `Proxy.newProxyInstance`, which constructs a proxy class for those interfaces.[1] Next, a `TracingIH` is constructed with the argument as its target. Finally, `create-Proxy` constructs and returns a new proxy that forwards its calls to the `TracingIH`. This proxy implements all of the interfaces of the target object and is assignment-compatible with those types.

The delegation part of George's solution happens in the `invoke` method. The `invoke` method in listing 4.3 first records the method name to a `java.io.Print-Writer`. A more complete facility would also include the arguments, but we omit them for brevity. Then the `invoke` method forwards the call to the target and, subsequently, stores the return value. If an exception is thrown, the exception is recorded with the print writer; otherwise, the return value is recorded. Finally, the result of the call is returned.

When a proxied method is called on a proxy instance, control first passes to the `invoke` method with the following arguments:

- *proxy*—The proxy instance on which the method was invoked. `TracingIH` happens to make no use of this parameter.

- *method*—A `Method` object for the invoked method.

- *args*—An array of objects containing the values of the arguments passed in the method invocation on the proxy instance. `args` is `null` if the `method`

---

[1] The `getInterfaces` method returns only the direct interfaces of a class. As George has written the invocation handler, only methods declared by direct interfaces are traced. In chapter 8, we present a method, `Mopex.getAllInterfaces`, that finds all of the interfaces implemented by a class. What about methods that are not implemented in an interface? George might be asked to supply a tool that finds those methods and puts them in an interface. Reflection can help here, too, but you will have to wait until chapter 7 to read how.

takes no arguments. Arguments of primitive types are wrapped in instances of the appropriate primitive wrapper class; for example, `java.lang.Integer` wraps an `int`.

The declared return type of `invoke` is `Object`. The value returned by `invoke` is subject to the following rules:

- If the called method has declared the return type void, the value returned by `invoke` does not matter. Returning `null` is the simplest option.

- If the declared return type of the interface method is a primitive type, the value returned by `invoke` must be an instance of the corresponding primitive wrapper class. Returning `null` in this case causes a `NullPointerException` to be thrown.

- If the value returned by `invoke` is not compatible with the interface method's declared return type, a `ClassCastException` is thrown by the method invocation on the proxy instance.

The exception `UndeclaredThrowableException` may be thrown by the execution of the `invoke` method. `UndeclaredThrowableException` wraps non-runtime exceptions that are not declared by the interface for the method being called. The cause of the wrapped exception may be accessed with `getCause`. This wrapping of an exception may seem odd, but it is necessary when you consider the difficulty of programming invocation handlers that are limited to throwing just those exceptions known at the origin of the call.

To fully understand the class `TracingIH` in listing 4.3, it is best to understand how a using application is changed by the execution of the statement

```
Dog proxyForRover = (Dog) TracingIH.createProxy( rover );
```

where `Dog` is a Java interface and `rover` contains an instance of a class `DogImpl` that implements that interface. Note that the proxy facility ensures that the proxy instance returned by `createProxy` can be cast to `Dog`. Figure 4.3 presents a diagram that shows all of the objects and classes that are relevant to the previous line of code. The objects created by that line of code are in the gray area.

This invocation handler in listing 4.3 provides the module that George wants. Instead of having to change source code, he can wrap objects with proxies and have the users of the objects reference the proxies. This technique avoids all of the shortcomings of the process George would have to follow without `Proxy`.

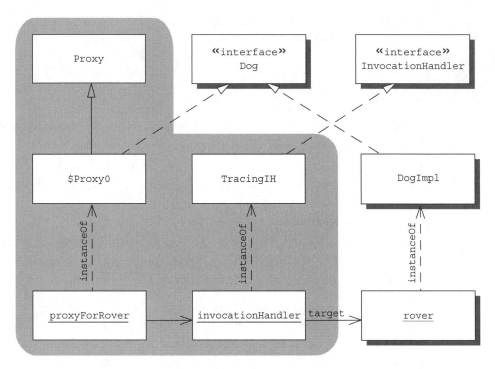

Figure 4.3   A class diagram illustrating the execution of the `createProxy` factory method from listing 4.3.

4.5 *A note on factories*

As mentioned earlier, the tracing invocation handler of listing 4.3 is missing a test to turn tracing on and off dynamically. Instead, the application uses either traced or nontraced versions of its classes. This is accomplished by applying the Abstract Factory pattern for construction of the potentially traced objects. That is, a class is declared that contains a method for creating new instances of Dog. This method chooses whether to create instances of the Dog class that traces or instances of the one that does not trace. An example factory for implementations of the Dog interface is shown in listing 4.4.

Listing 4.4   A factory that chooses between traced and untraced versions of a class

```
import java.lang.reflect.*;
import java.io.PrintWriter;

public class DogFactory {
```

```
private Class dogClass;
private boolean traceIsOn = false;

public DogFactory( String className, boolean trace ) {
    try {
        dogClass = Class.forName( className );
    } catch (ClassNotFoundException e){
        throw new RuntimeException(e); // or whatever is appropriate
    }
    traceIsOn = trace;
}

public Dog newInstance( String name, int size ) {
    try {
        Dog d = (Dog)dogClass.newInstance();
        d.initialize(name,size);
        if ( traceIsOn ) {
            d = (Dog)TracingIH.createProxy( d,
                                    new PrintWriter(System.out) );
        }
        return d;
    } catch(InstantiationException e){
        throw new RuntimeException(e); // or whatever is appropriate
    } catch(IllegalAccessException e){
        throw new RuntimeException(e); // or whatever is appropriate
    }
}
}
```

Notice that the factory method `newInstance` is enhanced reflectively by using the class object to create a new instance the same way as the factory method in the previous chapter. The lines

```
if (traceIsOn) {
    d = (Dog) TracingIH.createProxy(d, new PrintWriter(System.out));
}
```

assure that each `Dog` is wrapped in a tracing proxy when required. This puts the tests for tracing at construction time rather than during execution of the methods of `Dog`.

The factory method also conforms to design recommendations presented in section 3.4.2. The `newInstance` method constructs instances using the `newInstance` method of `Class`. After construction, the new `Dog` is made ready for use with a call to `initialize`.

4.6 Chaining proxies

One of the strengths of using proxies is that they can be arranged in a chain, with each proxy but the last having another proxy as its target. The last target in the chain is the real target object. When done properly, this chaining has the effect of composing the properties implemented by each proxy.

4.6.1 Structuring invocation handlers for chaining

Ensuring that proxies can be chained requires careful design. For example, the invocation handler for tracing is programmed with the assumption that its target is the real target and not another proxy. If the target is another proxy, the invocation handler may not perform the correct operation. To remedy this problem, we present InvocationHandlerBase, an abstract class for deriving invocation handlers for chainable proxies. The source code for InvocationHandlerBase is shown in listing 4.5.

Listing 4.5   InvocationHandlerBase

```java
import java.lang.reflect.*;
import mopex.*;

public abstract class InvocationHandlerBase implements InvocationHandler {

    protected Object nextTarget;
    protected Object realTarget = null;

    InvocationHandlerBase( Object target ) {
        nextTarget = target;
        if ( nextTarget != null ) {
            realTarget = findRealTarget(nextTarget);
            if (realTarget == null)
                throw new RuntimeException("findRealTarget failure");
        }
    }

    protected final Object getRealTarget() { return realTarget; }

    protected static final Object findRealTarget( Object t ) {
        if ( !Proxy.isProxyClass(t.getClass()) )
            return t;
        InvocationHandler ih = Proxy.getInvocationHandler(t);
        if ( InvocationHandlerBase.class.isInstance( ih ) ) {
            return ((InvocationHandlerBase)ih).getRealTarget();
        } else {
            try {
                Field f = Mopex.findField( ih.getClass(), "target" );
                if ( Object.class.isAssignableFrom(f.getType()) &&
                    !f.getType().isArray() ) {
```

```
                    f.setAccessible(true); // suppress access checks
                    Object innerTarget = f.get(ih);
                    return findRealTarget(innerTarget);
                }
                return null;
            } catch (NoSuchFieldException e){
                return null;
            } catch (SecurityException e){
                return null;
            } catch (IllegalAccessException e){
                return null;
            } // IllegalArgumentException cannot be raised
        }
    }
}
```

The service provided by InvocationHandlerBase is the recursive search findReal-Target that traverses the chain of proxy instances and invocation handlers to find the real target at the end of the chain. If each invocation handler in the chain extends InvocationHandlerBase, the traversal is simply accomplished with calls to getRealTarget, because findRealTarget is used in the constructor to initially set realTarget.

However, it is rather inflexible to assume that all of the invocation handlers encountered will extend InvocationHandlerBase. For invocation handlers that do not extend InvocationHandlerBase, we attempt to find a target using reflection. The findRealTarget method searches the target proxy instance's invocation handler for an Object field named target. The search for the target field is accomplished using Mopex.findField, defined in listing 4.6. If that field exists and has a non-array type assignable to Object, it is assumed that the field contains the next link in the chain of proxies.

Listing 4.6 The findField method in Mopex

```
public static Field findField( Class cls, String name )
                            throws NoSuchFieldException {
    if ( cls != null ) {
        try {
            return cls.getDeclaredField( name );
        } catch(NoSuchFieldException e){
            return findField( cls.getSuperclass(), name );
        }
    } else {
        throw new NoSuchFieldException();
    }
}
```

The interface in the Java Reflection API for querying a class object for its members is not always ideal. For example,

```
X.class.getDeclaredField("foo")
```

throws a `NoSuchFieldException` if the sought field `foo` is declared by a superclass of the target `X`. Mopex contains `findField` to make queries for fields more convenient. It recursively searches up the inheritance hierarchy and returns the first field with the specified name. This search furthers our goal of chaining invocation handlers that do not extend `InvocationHandlerBase` with those that do. Let's use it.

4.6.2 *Implementing a synchronized proxy*

To illustrate the concept of proxy chaining, we need another kind of proxy to chain with the tracing proxy. In this section, we present a proxy for making an object synchronized. This proxy has the effect of using the `synchronized` modifier on a class declaration if Java allowed such a combination. Listing 4.7 presents an invocation handler for synchronized access to its target object. All method forwarding occurs inside a `synchronized` statement.

Listing 4.7   An invocation handler for synchronized access

```java
import java.lang.reflect.*;

public class SynchronizedIH extends InvocationHandlerBase {

    public static Object createProxy( Object obj ) {
        return Proxy.newProxyInstance( obj.getClass().getClassLoader(),
                                       obj.getClass().getInterfaces(),
                                       new SynchronizedIH( obj ) );
    }

    private SynchronizedIH( Object obj ) { super( obj ); }

    public Object invoke( Object proxy, Method method, Object[] args )
        throws Throwable
    {
        Object result = null;
        synchronized ( this.getRealTarget() ) {
            result = method.invoke( nextTarget, args );

        }
        return result;
    }
}
```

The lock acquired by the synchronized statement in listing 4.7 is the one belonging to the real target, which is the better design decision. The alternative decision is acquiring the lock associated with the proxy instance. This alternative is likely the wrong design decision. For example, if there were multiple proxy instances for a single target, each proxy instance would be acquiring a different lock. For this reason, it is vital to discover the real target.

4.6.3 *Chaining the two proxies*

As mentioned previously, chaining is one of the more elegant properties of Proxy. That is, by using a synchronizing proxy in front of a tracing proxy, we achieve the effect of an object that both synchronizes and traces. As we did earlier, suppose Dog is a Java interface and DogImpl is an implementation of that interface. The statement

```
Dog rover = (Dog)SynchronizedIH.createProxy(
                TracingIH.createProxy( new DogImpl(),
                                new PrintWriter(System.out) ) );
```

constructs a synchronized proxy instance for a tracing proxy instance for a Dog object. For all practical purposes, this is a Dog object that synchronizes and traces. This is illustrated in figure 4.4, which shows that a call is passed from one proxy to the next until the call reaches the target.

When you chain proxies, the order usually makes a difference. That is, there is a difference between a synchronized tracing object and tracing synchronized object. The difference is whether or not the synchronization applies to the printing of the trace. In any multithreaded application, this is an important nuance because if the tracing is not conducted inside the synchronization, the trace output of two threads might be mixed so as to appear that the synchronization were not working. That is, the trace would not reflect the true behavior of the application, which would be a poor outcome of the chaining of the proxies.

The chaining of proxies is one way to address the problem of exponential growth in the size of the class hierarchy when you need to mix properties and classes. More concretely, the above proxy constructions are much more convenient than maintaining a synchronized version, a tracing version, and a synchronized tracing version of each class that requires these properties. Chapter 7 discusses another way to address this problem.

Irrespective of the approach taken, the importance of the problem and the fundamental reliance of the various solutions on reflection cannot be stressed

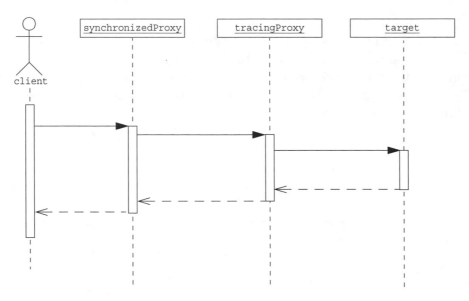

Figure 4.4   Sequence diagram illustrating the chaining of the synchronized proxy and the tracing proxy

enough. In order to be the most flexible, both adaptive and reusable, software must be able to examine itself and its environment (introspection), change itself (intercession), and combine with that environment.

4.7   Stubbing interfaces for unit testing

In each of the previous proxy examples, the proxy-instance-invocation-handler combination had a target to which to forward the method call. Having a target is not necessary; there are some situations where the invocation handler implements the methods entirely. Let's focus on one such example.

4.7.1   Examining stubs

A **test stub** is an implementation of an interface that is used to perform testing during development prior to full implementation. In topdown development, test stubs allow the development and testing of the upper levels of the system without requiring all of the lower-level code to be written. For example, an application developer may validate the behavior of a GUI while using test stubs for the business logic, which is concurrently being designed by a business analyst.

While essential for good testing, stubbing often makes life more difficult for developers. First of all, stubs are classes, which means more code to write and maintain. During development, interfaces change more, which means stubs need to be changed with them, thus increasing the cost of change.

Second, the implementation of stubs is mechanical and tedious work. Each stub should do two basic things. The stub needs to record incoming method invocations as the test is run so that the behavior can be validated. Also, the stub needs to script return values and exceptions. This scripted behavior is used by the test to sensitize paths through the code being tested. These two actions need to be taken for each method call, regardless of which methods are implemented by the stub.

Stub generation facilitates early forms of testing such as unit testing. Unit testing isolates small units of code, allowing validation of their behavior without interaction with other parts of the application. This isolation helps locate defects and yields higher confidence during integration.

Without unit testing, defects are much more difficult to locate during integration, and changes that break units may go unnoticed. However, many organizations do not unit test thoroughly because of the heavy burdens associated with maintaining the tests and the stubs. Stub generation is of extremely high value because it removes much of the maintenance burden, allowing developers to test more easily.

4.7.2 *Design for stubbing with Proxy*

Here we design and implement a test stub facility based on `Proxy`. Given a Java interface or set of interfaces, this facility creates test stub proxy instances. The facility obviates the need to hand-implement test stubs when doing topdown development. The use of `Proxy`-generated stubs in testing also promotes the practice of programming to interfaces.

Figure 4.5 shows the class diagram for the design of the test stub facility. The facility has three interfaces and four classes, whose purposes are defined as follows:

- *Stub*—This interface adds convenience methods to the proxy, for example, methods to get information from inside the invocation handler without calling `Proxy.getInvocationHandler`.

- *History*—The test stub facility allows for a history object to be defined that remembers methods called on the stub during a test case. This history can be queried to validate the behavior of the unit being tested.

- *DefaultHistory*—This class implements a `History` that does nothing (this is not shown is the class diagram in figure 4.5).

- *ReturnValueStrategy*—An application of the Strategy pattern that allows scripting of return values and thrown exceptions. This ability allows stubs to sensitize many paths through the unit being tested.

- *DefaultReturnValueStrategy*—This class implements the `ReturnValue-Strategy` that is used if none is specified.

- *WrappedException*—A `ReturnValueStrategy` may wish to throw an exception. It does so by wrapping that exception in a `WrappedException`. This enables the stub facility to tell the difference between a real exception, a scripted exception, and an exception as a return value.

- *StubIH*—This is the invocation handler for the test stub facility. It is responsible for using the return value strategy to determine the return value and for using the history object to record the method invocation.

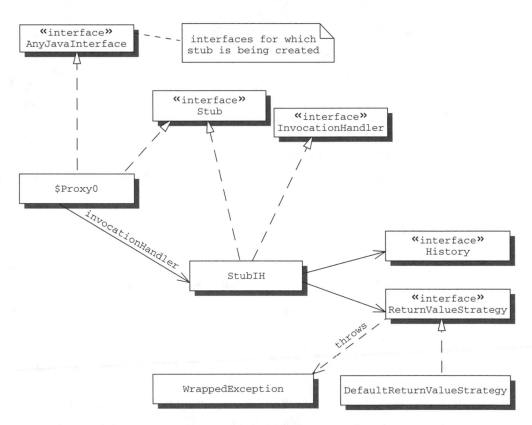

Figure 4.5   Design for the test stub proxy

4.7.3 *Implementation of stubbing with Proxy*

Listing 4.8 shows the `Stub` interface. This interface is dynamically added to the set of interfaces supported by the stub proxy class. The methods of `Stub` are implemented by the stub invocation handler, `StubIH`. This interface is for convenience methods.

In this case, there is just one method, `getHistory`, that allows the users of a proxy instance to easily get the history object without having to call `Proxy.get-InvocationHandler` first. Note that `Stub` extends `Serializable`, which permits the proxy instances and the invocation handler to be saved.

Listing 4.8 Stub interface

```
public interface Stub extends Serializable {
    /**
     * Returns the history object for the stub.
     */
    History getHistory( );
}
```

Listing 4.9 presents the `History` interface. The methods defined are used only to add information to the history object. The return value of `recordMethodCall` is an identifier that is used in the other methods to match the result with the call. It is the obligation of the implementor of `History` to add methods that allow the history to be examined. We choose not to present such an implementation, because it does not add value to our study of Java reflection.

Listing 4.9 History interface

```
public interface History extends java.io.Serializable {

    long recordMethodCall( Proxy p, Method m, Object[] args );
    void recordReturnValue( long callID, Object returnValue );
    void recordException( long callID, Throwable cause );

}
```

The class displayed in listing 4.10 is the default implementation for `History`. This implementation does nothing, and its only purpose is to make the code clearer by obviating many checks for null (the pattern for this class is called Null Object [77]).

Listing 4.10   DefaultHistory class

```java
public class DefaultHistory implements History {

    public long recordMethodCall( Proxy p, Method m, Object[] args ) {
        return 0;
    }
    public void recordReturnValue( long callID, Object returnValue ) {}
    public void recordException( long callID, Throwable cause ) {}
}
```

Listing 4.11 shows the interface ReturnValueStrategy that is used to substitute a return value in place of executing the real, yet-to-be-implemented method. The only hard requirement for getReturnValue is that a value of the expected type must be produced. Here, a matter of quality comes into play: the more real the return values look, the easier it is to test the units that use the stub. Note that the history is also passed to getReturnValue. This can be valuable in producing a real-looking stream of return values.

Listing 4.11   ReturnValueStrategy interface

```java
public interface ReturnValueStrategy {

    /**
     * Note that getReturnValue is expected to produce the return values
     * for calls to Object.equals, Object.toString, and Object.hashCode.
     */
    Object getReturnValue( Proxy p, Method m, Object[] args, History h )
        throws WrappedException;

}
```

Listing 4.12 contains the default implementation for ReturnValueStrategy. Unlike DefaultHistory in listing 4.10, DefaultReturnValueStrategy is not a null object because it really tries to fulfill the role of a ReturnValueStrategy.

Listing 4.12   DefaultReturnValueStrategy class

```java
public class DefaultReturnValueStrategy implements ReturnValueStrategy {

    public Object getReturnValue( Proxy p,
                                  Method m,
                                  Object[] args,
                                  History h ) {
        if ( !m.getReturnType().isPrimitive() ) {
```

```
            try {
                return m.getReturnType().newInstance();
            } catch(InstantiationException e){
                return null;
            } catch(IllegalAccessException e){
                return null;
            }
        } else if ( m.getReturnType() == void.class ) {
            return null;
        } else if (m.getReturnType() == boolean.class) {
            return new Boolean(false);
        } else if ( m.getReturnType() == short.class ) {
            return new Short((short)0);
        } else if ( m.getReturnType() == int.class ) {
            return new Integer(0);
        } else if ( m.getReturnType() == long.class ) {
            return new Long(0);
        } else if ( m.getReturnType() == double.class ) {
            return new Double(0);
        } else if ( m.getReturnType() == byte.class ) {
            return new Byte((byte)0);
        } else if ( m.getReturnType() == char.class ) {
            return new Character((char)0);
        } else if ( m.getReturnType() == float.class ) {
            return new Float(0);
        }
        throw new Error("Unknown return type: " + m.getReturnType());
    }
}
```

This default implementation of `ReturnValueStrategy` provides several interesting lessons about the use of reflection:

- The `newInstance` statement is used to call the constructor with no parameters, which may not exist or may not be accessible. If such a constructor exists and is accessible, its result is assumed to be a reasonable return value for a test stub. If no such constructor exists, `null` is a reasonable return value. The lesson in this case is that simply calling `m.getReturnType().newInstance()` achieves the desired result—no `Constructor` objects are necessary.

- Each value of a primitive type is returned wrapped exactly in an object of its associated wrapper. Wrapper objects are not coerced. For example, an `Integer` object may not be used as a return object when `invoke` is called for a method that returns a `long`.

- The sieve of nested if statements ends with the throwing of an error. This ensures that if some future version of Java adds additional primitive types, the problem code can be immediately identified.

It is possible that a method is supposed to return an object of type `Throwable` rather than throw the object as an exception. In order for the return value strategy to distinguish between these two cases, the exception in listing 4.13 is defined. If the stub is to merely return a `Throwable` object, then the return value strategy returns the `Throwable` object. However, if the stub is to throw the object, the return value strategy wraps the `Throwable` object in a `WrappedException` and throws it to the stub.

Listing 4.13   WrappedException class

```java
public  class WrappedException extends Exception {
    public WrappedException( Throwable cause ) { super(cause); }
}
```

Finally, we come to the center of the test stub facility, the invocation handler in listing 4.14. This class implements both `Stub` and `InvocationHandler`. The static `createStub` factory methods are responsible for constructing proxy instances that serve as test stubs. These methods are similar to the previous factory methods in this chapter except in two respects. First, `StubIH` does not allow the construction of stubs for the `Stub` or `InvocationHander` interfaces. Second, the `Stub` interface is added to the array of proxied interfaces. This addition allows stub users to invoke `Stub` methods directly on a stub proxy instance instead of having to get the invocation handler.

The heart of the facility is the implementation of the `invoke` method. If the method is declared by the `Stub` interface, `invoke` calls its `StubIH` implementation. Otherwise, it records the invocation to history and determines the return value using the return value strategy. As with all other proxy instances, `invoke` handles `toString`, `equals`, and `hashCode`, and may handle `clone` and `finalize`, while all the other methods declared by `java.lang.Object` are called directly on the proxy instance.

Listing 4.14   StubIH invocation handler

```java
public class StubIH implements InvocationHandler, Stub {
    private ReturnValueStrategy retValStrategy
        = new DefaultReturnValueStrategy();
```

```
private History history = new DefaultHistory();

public static Stub createStub( Class[] interfaces,
                               ReturnValueStrategy rvs ) {
    return createStub( interfaces, rvs, null );
}

public static Stub createStub( Class[] interfaces,
                               ReturnValueStrategy rvs,
                               History h )
{
    for ( int i = 0; i < interfaces.length; i++ )
        if ( interfaces[i] == Stub.class
             || interfaces[i] == InvocationHandler.class )
            throw new RuntimeException( "Cannot stub " + interfaces[i] );

    Class[] newInterfaces = new Class[interfaces.length+1];
    newInterfaces[0] = Stub.class;
    System.arraycopy( interfaces,
                      0,
                      newInterfaces,
                      1,
                      interfaces.length);

    return (Stub)Proxy.newProxyInstance( Stub.class.getClassLoader(),
                                         newInterfaces,
                                         new StubIH( newInterfaces,
                                                     rvs,
                                                     h ) );
}

private StubIH( Class[] interfaces,
                ReturnValueStrategy rvs,
                History h  )
{
    if ( h != null )
        history = h;
    if ( rvs != null )
        retValStrategy = rvs;
}

public final History getHistory() { return history; }

public Object invoke( Object p, Method m, Object[] args )
    throws Throwable
{
    if ( m.getDeclaringClass() == Stub.class ) {
        // for calls to methods declared in Stub interface
        return m.invoke( this, args );
    }

    long callId = history.recordMethodCall( (Proxy)p, m, args );

    try {
```

```
                    Object result = retValStrategy.getReturnValue( (Proxy)p,
                                                                   m,
                                                                   args,
                                                                   history );
                history.recordReturnValue( callId, result );
                return result;
            } catch(WrappedException e){
                history.recordException( callId, e.getCause() );
                throw e.getCause();

            } catch(Exception e){
                history.recordException( callId, e );
                throw e;
            }
        }
    }
}
```

The proper use for this test stub is as follows:

1 Construct the object being tested and the stubs that it needs. Set the stubs
   on the object being tested.

2 In the return value strategies of each of the stubs, script the return values
   or exceptions that guide execution along the desired path through the
   class being tested.

3 Invoke the method being tested on the object.

4 Test the correctness of the return value of the method.

5 Query the history in each of the stubs for the behavior of the object and
   test its correctness.

Given sufficient history and return value strategy implementations, this test facility can be highly effective. It provides the benefits of test stubbing without the burdens of implementing and maintaining a stub class for each interface.

   To better understand the stub proxy, consider George's deployment problem
from section 3.1. George began with an interface for the customer database that
he wanted to stub. With the stub proxy, he may start by merely writing

```
CustomerDatabase db
        = (CustomerDatabase)StubIH.createStub(
                        new Class[]{CustomerDatabase.class},
                        null,
                        null );
```

which creates the database facade object. As he progresses, he can enhance the stub by providing a return value strategy or a specialized history object.

This completes the presentation of the test stub proxy. It is based on a similar facility that was implemented and used by one of the authors in the development of a commercial product. Our presentation used `History` and `ReturnValueStrategy` to abstract away many details of that implementation so that the quintessential idea remains. In all other respects, the code presented is ready for you to use.

4.8 *Generating SOAP remote proxies*

The classic application of proxies is in the implementation of remote services. A proxy can make remote objects seem local to the rest of an application. The application calls methods on the proxy as if it were the remote object. The proxy forwards method calls to the remote object using the appropriate protocol.

The specifics of the remote protocol can become tangled with the application, cluttering the business logic. This tangling makes the application less flexible. Fortunately, `Proxy` can be used to separate this concern into its own class. This design allows the remote protocol to vary independently from the rest of the application. Let's examine how `Proxy` can help apply this classic pattern to a new technology.

Web services are the most recent trend in remote protocols. The Web Services Architecture technical report [94] states the following:

> A Web service is a software system designed to support interoperable machine-to-machine interaction over a network. It has an interface described in a machine-processable format (specifically WSDL). Other systems interact with the Web service in a manner prescribed by its description using SOAP-messages, typically conveyed using HTTP with an XML serialization in conjunction with other Web-related standards.

An important building block of Web services is SOAP, the Simple Object Access Protocol. Here we construct an invocation handler that allows you to easily write code to access remote objects using SOAP. Furthermore, the combination of `Proxy` and other reflective capabilities enables the writing of an invocation handler that works for all simple Web services. We demonstrate the effectiveness of this invocation handler and the Web services standards with a very small test program that retrieves the price of *The Three Musketeers* from the Barnes and Noble Quote Service on the XMethods web site (www.xmethods.org).

To start, we need to cover a few basic facts about SOAP (more information is available at www.w3.org/TR/SOAP). SOAP is a lightweight protocol for making method invocations on remote objects and receiving return values. For our example we use the original Apache implementation as our SOAP API. Although by the time this book is printed the Apache Axis project will probably have subsumed the Apache SOAP project, the example is still relevant and illustrative.

In the original Apache implementation of SOAP, there are three classes that will concern us: Call, Parameter, and Response (see ws.apache.org/soap/docs for the documentation). Basically, you construct a Call object with the URI of the service, the name of the method, and a Vector of Parameter objects. After a call is constructed, the Call class has an invoke method to start remote access. The invoke method returns a Response object, which contains the return value.

Listing 4.15 shows the invocation handler for our SOAP proxies.

Listing 4.15   An invocation handler for SOAP remote proxies

```java
import org.apache.soap.rpc.Call;
import org.apache.soap.rpc.Parameter;
import org.apache.soap.rpc.Response;

import java.lang.reflect.*;
import java.net.URL;
import java.util.Vector;

public class SoapInvocationHandler implements InvocationHandler {

    public static Object createSoapProxy( Class[] interfaces,
                                           URL serverURL,
                                           String serviceName,
                                           String encoding )
    {
        SoapInvocationHandler handler = new SoapInvocationHandler();
        handler.serverURL = serverURL;
        handler.serviceName = serviceName;          // Creates proxy and its
        handler.encoding = encoding;                // invocation handler ❶

        return Proxy.newProxyInstance(
                   SoapInvocationHandler.class.getClassLoader(),
                   interfaces,
                   handler );
    }

    private URL serverURL;
    private String serviceName;       // Declares networking ❷
    private String encoding;          // parameters required by SOAP

    private SoapInvocationHandler() {}

    public Object invoke( Object proxy, Method method, Object[] args )
        throws Throwable
    {                                 // Creates, populates, and
                                      // invokes a Call object ❸
```

```
Call call = new Call();                          Constructs the
call.setTargetObjectURI( serviceName );          Call object
call.setMethodName( method.getName() );

Vector params = new Vector();                          Creates a Vector
Class[] types = method.getParameterTypes();             of Parameter
for ( int i = 0; i < args.length; i++ ) {                    objects
    params.add(
           new Parameter( "p"+i, types[i], args[i], encoding )
           );
}                                               Invokes the Call to
call.setParams( params );                       send a SOAP remote call

Response resp = call.invoke( serverURL, "" );

if ( resp.generatedFault() ) {
    throw new RuntimeException( resp.getFault().toString() );
}
else {
    return resp.getReturnValue().getValue();
}                                                   Checks the
    }                                               Response object
}
```

Let's take a tour:

❶ The static createSoapProxy factory method creates an invocation handler, populates its instance variables, and creates and returns a new proxy instance. Using the Java Proxy implies that if a proper Java interface is declared for any Web service, a usable proxy object for the Web service is constructed.

❷ These are the networking parameters required by SOAP. The first is the URL for finding the Web service. The second is the name of the Web service. The third is the kind of encoding for the invocation parameters.

❸ The invoke method of the invocation handler is used to create, populate, and invoke a Call object.

❹ Here the Call object is constructed and the names of the Web service and remote method are set.

❺ A Vector of Parameter objects is created. Notice how nicely the arguments to the invoke method of InvocationHandler support the SOAP implementation. For example, the Method argument facilitates the marshalling of the parameters for the remote call.

❻ The invoke method of Call is used to send a SOAP remote call to the server specified by the URL stored in serverURL.

❼ After the invocation, the `Response` object is checked. If a fault occurred, an exception is thrown. Otherwise, the return value that is embedded in the `Response` object is returned.

Now that you understand the invocation handler for creating a SOAP proxy, let's put it to use. Listing 4.16 contains an interface for using the Barnes and Noble Quote Service. The quote service simply returns the price (in U.S. dollars) of a book, given its ISBN. We discovered this service by scanning the web site services.xmethods.net. Using the Web Services Description Language (WSDL) specification of the service, an interface was written for the Barnes and Noble Quote Service. A description of WSDL may be found at www.w3.org/TR/wsdl.

Listing 4.16 A Java interface that corresponds to the Barnes and Noble Quote Service

```
public interface BNQuoteService {

    float getPrice( String isbn );
}
```

With the interface declared and with our general SOAP invocation handler, the test program to acquire the price of *The Three Musketeers* is easy to write. Listing 4.17 shows such a program. The arguments for the call to `createSoap-Proxy` come from the WSDL description of the Quote Service.

Listing 4.17 Checking a price through the Barnes and Noble Quote Service

```
import org.apache.soap.rpc.*;
import java.net.URL;
import java.util.Vector;

public class SoapClientTest {

    public static void main( String[] args ) {
        String servicesURL
            = "http://services.xmethods.net:80/soap/servlet/rpcrouter";
        try {
            BNQuoteService quoter
                = (BNQuoteService) SoapInvocationHandler.createSoapProxy(
                    new Class[] {BNQuoteService.class},
                    new URL(servicesURL),
                    "urn:xmethods-BNPriceCheck",
                    "http://schemas.xmlsoap.org/soap/encoding/" );

            System.out.println( "Price is: "
                                + quoter.getPrice("0192835750") );
        }
```

```
        catch (Exception ex) {
            ex.printStackTrace();
        }
    }
}
```

Of course, to write the test program, we got the ISBN from a copy of *The Three Musketeers* in our bookcase. A shopping program that retrieves that price from several suppliers given the title of the book would require the use of more Web services. However, it should be clear that the use of Web services need not be arduous with the help of reflection.

4.9 *Pitfalls of using Proxy*

With respect to ease of use of Proxy, this chapter has painted a pretty picture. However, there are situations for which you must be alert. A tricky situation arises when proxy instances are passed as arguments into contexts that are expecting a real object.

Consider the Point interface and its implementation shown in listing 4.18. Suppose there is a proxy instance for a Point where the invocation handler merely forwards the method call. That is, invoke for the invocation handler is written as follows:

```
public Object invoke( Object proxy, Method method, Object[] args )
                        throws Throwable {
    return method.invoke( target, args );
}
```

When this invoke method forwards the call p.equals(p) where p contains a reference to a proxy instance with a target of type PointImpl1, the return has the value false. This happens because the argument is a proxy instance, which is not of type PointImpl1.

Listing 4.18   Point class

```
public interface Point {
        float getX();
        float getY();
}

public class PointImpl1 implements Point {

    private float x, y;

    public PointImpl1( float x, float y ) { this.x = x; this.y = y; }
```

```
public float getX() { return x; }
public float getY() { return y; }

public boolean equals( Object obj ) {
    if ( obj instanceof PointImpl1) {
        PointImpl1 p = (PointImpl1)obj;
        return p.x == x && p.y == y;
    }
    else
        return false;
}
}
```

Now, consider another `Point` implementation shown in listing 4.19. Using this implementation, `p.equals(p)` returns the expected value, `true`. The difference between the two implementations is that while the first accesses values through the concrete implementation, the second accesses these same values but through the interface. The second succeeds because the proxy instance understands how to respond to the interface.

Listing 4.19 `PointImpl2` **class**

```
public class PointImpl2 implements Point {

    private float x, y;

    public PointImpl2( float x, float y ) { this.x = x; this.y = y; }
    public float getX() { return x; }
    public float getY() { return y; }

    public boolean equals( Object obj ) {
        if ( obj instanceof Point) {
            Point p = (Point)obj;
            return p.getX() == x && p.getY() == y;
        }
        else
            return false;
    }
}
```

The general rule is if a class is expected to be proxied, a method parameter that has that class as its type should be accessed through the interface. This can be problematic if the interface does not provide the necessary access (as would be the case if `Point` interface did not have both accessors).

4.10 Summary

In addition to creating a substitute for an individual object, Proxy is an effective tool for adding properties to objects. Separating wrapping code, such as tracing, into an invocation handler gives developers one place to write, test, debug, and modify the code that implements the property. Proxy keeps concerns from becoming entangled with the business logic. Proxy also allows developers to reuse code in other applications. Proxy can be profitably used any time code needs to execute before or after some or all methods of an interface.

Further, Proxy relieves developers from the tedium of repeatedly writing the same code all over an application. With its programmatic introspection of argument interfaces, Proxy is not error-prone. Proxy is not fragile to interface updates because it binds to interfaces at runtime.

Proxy is also the only way to dynamically create classes from inside the Java programming language. Dynamic class creation yields several benefits. Without Proxy, developers are required to maintain hierarchies of proxy implementation classes. Proxy allows developers to specify, in Java, how to create a proxy implementation given some interfaces. All of the implementation classes are created at runtime, leaving only the specification to be maintained by the developers.

This specification also allows the creation of proxy classes for interfaces that were not available when the application was compiled. This means that Proxy can work with dynamic loading to enhance application flexibility.

The use of Proxy increases flexibility by creating modules that concentrate the code needed to give properties to an object and that may be easily reused in other contexts. Such increases in flexibility can be translated into increased profits. There is a performance impact for the extra level of indirection, which can be measured with the techniques presented in chapter 9. In addition, chapter 7 presents additional techniques for attaining flexibility when interfaces are not available.

Call stack introspection

In this chapter

- Examining the call stack
- Using call stack introspection
- Avoiding infinite recursion during method intercession
- Checking class invariants

Introspection includes more than the structure of an application. Information about the execution state of the running application is also useful for increasing flexibility. Java has metaobjects that represent the execution state of the running program, including metaobjects that represent the call stack.

Each thread of execution has a call stack consisting of stack frames. Each frame in the call stack represents a method call. Stack frames contain information such as an identification of the method, the location of the statement that is currently executing, the arguments to the method, local variables and their values, and so on. Each stack frame represents the method last called by the method in the frame below it. In Java, the frame at the bottom of a call stack represents the main method of an application or the run method of a thread.

Call stack introspection allows a thread to examine its context. This context includes the name of the method that it is currently executing and the series of method calls that led to that method. This information is useful in several ways:

- *Logging*—An application can log more precise messages given this information.

- *Security*—An API can decide whether or not to proceed based upon its caller's package or class.

- *Control flow*—A reflective facility can avoid situations such as infinite recursion.

These and other applications make call stack introspection a useful tool for programmers.

Java supports call stack introspection though an indirect facility. There is no facility to directly modify a call stack or any of its constituent frames. You can consider methods for thread management to be indirect ways to modify the call stack. The rest of this chapter further motivates the use of call stack introspection and details its mechanics in Java.

5.1 George's logging problem

When George first came to WCI, he was given the project of designing and implementing their approach to logging.[1] Logging, as an individual feature, was seen as

---

[1] In JDK 1.4, Java added the logging facility, `java.util.logging`. This facility is useful and flexible. We exclude it here to concentrate on illustrating the details of call stack introspection. In general, the Java logging facility is fairly advanced, providing class name and method name information about the caller. However, it does not provide line numbers or a full stack trace. The scenario in this chapter comes from a real situation faced by a development organization using JDK 1.3, before the release of JDK 1.4.

an opportunity for George to work independently. Because logging is a concern that cuts across all modules, this task was also an opportunity for him to become familiar with the whole code base.

Logging is an important tool for both diagnosing problems and rollback and recovery in an operational application. We concentrate on the mechanics and information flow for a logging API. There are many good resources on the uses for logging, for example, see the *ACM Computing Surveys* article by Elnozahy et al [26].

Tracing, as we presented it in section 4.4, records the entry and exit to a method. As such, tracing is a special kind of logging. Logging is more general because it can record the passing of other control points than method entry and exit, and it records special kinds of events.

Good applications can do quite a bit of logging. For example, figure 5.1 (from [45]) depicts the logging code in Tomcat, which is the servlet container that is the official reference implementation for Java Servlet and Java Server Pages technologies (see jakarta.apache.org/tomcat). The figure is a bar graph where each bar represents the size of a module in the Tomcat implementation. The stripes in each bar represent logging code.

George knows that to be effective, a logging facility must provide metadata in the records that are logged. He decides to log the name of the calling class, the name of the calling method, and the line number where the call was made. The resulting interface to his logging facility is shown in listing 5.1.

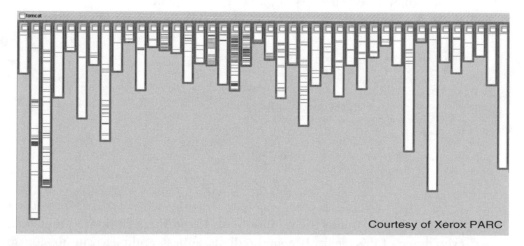

Courtesy of Xerox PARC

Figure 5.1 **The amount of logging in Apache Tomcat. Each vertical bar represents a module. The stripes represent logging code.**

Listing 5.1   Interface to an overly simple logging facility

```
public interface Logger {
    // Types for log records
    public static final int ERROR = 0;
    public static final int WARNING = 100;
    public static final int STATUS = 200;
    public static final int DEBUG = 300;
    public static final int TRACE = 400;

    void logRecord( String className,
                    String methodName,
                    int lineNum,
                    String message,
                    int logRecordType );

    void logProblem( String className,
                     String methodName,
                     int lineNum,
                     Throwable problem );

}
```

In listing 5.1 the five constants are for classifying the log records. The method
`logRecord` writes a log record to whatever medium is used to store such records.
The method `logProblem` does the same for a `Throwable`. The line number argument for each method is a nice bit of metadata to have when examining the program with an interactive development environment.

Here is an example of how George's coworkers would use this facility:

```
public class Dog {
    private Logger log = new LoggerImpl();

    public void bark() {
        ...
        this.log.logRecord( "Dog",
                            "bark",
                            23,
                            "Execution point A passed",
                            Logger.STATUS );
        ...
    }
}
```

George's facility fulfills the requirements for storing the desired metadata. However, usage of this facility becomes tedious, at best, and nearly impossible to maintain, at worst. Typing all of that metadata is fragile. Changes to the surrounding
code can cause changes in the logging calls. The class name and method name

can easily be incorrect if code is copied and pasted or if a class or method is renamed. In addition, if a subclass inherits code that does logging, the logging call still records the name of the superclass. The line number argument is so unstable that this particular interface is not really practical.

Clearly, this metadata should be available without needing to pass it as parameters. Before JDK 1.4, this information was virtually unavailable programmatically. However, JDK 1.4 provides a set of introspective features to make this metadata available. Next we explore call stack introspection and demonstrate how to simplify George's interface.

5.2 *Performing call stack introspection*

To achieve call stack introspection, we are going to need a little programming trick, because there is no accessible call stack metaobject in Java. Instead, when an instance of `Throwable` is created, the call stack is saved as an array of `StackTrace-Element`. By writing

```
new Throwable().getStackTrace()
```

we have access to a representation of the call stack when the `Throwable` was created. Table 5.1 shows the part of the public interface to the Java `Throwable` class relevant to call stack introspection. `Throwable` has always supported the printing of stack traces. In the past, some ingenious developers would turn this into call stack introspection by capturing the output of `printStackTrace`, parsing it, and making it available programmatically. JDK 1.4 alleviates the need for such solutions by including `StackTraceElement` objects that can be obtained from a `Throwable`.

`Throwable` supports a method named `getStackTrace` that returns an array of `StackTraceElement`. These objects provide access to the same information printed by `printStackTrace`. The array returned by `getStackTrace` represents the call

Table 5.1   Relevant interface to `Throwable`

Method	Description
void **printStackTrace**()	Prints this throwable and the call stack to the standard error stream
void **printStackTrace**(PrintStream s)	Prints this throwable and the call stack to the specified print stream
void **printStackTrace**(PrintWriter s)	Prints this throwable and the call stack to the specified print writer
StackTraceElement[] **getStackTrace**()	Returns the call stack as an array of stack trace elements

stack, with each element representing one stack frame and the first representing the most recent method invocation.

Table 5.2 shows the primary interface to a StackTraceElement. Each StackTrace-Element provides information on the class name, method name, and line number for the execution point that it represents, the name of the file that contains the source code, and an indication as to whether or not the method is native.

Table 5.2   The methods defined by StackTraceElement

Method	Description
String **getFileName**()	The name of the source file containing the execution point represented by this stack trace element is returned.
int **getLineNumber**()	The line number of the source line containing the execution point represented by this stack trace element is returned.
String **getClassName**()	The fully qualified name of the class containing the execution point represented by this stack trace element is returned.
String **getMethodName**()	The name of the method containing the execution point represented by this stack trace element is returned.
boolean **isNativeMethod**()	If the method containing the execution point represented by this stack trace element is a native method, true is returned.

By creating a new Throwable, you can perform call stack introspection. Here is a simple example. In Java, instance methods can easily obtain the name of their class with the following line:

```
this.getClass().getName();
```

However, trying to use this code in a static method or initializer yields a compiler error. This error occurs because this cannot be used in a static context. It is necessary to use call stack introspection to obtain the class name from a static context. The following line of code accomplishes that task:

```
(new Throwable()).getStackTrace()[0].getClassName();
```

This is just one problem solved by call stack introspection.

5.3 Logging with call stack introspection

Now let's improve George's logging facility by using call stack introspection. First, we present a better interface in listing 5.2. This interface eliminates those parameters that can be determined reflectively.

Listing 5.2   A better Logger

```
public interface Logger {
    // Types for log records
    public static final int ERROR = 0;
    public static final int WARNING = 100;
    public static final int STATUS = 200;
    public static final int DEBUG = 300;
    public static final int TRACE = 400;

    void logRecord( String message, int logRecordType );

    void logProblem( Throwable problem );
}
```

Listing 5.3 contains an implementation of the `Logger` interface. The second line of `logRecord` constructs a new `Throwable`, making its stack trace information available. Subsequent lines query the stack frame of the caller of `logRecord` to get the necessary metadata.

Listing 5.3   Partial implementation of reflective Logger

```
public class LoggerImpl implements Logger {

    public void logRecord( String message, int logRecordType ) {
        Throwable ex = new Throwable();
        StackTraceElement ste = ex.getStackTrace()[1];

        String callerClassName = ste.getClassName();
        String callerMethodName = ste.getMethodName();
        int callerLineNum = ste.getLineNumber();

        // write of log record goes here
    }

    public void logProblem( Throwable t ) {
        // write of log record goes here
    }
}
```

The implementation is straightforward except for the index into the `StackTrace-Element` array. Remember that the top of the stack contains the call to `logRecord`. Consequently, `logRecord` uses the second element in the array. The change to the logger implementation is only a few lines of code. However, the addition of introspection changes its usability dramatically.

5.4 *Pitfalls*

When an application uses call stack introspection, which stack frame to use becomes an issue. Recall that in the previous example, the logRecord method uses the second stack frame. This works correctly. However, imagine if the other method in the interface is implemented as follows:

```
public void logProblem (Throwable problem) {
    this.logRecord( problem.toString(), ERROR );
}
```

Although this looks like an effective implementation, it is defective because log-Problem adds a stack frame that is unanticipated by logRecord. Therefore, the log entry looks like it was entered by the logProblem method in the Logger class.

This problem may be addressed in several ways according to the circumstances. Enabling the log methods to search the entire call stack for the appropriate frame would be the most general solution. You might think this is simple; however, it presents several difficulties. You could search for the first frame that does not occur in the LoggerImpl class. This search might yield another logger that is delegating to the LoggerImpl. You could search for the first class that does not exist in the logging package. This search prevents the application from providing logging functionality in another package's facade.

A simpler approach is to ensure that the correct stack element is captured when a call enters the facility. This may be done as follows:

```
public void logRecord( String message, int logRecordType ) {
    logMessage( message,
                logRecordType,
                (new Throwable()).getStackTrace()[1]);
}
public void logProblem( Throwable t ) {
    logMessage( t.toString(),
                ERROR,
                (new Throwable()).getStackTrace()[1] );
}
public void logMessage( String message,
                        int logRecordType,
                        StackTraceElement ste )
{
    String callerClassName = ste.getClassName();
    String callerMethodName = ste.getMethodName();
    int callerLineNum = ste.getLineNumber();

    // write of log record goes here
}
```

The implementations of `logRecord` and `logProblem` each pass the correct stack trace element to `logMessage`, which does the actual recording of the log entry. The `logMessage` method is public to allow explicit specification of the stack frame in problematic situations. This arrangement ensures that the correct information is entered into the log.

5.5 *Class invariant checking*

George has been presented with another problem. A major wildlife service wants to track the lifecycles of animals. Life spans, diseases, and pregnancies are just some of the conditions that the service wants to track. George is responsible for implementing the class of time intervals used to track the start and end of these conditions. Listing 5.4 presents George's interface, `TimeInterval`, and his first draft of an implementation.

Listing 5.4   The draft implementation of `TimeInterval`

```
import java.util.Date;

/**
 * Class invariant: start() <= end()
 */
interface TimeInterval {
    Date getStart();
    Date getEnd();
}
```

```
import java.util.Date;

public class TimeIntervalImpl1 implements TimeInterval {

    private final Date start;
    private final Date end;

    public TimeIntervalImpl1( Date s, Date e ) {
        start = s;
        end = e;
        assert invariant() : "start>end";
    }

    public Date getStart() { return start; }

    public Date getEnd() { return end; }

    public boolean invariant() { return start.compareTo(end) <= 0; }
}
```

George recognizes that to operate properly, implementations of `TimeInterval` are required to have their start date on or before their end date. He dutifully records this in the comment describing the class. This requirement for implementations of `TimeInterval` is called a class invariant. An **invariant** is a logical condition of the state of a program that is always true, or always true except if control is in some particular piece of code. A **class invariant** is a logical condition that is true for each instance of the class after the instance is constructed and whenever no method of the class is executing. Note that a method is considered to be executing if it is on the call stack, even if that method has passed control by calling another method in the application.

The class invariant for `TimeInterval` is established by the constructor of `TimeIntervalImpl1` and seems to be inviolate. After all, there are only accessor methods and no methods to change the private fields. However, examining the implementation, shows that this invariant can be violated easily from outside the class by any caller that maintains a reference to one of the internal date objects or any caller to one of the accessors.

The problem is that `TimeIntervalImpl1` does not fully encapsulate its components. In this respect, there are two distinct defects. First, in the constructor, `TimeIntervalImpl1` merely assigns the arguments to its private fields rather than making defensive copies. The caller of the constructor may retain access to what becomes the internal parts of a time interval object. Second, the accessors return object references to the internal parts of a time interval. Again, defensive copies should be made.

George quickly fixes the problem with `TimeIntervalImpl2` shown in listing 5.5.[3] `TimeIntervalImpl2` makes defensive copies in both the constructor and the accessors, which means that no outside object holds a reference to the parts of the time interval. Note that in the constructor, a copy constructor is used rather than `clone`, because the incoming arguments may belong to a subclass of `Date` that overrides `clone` in an undesirable manner. `TimeIntervalImpl2` ensures that its instances are fully encapsulated and that the class invariant is inviolate.

Listing 5.5   A fully encapsulated implementation of `TimeInterval`

```
import java.util.Date;

public class TimeIntervalImpl2 implements TimeInterval {

    private final Date start;
```

---

[3] This implementation is based on one we saw in *Effective Java* [7], a book containing many worthwhile lessons for Java programmers.

```
    private final Date end;

    public TimeIntervalImpl2( Date s, Date e ) {
        start = new Date(s.getTime());
        end = new Date(e.getTime());
        assert invariant() : "start>end";
    }

    public Date getStart() { return (Date)start.clone(); }

    public Date getEnd() { return (Date)end.clone(); }

    public boolean invariant() { return start.compareTo(end) <= 0; }
}
```

Writing down the invariants is an important aspect of documenting a class. Maintenance programmers must be informed of the quintessential properties of a class. Classes that are not fully encapsulated need class invariant checking to protect themselves from external code that violates the invariant. A fully encapsulated class can ensure that its class invariants hold based solely on its own code. Nonetheless, checking invariants is useful for fully encapsulated classes to prevent maintenance from inserting code that invalidate invariants.

On recognizing the importance of checking invariants, George decides to provide a facility for his team. First, he specifies an interface, shown in listing 5.6, that all classes using his facility must implement.

> **Listing 5.6 The InvariantSupporter interface**

```
public interface InvariantSupporter {
    boolean invariant();
}
```

George envisions writing a class InvariantChecker with a static method checkInvariant that calls the invariant and provides other services (for example, bypassing invariant checks for customers that require higher performance). With these services in mind, George's facility is a better alternative than establishing a coding standard in which the invariant method is called directly. His teammates would write calls to InvariantChecker.checkInvariant at the beginning and end of every method (remember all return statements count as being the end of a method).

George prototypes the facility with a checkInvariant that merely calls the invariant method and throws IllegalStateException if the class invariant does not hold. His first case is shown in listing 5.7. It contains a problem that demonstrates the wisdom of the decision to write an invariant-checking facility.

Listing 5.7 The Monkey class

```java
public class Monkey implements InvariantSupporter {

    public void hang() {
        InvariantChecker.checkInvariant( this );
        // ...
        // implementation of hang
        // ...
        InvariantChecker.checkInvariant( this );
    }

    public boolean invariant(){
        screech();
        return true;
    }

    public void screech() {
        InvariantChecker.checkInvariant( this );
        // ...
        // implementation of screech
        // ...
        InvariantChecker.checkInvariant( this );
    }
}
```

Monkey is an invariant supporter that exhibits one of the potential pitfalls involved in invariant checking. Its invariant method uses another instance method of Monkey. This causes an infinite recursion, because the invocation of screech immediately calls InvariantChecker.checkInvariant, which calls screech, and so on. Clearly, this is unacceptable.

We could adopt a programming convention that invariants may not call methods on the target object. But such programming conventions are easily forgotten or misunderstood. It is better to avoid programming conventions in favor of more flexible programs. This is accomplished by using call stack introspection to check for the infinite recursion and break it.

Listing 5.8 show the actual implementation of checkInvariant. This implementation looks back in the call stack to see if InvariantChecker.checkInvariant is present. If so, there is an infinite recursion that must be broken by immediately returning. If not, invariant may be called safely.

Listing 5.8   The `InvariantChecker` class

```
public class InvariantChecker {

    public static void checkInvariant( InvariantSupporter obj ) {
        StackTraceElement[] ste = (new Throwable()).getStackTrace();
        for ( int i = 1; i < ste.length; i++ )
            if ( ste[i].getClassName().equals("InvariantChecker")
                    && ste[i].getMethodName().equals("checkInvariant") )
                return;
        if ( !obj.invariant() )
            throw new IllegalStateException("invariant failure");
    }
}
```

The expense of call stack introspection can be avoided with a simpler check. Listing 5.9 shows a different invariant checker that avoids the call stack introspection with a test of a static boolean field. This is accomplished at the expense of funneling all of the class invariant checking in the application into one synchronized static method.

Listing 5.9   The `SynchronizedInvariantChecker` class

```
public class SynchronizedInvariantChecker {

    private static boolean invariantCheckInProgress = false;

    synchronized public static void checkInvariant( InvariantSupporter obj )
    {
        if ( invariantCheckInProgress )
            return;
        invariantCheckInProgress = true;
        if ( !obj.invariant() )
            throw new IllegalStateException("invariant failure");
        invariantCheckInProgress = false;
    }
}
```

If the application is not multithreaded, the `synchronized` modifier may be removed to get a better performing solution. For multithreaded applications, it is not clear which choice for invariant checking (listing 5.8 or listing 5.9) is better. To make the design choice even more complex, the near future will bring us personal computers with multiple processors. Consequently, a faster test at the expense of greater synchronization may not be a good trade-off.

For Java reflective programming, the complexity of multithreading usually has no impact because of the design of the Java Reflection API. This is not true for reflection in general. In languages that have the capability to make dynamic changes to the running program, multithreading can be more problematic. Java reflective programs may only introspect (in particular, a class object may not be changed dynamically and an object may not change the class to which it belongs). Certainly, call stack introspection is one area where the multithreading issues must be addressed. We will see another area in the next chapter (section 6.4).

5.6 *Summary*

Call stack introspection allows a program to obtain information about its static context including class name, method name, and program line number. It also makes dynamic context available such as the sequence of method calls leading to the current one. This information is accessed by examining metaobjects that represent the program's call stack.

Java's call stack introspection facility is somewhat improvised in JDK 1.4. `Throwable` objects are populated with programmatic representation of the call stack when constructed. This representation can be introspected over, but it cannot be changed.

Though improvised, this facility is still useful. Logging components and similar applications can use call stack introspection to obtain context information for recording. Without this ability, context information must be provided by hand, which becomes difficult to maintain.

Using the class loader 6

In this chapter

- What the class loader does
- How to override the class loader and why
- Examples of specialized class loaders

Chapter 3 introduced dynamic loading, the mechanism that allows you to bring new code into a running system. The examples in chapter 3 use `Class.forName` to load new classes. Each class in a Java application is loaded by a **class loader**, an object that constructs a class object from Java bytecodes. The class `java.lang.ClassLoader` is an abstract base class for all Java class loaders. There is a default **system class loader**, which loads class files from the local file system only. However, you can create subclasses of `ClassLoader` that can be very useful.

In this chapter, you will learn that Java provides the capability to define your own class loader and thus intercede in the class-loading process. During that intercession, some metadata is available that is not available from any of the Java metaobjects. With your own specialized class loader, you can record that metadata and use it later. Class loaders also define namespaces, which provides an additional degree of access control. A class loader can vary the location and format of the class files it loads. These considerations make the Java class loader a powerful tool, but also a complicated one. This chapter concentrates on explaining the Java class loader and exposing its practical uses.

Although you may be a bit surprised to find a chapter on class loading in a book about reflection, subclassing the class loader is a form of reflection. The ability to intercede in the loading process unequivocally implies that the class loader is a reflective facility. As this chapter unfolds, the value of specialized classes to the programmer of reflective applications will become clear.

6.1 *George's test problem*

All software development teams, including George's, must plan for and implement regression testing. According to *The Hacker's Dictionary* [83], **software rot** is:

> A hypothetical disease the existence of which has been deduced from the observation that unused programs and features will stop working after sufficient time even if nothing has changed.

Regression testing is intended to stop software rot by exercising parts of an application and validating the results against expected behavior.

Good test practice mandates that you should be able to automatically run the full suite of regression tests (for a unit, component, or product). Rather than creating a shell script for the suite that runs test case after test case, there are considerable advantages to writing a Java program to run the entire suite. For example, you can more easily test whether the correct exceptions are raised when the test program is written in Java. Although this solution is attractive, there is a subtle problem that accompanies using a Java program run the test suite: after running the first test case, all the static fields in the loaded classes must be reinitialized before running the next test case.

One day, the test manager for George's test team comes to him with a request. For each class that has static fields, he wants George to write a static method that reinitializes their values. The test manager has assumed that this is the best way to be certain that his team's test cases begin execution with the static fields having the correct values.

Upon considering the test manager's request, George realizes that the task will be tedious and involve a great deal of upkeep. He also realizes that although a static method has been requested, the true goal is to reinitialize the static fields. George decides to employ his knowledge of reflection to create a better solution.

George knows that static fields are initialized each time a class is loaded. Reloading the classes solves the problem without writing and maintaining additional static initializer methods. He therefore pursues a solution that involves specializing `ClassLoader`. Let's examine `ClassLoader` to see how George can solve his problem.

6.2 Essentials of ClassLoader

At startup, the Java virtual machine loads programs using the system class loader. The system class loader obtains classes in a platform-dependent manner from the local file system. Typically, the `CLASSPATH` environment variable directs the system class loader's search for `.class` files.

Our eventual goal in this chapter is to create specialized class loaders that accomplish useful tasks. However, before specializing class loaders, it is important to understand certain fundamentals. Let's examine how specialized class loaders fit in with the rest of the system.

6.2.1 Understanding the delegation model

Specialized class loaders usually work cooperatively with existing class loaders. Before attempting to load a class, a specialized class loader usually delegates to another loader called its **parent class loader**. The ultimate parent in this loading chain of responsibility is almost always the system class loader.

Figure 6.1 depicts the structure of the delegation model. The class of the system class loader is represented by an unnamed box because the Java documentation does not specify a name for this class. Despite the drawing, it need not be a direct subclass of `ClassLoader`.

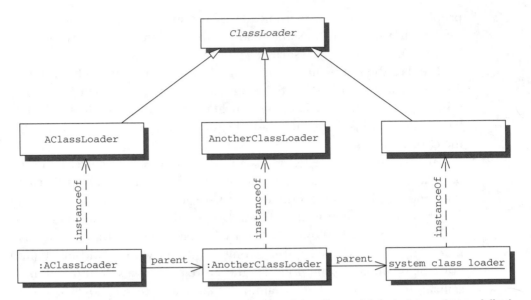

Figure 6.1   UML diagram illustrating the `ClassLoader` delegation model. An instance of a specialized class loader is created with a constructor that allows the specification of a parent class loader. The name of the class of the system class loader is platform-dependent and, consequently, that box is left blank.

ClassLoader is the abstract base class for all class loader objects. It offers two constructors:

```
protected ClassLoader()
protected ClassLoader( ClassLoader parent )
```

Both constructors support the delegation model. The first constructor sets the parent class loader to the system class loader. The second constructor directly supports the delegation model with an extra parameter. The parameter to the second constructor can be null, in which case the constructed loader uses the system class loader as its parent.

ClassLoader introduces methods for supporting class loading and the delegation model. For example, getParent returns the parent loader for a class loader. The system class loader may be retrieved using the static method getSystemClass-Loader. Table 6.1 summarizes the important methods of ClassLoader.

The public method loadClass is where the loading process starts. The JVM loads all classes by making a call to loadClass. The default implementation of loadClass performs the following actions:

1   Calls `findLoadedClass` to check if the class has been loaded already. `ClassLoader` tracks classes that it has already loaded. Subclasses inherit this behavior.

2   If step 1 does not find a loaded class, calls `loadClass` on the parent class loader. In this way, the default implementation of `loadClass` supports the delegation model.

3   If the previous two steps do not produce a class, calls `findClass` to find the class, read its bytecodes, and create the class object using `defineClass`.

4   If the above steps fail to produce a class, throws a `ClassNotFoundException`.

Most class objects are created by executing `defineClass` on a bytecode array. Even `Proxy` classes are created this way. Figure 6.2 illustrates the arrangement of calls in the class loader delegation model.

The class loader that produces a class using `defineClass` is called the class's **defining loader**. A reference to the defining class loader can be obtained with the `getClassLoader` method defined by `Class`. Any class loader that participates in the `loadClass` process for a class is an **initiating loader** for that class. Because of the delegation model, there can be one or more initiating loaders.

Class objects for array classes are created automatically as required by the Java virtual machine (that is, array class objects are not created by class loaders). The

Table 6.1   Methods of `ClassLoader` essential for writing your own class loader

Method	Description
ClassLoader **getParent**()	Final method that returns the parent class loader for the target class loader.
ClassLoader **getSystemClassLoader**()	Static method for accessing the system class loader.
Class **findClass**(String name)	Protected method that obtains the class object for the specified class.
Class **loadClass**(String name)	The public method for loading a class with a specified name—all class loading starts with a call to this method.
Class **defineClass** (String name, byte[] b, int off, int len)	Protected final method that converts an array of bytecodes (having the format of a valid class file as defined by the Java Virtual Machine Specification [60]) into an instance of `Class`. Note that a `SecurityException` is thrown if the name begins with "`java.`"
Class **findLoadedClass**(String name)	Protected final method that finds the class with the given name if it had been previously loaded through this class loader.

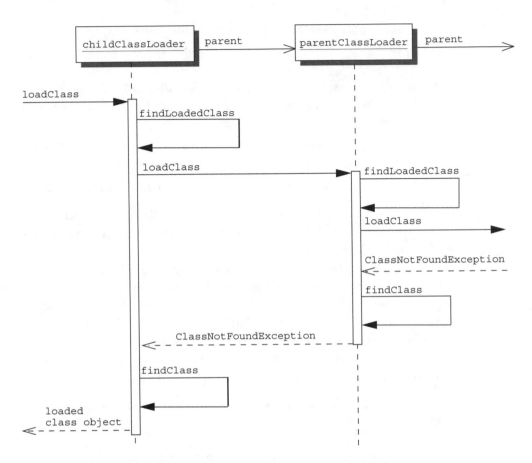

Figure 6.2 Sequence diagram that illustrates the ClassLoader delegation model. All loading begins with a call to loadClass. If the class has not been loaded, the loadClass call is delegated to the parent. If the parent does not load the class (as shown in the diagram), findClass is called to load the class. Note that loadClass implements this sequence diagram.

class loader for an array class, as returned by getClassLoader, is the same as the defining class loader for its element type. If the element type is a primitive type, then the array class object has no class loader and getClassLoader returns null.

Java programmers are strongly encouraged to override findClass rather than loadClass, because the implementation of loadClass defined by ClassLoader supports the delegation model. It is possible to override loadClass, but this is bad form.

6.2.2 *Programming a simple class loader*

Now that you understand the basics of the delegation model, let's examine a simple example of a specialized class loader. If its parent loader cannot find the class, our simple loader searches an auxiliary path to find the class file. In this way, it enables runtime extension of the class path.

This class loader, SimpleClassLoader, is implemented in listing 6.1. The auxiliary path is provided to the constructor and is stored in the string array dirs. Notice that findClass is overridden rather than loadClass. This override reads the .class file with the protected method getClassData, which simply appends to the directory the name of the class being sought.

Listing 6.1 SimpleClassLoader

```java
package simpleclassloader;
import java.io.*;

public class SimpleClassLoader extends ClassLoader {

    String[] dirs;

    public SimpleClassLoader( String path ) {                    ❶
        dirs = path.split(System.getProperty("path.separator") );
    }

    public SimpleClassLoader( String path, ClassLoader parent ) {
        super( parent );
        dirs = path.split(System.getProperty("path.separator") );
    }

    public void extendClasspath( String path ) {
        String[] exDirs = path.split(System.getProperty("path.separator"));
        String[] newDirs = new String[ dirs.length + exDirs.length ];
        System.arraycopy( dirs, 0, newDirs, 0, dirs.length );
        System.arraycopy( exDirs, 0, newDirs, dirs.length, exDirs.length );
        dirs = newDirs;                                          ❷
    }

    public synchronized Class findClass( String name )
        throws ClassNotFoundException
    {
        for ( int i = 0; i < dirs.length; i++ ) {
            byte[] buf = getClassData( dirs[i], name );
            if ( buf != null )
                return defineClass( name, buf, 0, buf.length );   ❸
        }
        throw new ClassNotFoundException();
    }

    protected byte[] getClassData( String directory, String name ){
        String classFile = directory + "/" + name.replace('.','/') + ".class";
```

Constructors correspond to those of `ClassLoader` ❶

Method allows dynamic addition of new paths ❷

`defineClass` is called to create the class object ❸

```
        int classSize
            = (new Long((new File( classFile )).length()))).intValue();
        byte[] buf = new byte[classSize];
        try {
            FileInputStream filein = new FileInputStream( classFile );
            classSize = filein.read ( buf );
            filein.close();
        } catch(FileNotFoundException e){
            return null;
        } catch(IOException e){
            return null;
        }
        return buf;
    }
}
```

Here are some points to note about `SimpleClassLoader`:

❶ The two constructors correspond to those of `ClassLoader`.

❷ The `extendClasspath` method allows the dynamic addition of new paths.

❸ When `findClass` has the desired bytecode array, `defineClass` is called to create the class object.

`SimpleClassLoader` is actually quite a useful alternative to the use of `Class.for-Name`. The system class loader caches the class path at startup, so you cannot change the behavior of the system class loader by performing a `System.setProperty` in `java.class.path` at runtime (see [13]). This means that runtime changes to the class path have no effect on the system class loader. Consequently, `Simple-ClassLoader` is handy for loading from directories known only after the program is loaded.

6.2.3 *Reinitializing static fields: a solution*

George now has the tools to solve his problem: the use of distinct class loaders and of reflective method invocation. He writes the very simple program in listing 6.2 to present to his project's test team. This program loads each test case in a test suite using its own `SimpleClassLoader`.

Listing 6.2   SimpleSuiteTestProgram

```
import java.lang.reflect.*;
import simpleclassloader.*;
public class SimpleSuiteTestProgram {
```

```
        static Class[] formals = { String[].class };
        static Object[] actuals = { new String[]{ "" } };

        public static void main( String[] args ) {
            try {
                for ( int i = 0;; i++ ) {
                    ClassLoader aClassLoader
                        = new SimpleClassLoader( "testcases" );
                    Class c = aClassLoader.loadClass( "TestCase" + i );
                    Method m = null;
                    try {
                        m = c.getMethod( "main", formals );
                    } catch(NoSuchMethodException e){
                        System.out.println( "TestCase" + i
                                        + ": no main in test case" );
                        break;
                    }
                    try {
                        m.invoke( null, actuals );
                    } catch (Exception e) {
                        e.printStackTrace();
                    }
                }
            } catch(ClassNotFoundException e){ } // testing completed
        }
    }
```

The program `SimpleSuiteTestProgram` expects the test cases to be programs in the `testcases` directory. The program also expects test cases named `TestCase0`, `TestCase1`, and so on. No gaps are allowed in the numbering.

Each test case is loaded by a new `SimpleClassLoader` from listing 6.1. After loading a test case with its own loader, the program executes it by finding its static `main` method. This is all that is necessary to install the new loader for the test case, which subsequently loads all of the classes that the test case references. Therefore, the loader for the test case has its own copy of each class, and the statics all get reinitialized.

The simple program to run a test suite in listing 6.2 is far from a production-quality tool, but it does illustrate how such a tool should work. There are publicly available tools, such as JUnit [6], that are much more capable than this simple program. To be sure, the ability to specify the class loader is a consideration in choosing such a tool because of the issue of reinitializing static fields. Let's take a closer look at why George's solution works.

6.3 *Multiple namespaces*

Although a class in the Java language is identified by its fully qualified name, a class object in the virtual machine is actually identified by both its fully qualified name and defining loader. This means that a class loader defines a runtime namespace, which implies the following:

- Your application may use multiple class loaders to load multiple classes that have the same name.
- Two class objects that have different defining loaders are different types even if they are generated from the same class file.

In addition, when a class is loaded by executing defineClass, all classes that it references are also loaded by its defining loader. That is, the JVM loads each referenced class using loadClass on the referencer's defining loader. Note that a call to Class.forName uses the defining loader for the calling object to perform the load.

Let's demonstrate this concretely with the example in listing 6.3. Two class loaders each load the same class, resulting in two distinct class objects. The class, ConstructOnce, is written so that only the first call to its constructor succeeds. Subsequent calls to the constructor result in an IllegalStateException. Successful execution of the newInstance call on the class loaded by second class loader confirms that the two class objects are distinct.

Listing 6.3 SimpleClassLoaderTest

```
import simpleclassloader.*;
public class SimpleClassLoaderTest {

    public static void main( String[] args )
        throws ClassNotFoundException,
               InstantiationException,
               IllegalAccessException
    {
        SimpleClassLoader firstClassLoader
            = new SimpleClassLoader( "testclasses" );
        Class c1 = firstClassLoader.loadClass( "ConstructOnce" );

        SimpleClassLoader secondClassLoader
            = new SimpleClassLoader( "testclasses" );
        Class c2 = secondClassLoader.loadClass( "ConstructOnce" );

        Object x = c1.newInstance();

        try {
            Object y = c1.newInstance();
            throw new RuntimeException("Test fails");
```

```
        } catch( IllegalStateException e ) { }
        Object z = c2.newInstance();
    }
}
```

The test program in listing 6.3 loads the class ConstructOnce in listing 6.4 twice. The test program uses the SimpleClassLoader (listing 6.1) to load ConstructOnce from the directory testclasses. The constructor of ConstructOnce is invoked by the call to newInstance. The constructor fails if it is run more than once, as is illustrated by the try statement in the middle of the main method. The test program successfully completes the try block, because the second newInstance for the class object loaded by c1 throws an IllegalStateException.

Now for the main point of this example. When another class loader (c2) is used to load ConstructOnce, a second class object for ConstructOnce is created that may construct one instance. This shows that the class loaders created distinct class objects and, consequently, separate namespaces.

Listing 6.4 ConstructOnce

```
public class ConstructOnce {
    static private boolean runOnce = false;
    public ConstructOnce() {
        if ( runOnce )
            throw new IllegalStateException("run twice");
        runOnce = true;
    }
}
```

Note that for the test program in listing 6.3 to work, there must be no references to ConstructOnce. The constructors are called using newInstance rather than writing new ConstructOnce(). A reference to ConstructOnce would cause the ConstructOnce class file to be loaded by the system class loader, the defining loader of the test program. Such a reference in SimpleClassLoaderTest causes subsequent references to be successfully handled by findLoadedClass, which implies that the specialized class loader never executes defineClass.

Similarly, ConstructOnce should not be in the class path of the program when run. If it appears in the class path as well as the SimpleClassLoader path, it is visible to the system class loader. This visibility causes the system class loader to load it during the parent call to loadClass, and the SimpleClassLoader never gets to call defineClass.

6.4 *Dynamic class replacement*

Some applications are intended for continuous operation. Taking the application down to change an algorithm may have serious consequences that you need to avoid. Let's stress our understanding of ClassLoader by attacking this challenging problem. A class has three states that may be termed as follows:

- *Unloaded*—An unloaded class exists only as a class file.
- *Loaded*—A loaded class is one for which a class object has been created, but the class object does not yet have either instances, loaded subclasses, or running methods.
- *Active*—An active class has either instances or loaded subclasses or running methods.

Replacing the implementation of an active class is a very challenging problem. This is an on-going area of Java research where complete solutions involve modification to either the compiler, the virtual machine, or both (for example, see [64]). Despite the difficulty of this problem, a Java program can be crafted so that the implementation of an active class may be replaced under reasonable circumstances. The following example demonstrates how to write a program so that you can replace the implementation of a loaded class that, for the sake of simplicity, may have instances but no loaded subclasses.

6.4.1 *Designing for replacement*

Replacement of active classes has two subrequirements. First, you must maintain references to all of its instances. Second, you must have a method for migrating instances from one implementation to another. During replacement, each instance is migrated and replaced. Figure 6.3 presents a design that enables us to replace the implementation of an active class. The design has the following notable features:

- AbstractProduct contains the code that is responsible for keeping track of the instances of the class.
- The replacement class resides in a different package than the original; this eliminates the need to change the name of the class. Each package is loaded with a different class loader.
- Each old instance needs to be mapped into an instance of the replacement class. This design specifies that the replacement class has a static method named evolve that produces a replacement object from an

original object. This isolates the details of evolution in the replacement class where they should be and serves as another example of the application of the Strategy pattern.

- The client code must not hold direct references to instances of the active class. Instead, indirect references are created using `Proxy`, as you learned to do in chapter 4. For this reason, `Product` is introduced as an interface.

The design in figure 6.3 uses the `newInstance` method in `AbstractProduct` to create instances of the implementation of `Product`, but the caller receives a proxy to

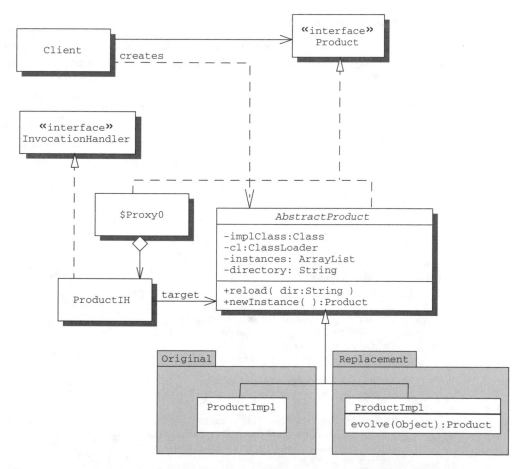

Figure 6.3   Design for dynamically replacing a class. The product is separated from its clients by a Java proxy. The client interface is implemented by the proxy class and an abstract class, which hides the class of the current implementation. Distinct implementations of the product can be loaded by different class loaders.

that instance. In addition, the proxy is stored in a static list of `AbstractProduct` named `instances`, which is used to locate each instance of the implementation of `Product`. The method reload is used initially to load the implementation and subsequently to change the implementation.

This design is another application of the Abstract Factory pattern. However, it is different from the ones described earlier in this book. In those earlier examples, the product implementation classes have distinct names. Here, because of the use of different class loaders, the product implementation classes have the same names. In some contexts, this can be an important advantage.

6.4.2 *Implementing replacement*

Listings 6.5 and 6.6 show the code for `AbstractProduct` and `ProductIH`. First, let's examine `AbstractProduct` in listing 6.5, which defines two static methods, `newInstance` and `reload`.

1 The `newInstance` method uses the class object of the current implementation (stored in `implClass`) to construct a new instance of the product, which is hidden behind a newly created proxy. Reloading the class involves evolving the instances. Consequently, all of the extant instances must be tracked, which is done by adding a weak reference to the proxy to a list named `instances`.

2 The `reload` method loads the new implementation and evolves each existing instance of the old implementation.

Listing 6.5 `AbstractProduct` for dynamic class replacement

```
abstract public class AbstractProduct implements Product {

    static private ClassLoader cl = null;
    static private String      directory = null;
    static private Class       implClass;
    static private List        instances = new ArrayList();

    public static Product newInstance( )
        throws InstantiationException, IllegalAccessException
    {
        AbstractProduct obj = (AbstractProduct)implClass.newInstance();
        Product anAProxy = (Product)ProductIH.newInstance( obj );
        instances.add( new WeakReference( anAProxy ) );
        return anAProxy;
    }

    public static void reload( String dir )
        throws ClassNotFoundException,
```

```
            InstantiationException,
            IllegalAccessException,
            NoSuchMethodException,
            InvocationTargetException
{
    cl = new SimpleClassLoader( dir );        ❶ Constructs new class
    implClass = cl.loadClass( "ProductImpl" );   loader and loads
                                                  implementation

    if (directory == null) {      ❷ If first
        directory = dir;            implementation,
        return;                     return
    }

    directory = dir;
    List newInstances = new ArrayList();

    Method evolve
        = implClass.getDeclaredMethod( "evolve",
                                    new Class[]{Object.class} );

    for ( int i = 0; i < instances.size(); i++ ) {
        Proxy x =(Proxy)((WeakReference)instances.get(i)).get();
        if ( x != null ) {
            ProductIH aih = (ProductIH)Proxy.getInvocationHandler(x);
            Product oldObject = aih.getTarget();
            Product replacement
                = (Product)evolve.invoke( null,
                                        new Object[]{oldObject} );
            aih.setTarget( replacement );
            newInstances.add( new WeakReference( x ) );   Evolves each ❸
        }                                                 instance of
    }                                                     the product
    instances = newInstances;   ❹ Replaces list of
}                                  instances
}
```

Let's look at the `reload` method in detail:

❶ Constructs a new class loader and loads the new implementation.

❷ If the `directory` instance variable is `null`, loads the first implementation. That is, `reload` is also used for the first load.

❸ For `reload` calls after the first, evolves each instance of the product. This is done by iterating through the `instances` list and invoking `evolve`. The `evolve` method returns a new object that is suitable for the new implementation. The new object is stored as the target of the proxy instance, which is known to the clients.

❹ The list of instances is replaced (this is further explained later).

AbstractProduct has an additional nuance to it. Its instances list does not contain direct references to the proxies. If it did, the garbage collector would never free an instance of Product when the client finishes with it.

Instead, weak references are stored in the instances list. WeakReference is part of java.lang.ref. Weak references are constructed with a reference to another object, its **referent**. The referent may be retrieved with a get method. Weak references do not prevent their referents from being garbage collected. After garbage collection of the referent, the get method on a weak reference returns null. When a class is reloaded, a new instances list is created with only weak references with non-null referents.[1]

This design also contains an application of the Proxy pattern (that is, two distinct objects are required). If java.lang.reflect.Proxy were being used to implement some other pattern, AbstractProduct might also implement the InvocationHandler interface. However, in this example, the invocation handler must be retargeted to different implementations of Product, which implies that the invocation handler must be distinct from the target.

Listing 6.6 presents the code for the invocation handler, ProductIH. This invocation handler is straightforward in that its invoke method merely delegates the call to the target. It has a setTarget method, which permits the product object to evolve after its class is replaced. The invocation handler adds value because it hides the real product, making the replacement transparent to clients that use the product.

Listing 6.6   ProductIH, the invocation handler for proxies for Product

```
import java.lang.reflect.*;

class ProductIH implements InvocationHandler {

    private Product target = null;
    static private Class[] productAInterfaces = { Product.class };

    public static Product newInstance( AbstractProduct obj ) {
        return (Product)
            Proxy.newProxyInstance( obj.getClass().getClassLoader(),
                                    productAInterfaces,
                                    new ProductIH( obj ) );
    }

    private ProductIH( AbstractProduct obj ) { target = obj; }
```

---

[1] This simple scheme for handling weak references with null referents may not be the best for all applications, because the data structure holding the weak references may grow large before being compacted.

```
public void setTarget( Product x ){ target = x; }
public Product getTarget( ){ return target; }

public Object invoke( Object t, Method m, Object[] args )
    throws Throwable
{
    Object result = null;
    try {
        result = m.invoke( target, args );
    } catch (InvocationTargetException e) {
        throw e.getTargetException();
    }
    return result;
}
}
```

There are two questions that need to be addressed:

1 The replacement of one implementation of Product with another could be accomplished with implementation classes that have different class names; why go to the bother of having packages to allow the names of the implementation classes to be the same?

2 The packages provide a compile-time namespace; why is it necessary to have distinct class loaders for each package?

Typically, we would like to replace a component rather than a single class. In this case, changing all the names of the classes in the component and the internal references to those classes is a tedious and error-prone process. It is best not to make all of those changes.

Now that we've answered the first questioned, the answer to the second question is apparent. If both the component and its replacement have a large number of common names, the use of distinct class loaders ensures that no reference to the original component can leak into the replacement.

6.4.3 *Simplifying assumptions*

Dynamic class replacement is a good example with which to end this chapter because of the number of concepts that are covered. These concepts include Proxy, the Proxy pattern, extent management (tracking the instances of a class), and the simple class loader. However, we've made a number of simplifying assumptions. Let us discuss them:

- The original class (the one being replaced) is assumed to have no loaded subclasses. Requiring it to be final is the easiest way to deal with this assumption. Barring this, subclasses of the original would have to be replaced, too. This leads to the problem of finding those subclasses, which is extrinsic to the Java reflection API. This subproblem may be solved with a specialized class loader that tracks the inheritance hierarchy of the classes it loads, an exercise we leave to you.

- The use of the proxy is not transparent to reflective code. In our example, three classes, `Product`, `AbstractProduct`, and `ProductImpl`, are used to implement the concept of a dynamically replaceable `Product`. Reflective code may not react as intended to the proxy-target combination. In addition, if an application does manage to obtain a reference to a nonproxied product, after class replacement, that reference becomes stale.

- The example assumes a single-threaded client. Consequently, when the client is reloading the active class, no method of the active class is running. A multithreaded client is much more problematic, depending on the nature of the invariants. If there are only class invariants involving `Product`, then by using a synchronized proxy (like the one programmed in section 4.6.2), you can have the reload method acquire the lock for each proxy before evolving the target object. Stronger invariants require more complex locking schemes.

- Additional capability comes with a cost. The use of the proxy to break the tight coupling between the client and the instances of `Product` has two performance impacts. First, the construction costs are higher because instances of `Proxy` must be constructed as well as instances of `ProductImpl`. Second, each method call to `Product` is implemented as two method calls, one to the proxy and one from the proxy to forward the call. Chapter 9 provides a quantitative discussion of these performance issues.

Despite these limitations, the ability to replace an active class can be great boon to software distribution and management.

6.5 *Additional considerations*

When pondering whether or not to write a specialized class loader, in addition to the issues already discussed in this chapter, there are a number of other considerations:

6.5.1 *Security*

Security in Java has four pillars:

- The Java language and the Java Virtual Machine
- The bytecode verifier
- The security manager
- The class loader architecture

The Java security model (see *Inside Java 2 Platform Security* [40] for a detailed description) is designed to control the execution of untrusted code. The effectiveness of Java security is evident from the innumerable times applets are downloaded with a web browser. This security is all for nought if you load classes from an untrustworthy source. `SimpleClassLoader` is a good base example for this chapter because of the separation of class loading from security.

If you are designing a specialized class loader that might load untrusted code, that design must use the Java security model to control the permissions of untrusted code. In particular, consider subclassing `java.security.SecureClass-Loader`, which is a concrete subclass of `ClassLoader` with protected constructors. `SecureClassLoader` supports the security model by ensuring that any call to its constructors is permitted by the supervising security manager.

Before leaving the topic of security, there is an important heuristic to convey. If your reflective code does not appear to be working according to the Reflection API specification, especially by throwing a `SecurityException`, check for a specialized security manager using `System.getSecurityManager`. Specialized security managers can bar your reflective program from performing its task, for example, when attempting to use `setAccessible` to provide access to private members of a class. This heuristic will help you avoid some vexing problems when debugging reflective code.

6.5.2 *Don't reinvent the wheel*

Although this chapter is a tutorial on how to write a specialized class loader, you should avoid doing this if you can. The JDK contains a usable concrete class loader, `java.net.URLClassLoader`, which is a subclass of `SecureClassLoader`. As its name implies, `URLClassLoader` permits you to specify a URL from which a class can be loaded.

Because a URL can specify a directory in the local file system, `URLClassLoader` subsumes the functionality of `SimpleClassLoader`. Also, `URLClassLoader` permits the use of a `URLStreamHandler` to control the protocol for obtaining class files.

This capability allows the loading of class files by means other than local file access, such as FTP, HTTP, or gopher. Before designing a specialized class loader, you should consider whether one of these two can do the job or serve as a base class.

6.5.3 *Modifying bytecode in a class loader*

Between the reading of the bytecodes and the call to `defineClass`, the bytecodes may be changed. You might wish to change the bytecodes of a class to superimpose a property on the class, similar to what was done with proxies in chapter 4. (Three good papers on this topic are [16], [48], and [52].)

To assist in modifying bytecodes, there is the Jikes toolkit available from IBM [47]. Doing this, of course, requires that you master the Java Virtual Machine specification [60]. A higher-level approach is taken by Javassist (from the Tokyo Institute of Technology [85]) where the bytecode array is converted into a set of Java objects that can be manipulated and then converted back to a bytecode array for `defineClass`. The next two chapters will show how to accomplish similar feats through the use of Java reflection and code generation.

6.5.4 *When not to invent a specialized class loader*

In addition to not duplicating existing class loaders, you should not invent a class loader for reasons that have been overtaken by the evolution of Java technology. The literature about Java is full of such examples of specialized class loaders. Here are a few examples:

- *Compression*—When secondary storage is an issue, class files can be compressed for shipment and decompressed by the class loader.
  Competition: Java has been extended to allow compressed JAR files. A decompressing class loader may offer a finer grained solution, but it may not be worth the development overhead to obtain. In addition, in the case of bulk loading, it may be less efficient than the JAR solution.
- *Security*—When security is an issue, a class loader may examine class files to ensure that they contain a proper digital signature.
  Competition: Signed applets and other prepackaged methods of performing this task have become more common.
- *Self-extracting programs*—If you store the class files of an application as an array of byte arrays, then you can run the application with a special class loader without installing it first.

Competition: A JAR file can be considered an entire application or library in one file. This file has the same portability benefits as the one mentioned previously.

- *Encryption*—If you ship encrypted class files so that they cannot be read by a decompiler, the secure place for the decryption is in the class loader.

  Problem: The decrypting class loader must be shipped unencrypted. Therefore, it can be decompiled and used to defeat the encryption. Another way to circumvent this scheme is claimed in Cracking Java Byte-Code Encryption [78].

6.5.5 *Additional examples*

Despite these examples, there are still many reasons to create a specialized class loader. For example, one of this book's authors worked on a team that developed a virtual file system inside a database for rapid deployment of data files to all system components connected to that database. It was a natural extension to put class files into that virtual file system and allow dynamic patching and extension to all connected system components. To do so, the team implemented a class loader that read from the database file system with SQL and JDBC.

Often, it is useful to know which classes have been loaded into the system and when they were loaded. However, this is beyond the metadata available from the Java Reflection API. This class object loading and timing information is available during the class-loading process, so it can be stored by a specialized class loader, thereby making it available. Java class loading is lazy, that is, a class is loaded when it is needed to resolve a link.

Knowing when a class is loaded may be the key to solving some performance problems. Consider the situation where a user of a graphical user interface (GUI) waits for a while and then starts a process. The classes for the process's objects may not have been loaded at the time when the user issued the command. If this is the case, the JVM must load the classes during the time when the user starts the process, slowing down the responsiveness of the command the first time it is issued.

Such a problem may be solved by preloading particular classes into an application. If those classes are known individually, they can be loaded when the program starts using `forName`. However, this set may change frequently or not all classes may be known at compile time. Writing a specialized class loader for preloading allows preloading of entire JAR files or directories, as well as other custom preloading tasks.

6.5.6 *Endorsed Standards Override*

An **endorsed standard** is an API defined through some standards process other than the Java Community Process. For example, `org.omg.CORBA` is such a package. An endorsed standard may be revised between releases of the Java 2 Platform. Revisions to endorsed standards are placed in JAR files in the `lib\endorsed` directory under the home directory for the Java installation. Depending on your application, your specialized loader may need to be cognizant of this convention in determining the proper class file to load. More information on this topic can be found at java.sun.com/j2se/1.4.2/docs/guide/standards/index.html.

6.6 *Summary*

A specialized class loader gives an application dynamic control over its classes. In particular,

- Which class file gets loaded and used
- Where to search for a class file
- What protocols to use when finding a class file
- When a class file gets loaded (if it is before the first use)

We have concentrated on the first two bullets in this chapter. In addition, a class loader establishes a namespace for the classes that it loads. George used the namespaces defined by class loaders to isolate each test case and force the initialization of static fields. Using a new class loader for each test case turned a difficult problem into an easy one.

`ClassLoader` is considered a reflective facility, because the ability to create a class loader is a form of intercession. When a class is loaded by a specialized class loader, it also loads (and intercedes) in the loading of all referenced classes. This kind of intercession permits a large increase in application flexibility, which ranges from deciding what code is used to implement a class to replacing that code even when the class is active. This degree of flexibility is not achieved with `ClassLoader` alone; it must be achieved in concert with the basic reflective features of Java. For example, when replacing an active class (section 6.4), no reference to the implementation class can be present in the client code. Successfully achieving this requires the dynamic proxy and dynamic invocation provided by `Method`.

Reflective code generation

7

In this chapter

- Why generating code with reflection is useful and easy to do
- A framework that makes code generation easy
- Examples of useful code generators

This chapter and the following chapter deal with the topic of reflective code generation. There are two reasons for taking up this topic:

- Code generation is the all-purpose workaround for the limitations of Java reflection.
- Code generation provides many good examples of the use of the reflection API.

The early chapters show that reflection in Java is basically limited to introspection and does not reach the full vision of reflective capabilities despite the usefulness of `Proxy`. This full vision requires the ability to change the behavior of a program. We can transcend these limitations by generating code. If an introspective program can generate code, compile that code, load that code, and then execute it, then behavior changing capabilities can be simulated.

Our presentation of code generation is accomplished with a framework for writing class-to-class transformations.[1] A **class-to-class transformation** takes a class as an input and generates another class as an output. This requires considerable use of introspective capabilities to examine the class object. This kind of code generation is different from some others you may have seen in that it is easier (for example, introspection obviates the need for a Java parser) and dynamic (generated classes can be loaded into a running program with `forName` or a specialized class loader).

To better understand why class-to-class transformations are valuable, consider the following linguistic interpretation of the evolution of computer programming. In the 1950s and 1960s, programming was about commanding the computer—verbs. In the 1970s, this approach proved deficient. A new paradigm arose in which the specification of abstract data types and then classes—nouns— became foremost for the programmer. This paradigm, object-oriented programming, evolved throughout the 1980s and 1990s.

Although powerful and useful, object-oriented programming has proved deficient in isolating properties of objects in a reusable way—adjectives, which are noun transformers. In other words, the industry has pushed object-oriented programming with only objects, classes, and inheritance to its limit, and out of its breakdown the need arises for a new kind of module. Such a module must play the role of an adjective, that is, the module may be composed with a class (noun)

---

[1] Code generation is a topic with greater breadth than what is discussed in this chapter. There are many books on the broader topic of code generation including [19] and [44].

to get a new class (compound noun) whose instances have the property denoted by the adjective.

Class-to-class transformations are a good way to introduce this new kind of module and teach Java reflection. Aspect-Oriented Programming also addresses this issue. We will come back to the relationship with Aspect-Oriented Programming in section 7.7. Meanwhile, let's check in on George.

A negotiation between Wildlife Components (WCI), George's employer, and a potential major customer is at an impasse. The business of the potential customer is animal population studies. Although each class in the WCI library is superb for modeling the behavior of individual animals, there is no capability to compute the set of all of the individual instances of each class—this set is called the **extent of the class**. Although the customer may program this capability into its application, the customer is demanding that Wildlife Components program this capability into the class library. The customer's goal is to transfer this cost (and the collateral maintenance costs) to Wildlife Components without increasing the contract price. Yielding to this demand is no small matter for Wildlife Components. On one hand, adding the capability to all classes in the library impacts the performance for all other customers. On the other hand, adding a extent-managed version of each library class doubles the size of the library—making it more complex and more costly to maintain.

The sale to this customer is large and important. The Wildlife Components' Vice President of Engineering gathers the development team to discuss the situation. After studying the issue, George proposes to end the impasse with the following compromise: Wildlife Components will create and maintain a code-generation tool that will create an extent-managed subclass of any of its library classes on demand. The customer can then use this tool to generate the classes it needs.

Once again, George is at the center of the action—he must now deliver a solution whereby Wildlife Components neither impacts the performance of its library for other customers nor doubles the size of its library. As George foresees, if properly implemented as a framework, the code-generation tool can provide the basis for many other code-generation tools.

7.1 Generating HelloWorld.java

To illustrate the process of generating and executing Java code, let's consider how to write a program that writes and executes a "Hello world!" program. The program in listing 7.1 writes a character stream to the `HelloWorld.java` file. It then uses `Runtime.exec` to compile[2] the file and loads the compiled class using `Class.forName`. Finally, the program runs the generated class using `invoke` to execute the `main` method of the generated class, which prints the "Hello world!" message.

Listing 7.1   A convoluted way to write a "Hello world!" program

```java
public class HelloWorldGenerator {

    public static void main( String[] args ) {

        try {
            FileOutputStream fstream
                = new FileOutputStream( "HelloWorld.java" );
            PrintWriter out = new PrintWriter( fstream );
            out.println(
                    "class HelloWorld {                              \n"
                + "     public static void main( String[] args ) { \n"
                + "         System.out.println( \"Hello world!\" );\n"
                + "     }                                           \n"
                + "}                                                "
                );
            out.flush();
            Process p
                = Runtime.getRuntime().exec( "javac HelloWorld.java" );

            p.waitFor();

            if ( p.exitValue() == 0 ) {
                Class outputClassObject = Class.forName( "HelloWorld" );

                Class[] fpl = { String[].class };
                Method m = outputClassObject.getMethod( "main", fpl );

                m.invoke( null, new Object[]{ new String[] {} } );

            } else {
                InputStream errStream = p.getErrorStream();
                for ( int j = errStream.available(); j > 0; j-- )
                    System.out.write( errStream.read() );
            }
        } catch(Exception e){
            throw new RuntimeException(e);
        }
    }
}
```

---

[2] The package `com.sun.tools.javac` in the `tools.jar` of the JDK is a direct interface to the Java compiler. There is a class named `Main` whose main method is invoked with the string argument array that you would give to `javac`. This book does not use that interface because it is not standard and not documented. In addition, note that prior to Java 1.4, the JDK license forbade redistribution of `tools.jar`.

The program in listing 7.1 is simple, but on some platforms, it may permanently block at the `waitFor` if there is a compilation error in the generated program. See the Java documentation on `Process` for more details. Appendix B presents another, longer version of this program that uses polling to avoid this blocking problem.

Listing 7.1 can only generate a single program. Instead, we might have a code generator that loads a class specified by a command-line parameter and, subsequently, generates a new class from information acquired by introspecting on the loaded class. Properly combining code generation with introspection leads to the notion of a class-to-class transformation.

7.2 Class-to-class transformation framework

We might produce a separate code-generation program that looks much like listing 7.1 for each class-to-class transformation. However, this would involve a large amount of repetition of the basic elements of the specialized code generators for class-to-class transformation. These basic elements include parameter processing as well as the management of the generated `.java` file, its compilation, and the loading of the corresponding `.class` file. A better idea is produce a framework that allows for succinct coding of transformations, because these basic elements of class generation are shared.

Figure 7.1 contains a class diagram for such a framework. The three abstract classes, `C2C` (for class-to-class), `C2CConstructor`, and `C2CTransformation`, are used to create transformations. `C2CException` is used to indicate that some exception has been encountered during the code-generation process (the framework is pedagogical, not production code; consequently, error handling is minimal). The other two auxiliary classes, `Args` and `UQueue`, are explained as we go along.

A class-to-class transformation is an object, specifically, an instance of a concrete subclass of `C2C`. Most transformations are created by subclassing `C2CTransformation`, which is given an **input class** from which it produces an **output class**. In some cases, you need to produce a particular output class without an input class. In such situations, you subclass `C2CConstructor`. There are also other command-line arguments that can be used to control a transformation. Some are general and defined by the framework, while others are specific to particular transformations.

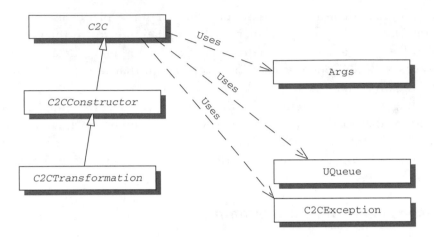

Figure 7.1 Class diagram for the class-to-class transformation framework

7.2.1 C2C

Listing 7.2 shows the C2C abstract class. It begins with a set of fields that are used to control the generation process. The principal part of the class is the method createClass, which is an application of the Template Method pattern [38]. The best way to explain the workings of the framework is to step through the code, especially the execution sequence of createClass describing the abstract methods, as we go along. Note that one of our framework conventions is that all abstract methods that begin with the prefixes check or generate are cooperative methods, that is, they must make a super call.

Listing 7.2 The C2C abstract class

```
package c2c;
import java.io.*;
import mopex.UQueue;

public abstract class C2C {
    protected String  classNamePrefix;
    protected Class   inputClassObject;
    protected String  inputClassName = null;
    protected String  outputClassName;
    protected Class   outputClassObject;
    protected String  packageName;
    protected String  qualifiedInputClassName = null;
    protected String  qualifiedOutputClassName;
```

❶ Instance variables that store the values of the command-line arguments

```
boolean isAbstract;
protected final void setAbstract() { isAbstract = true; }
protected final boolean isAbstract() { return isAbstract; }

boolean isFinal;
protected final void setFinal() { isFinal = true; }
protected final boolean isFinal() { return isFinal; }

boolean isInterface;
protected final void setInterface() { isInterface = true; }
protected final boolean isInterface() { return isInterface; }

boolean isNotPublic;
protected final void setNotPublic() { isNotPublic = true; }
protected final boolean isNotPublic() { return isNotPublic; }

public final Class createClass( String[] args ) {

    classNamePrefix = generateClassNamePrefix();

    Args myArgs = new Args(args);
    checkAndProcessArgs( myArgs );

    if ( !myArgs.complete() )
        throw new C2CException( "Usage: unprocessed flags: "
                                + myArgs.toString( ) );

    UQueue itQ = generateInterfaces();
    UQueue importQ = generateImports();

    String aClassString =
        (packageName==null ? "" : "package " + packageName + ";\n")
        + (importQ.isEmpty() ? "" : "import "
                                + importQ.toString(";\nimport ")
                                + ";\n")
        + getClassLevelJavadoc()
        + (isNotPublic?"":"public ")
        + (isFinal?"final ":"")
        + (isAbstract?"abstract ":"")
        + (isInterface?" interface ":" class ") + outputClassName + "\n"
        + (getSuperclass().equals("") ? "" : "    extends "
                                            + getSuperclass()
                                            + "\n")
        + (itQ.isEmpty() ? "" : "    implements " + itQ.toString(", ") )
        + "{\n//============ F I E L D S =====================\n"
        + generateFields()
        + "\n//============ C O N S T R U C T O R S ==========\n"
        + generateConstructors()
        + "\n//============ M E T H O D S ===================\n"
        + generateMethods()
        + "\n//============ N E S T E D   C L A S S E S =====\n"
        + generateNestedClasses()
        + "}\n";

    try {
```

② **Boolean instance variables that deal with class modifiers**

③ **Computes prefix for output class name**

④ **Handles arguments to the transformation**

⑤ **Accumulates information about imports and implemented interfaces**

⑥ **The heart of `createClass` is the string assignment**

```
                    FileWriter outputFile
                        = new FileWriter( outputClassName + ".java" );
                    outputFile.write( aClassString );
                    outputFile.close();

                    String cp = System.getProperty( "java.class.path" );
                    Process p =
                        Runtime.getRuntime().exec( "javac -source 1.4 -classpath \""
                                            + cp
                                            + "\" "
                                            + outputClassName
                                            + ".java");
                    p.waitFor();                                Writes output class to an  ❼
                                                               appropriate file and compiles it
                    if ( p.exitValue() == 0 ) {

                        outputClassObject =                            ❽ Loads
                            Class.forName(qualifiedOutputClassName);      output
                                                                         class
                    } else {
                        InputStream errStream = p.getErrorStream();
                        for ( int j = errStream.available(); j > 0; j-- )
                            System.out.write( errStream.read() );
                        throw new C2CException( "compile fails " + p.exitValue() );
                    }
                } catch(Exception e){ throw new C2CException(e); }

                checkPostconditions();   ❾ Checks for conflicts with other transformations

                System.out.println( outputClassName + " compiled and loaded" );

                return outputClassObject;
            }
        abstract protected String generateFlags();
        abstract protected String generateClassNamePrefix();
        abstract protected void   checkAndProcessArgs( Args args );
        abstract protected UQueue generateImports();
        abstract protected String getClassLevelJavadoc();       Declaration  ❿
        abstract protected String getSuperclass();              of the methods
        abstract protected UQueue generateInterfaces();         that concrete
        abstract protected String generateFields();             subclasses
        abstract protected String generateConstructors();       override
        abstract protected String generateMethods();
        abstract protected String generateNestedClasses();
        abstract protected void   checkPostconditions();
    }
```

Let's examine the **C2C** abstract class in detail:

❶ These are instance variables that store the values of the general command-line arguments defined by the framework. Concrete transformations may read these instance variables but must not change them. (A production version would make these variables private with protected accessors, but we have not done so here in order to make the framework more readable.)

❷ There are four boolean instance variables that deal with class modifiers. These may be set on the command line. In addition, they may be set by subclasses but not reset.

❸ generateClassNamePrefix is called in order to compute the default name of the output class, which is the prefix followed by the name of the input class. For example, if the input class is named Dog and the computed prefix is Synchronized, the default name of the output class is SynchronizedDog. There is a command-line argument (-output) for explicitly naming the output class.

❹ checkAndProcessArgs is called to handle the arguments to the transformation from a command line. The checkAndProcessArgs method is a cooperative method; that is, every subclass is given a chance to process elements of the argument array. See section 7.2.2 for the definition of the Args class and details of cooperative argument processing. checkAndProcessArgs is responsible for setting the instance variables declared in C2C. In particular, checkAndProcessArgs sets the input class name (inputClassName) and input class object (inputClassObject).

❺ The generateImports and generateInterfaces methods are called to generate data structures with the names of the packages to import and the interfaces that the output class is to extend. UQueue is a queue container class whose add operation does nothing if the element to be added is already in the queue. The UQueue class is not presented until section 7.5. Until then, the workings of its operations should be evident from their names except for toString(String). This operation returns a string of the entries in the queue where the separator is determined by the specified argument.

❻ The heart of createClass is the string assignment that mimics the Java syntax rules for creating a top-level class in a single file. The calls to generateFields, generateConstructors, generateMethods, and generateNestedClasses perform most of the work. For the sake of more readable code, we chose to use strings throughout the presentation of the class-to-class transformation framework. A production version would use StringBuffer to obtain better performance.

❼ The string for the output class is written to an appropriate file and that file is compiled. Note that the compilation uses the "-source 1.4" flag, which permits the use of assert statements. In addition, we have found that when there are compilation errors, the waitFor command does not terminate on all platforms. For this reason, we present an alternative that polls the compilation process for completion using exitValue in appendix B.

❽ The output class is loaded using Class.forName, and the object class object is stored in outputClassObject for use in the return statement. The use of Class.forName assumes that the qualified class name and the classpath combine to allow the loading of the class that was compiled a few statements earlier. For simplicity, this check has been omitted.

❾ checkPostconditions is called to execute checks on the output class object using the introspective operations of Java reflection. The purpose of checkPost-conditions is to allow a transformation writer to ensure than no other transformation (for example, implemented by a subclass) has generated code that is in conflict with the desired transformation. At times, such a check may be extrinsic to the Java reflection API.

❿ These are the methods that concrete subclasses of C2C override to fill out the template provided by createClass.

When programming a transformation (a subclass of one of the descendents of C2C), you usually create a static main to invoke createClass so that the transformation may be used from the command line. In addition, there are situations where invoking createClass directly is a very handy capability.

7.2.2 Args

The Args class contains a set of static methods for the cooperative processing of a command-line argument array. The fundamental idea is that a subclass of C2C scans the array for either a known flag or a flag followed by a parameter. Each known flag or flag-parameter pair is processed, and the flag is marked as processed. The methods of Args are used in implementing overrides of checkAndProcessArgs. An override of checkAndProcessArgs is required to perform a super call before looking for its own flags. The methods implemented in Args are defined as follows:

> *String **getFlagValue**(String flag)*—The args array is searched for flag. If found, the entry following the flag is returned and both the flag and the following entry are marked as processed. If the flag is not found in the args array, null is returned.

> *UQueue **getFlagValues**(String flag)*—At times, a flag-value pair may be repeated in the arguments (for example, -imports). The getFlagValues method returns a queue of all the values associated with flag. This is

accomplished with multiple calls to `getFlagValue`; consequently, the matching flag entries and the associated values are marked as processed. If no flags are found, an empty queue is returned.

boolean **hasFlagValue**(*String flag*)—The `args` array is searched for `flag`. If found, `true` is returned and the flag is marked as processed. If the flag is not found among the command-line arguments, `false` is returned.

String **getLast**( )—The last argument of the `args` array is returned. When `getLast` is used, the last argument is expected to be the name of the input class.

boolean **complete**( )—Returns `true` if all of the command-line arguments have been processed and `false` otherwise.

String **toString**( )—Returns a string that represents the command-line arguments.

For completeness, listing 7.3 contains the implementation of these methods.

Listing 7.3   The `Args` class

```java
package c2c;
import java.util.Vector;
import mopex.UQueue;

public class Args {

    private String[] args;
    private boolean[] argProcessed;

    Args( String[] cmdArgs ) {
        args = cmdArgs;
        argProcessed = new boolean[ args.length ];
    }

    public String getLast() {
        if ( args[args.length-1].charAt(0) == '-' )
            return null;
        String returnValue = args[args.length-1];
        argProcessed[args.length-1] = true;
        return returnValue;
    }

    public String getFlagValue( String flag ) {
        for ( int i = 0; i < args.length-1; i++ )
            if ( !argProcessed[i] && !argProcessed[i+1]
                              && args[i].equals(flag)
                              && args[i].charAt(0) == '-'
                              && args[i+1].charAt(0) != '-' ) {
```

```
                    String returnValue = args[i+1];
                    argProcessed[i] = true;
                    argProcessed[i+1] = true;
                    return returnValue;
            }
        return null;
    }

    public UQueue getFlagValues( String flag ){
        UQueue  values = new UQueue( String.class );
        String value = getFlagValue( flag );
        while ( value != null ) {
           values.add(value);
           value = getFlagValue( flag );
        }
        return values;
    }

    public boolean hasFlag( String flag ) {
        for ( int i = 0; i < args.length; i++ )
            if ( args[i] != null && args[i].equals(flag)
                            && args[i].charAt(0) == '-' ) {
                argProcessed[i] = true;
                return true;
            }
        return false;
    }

    public boolean complete(){
        for ( int i = 0; i < argProcessed.length; i++ )
            if ( !argProcessed[i] )
                return false;
        return true;
    }

    public String toString(){
        String result = "";
        for ( int i = 0; i < args.length; i++ )
            if ( !argProcessed[i] )
                result += args[i] + " ";
        return result;
    }
}
```

7.2.3 *C2CConstructor*

Some transformations require no input class, because the output class is generated from other parameters. The base class for such transformations is
C2CConstructor, whose implementation is contained in listing 7.4. C2CConstructor
also provides the default implementations for the abstract methods declared in

C2C. The most significant of these default implementations is checkAndProcess-Args, which defines the standard command-line flags for all transformations. These standard flags are defined as follows:

-abstract—This flag indicates that the output class is to be abstract.

-final—This flag indicates that the output class is to be final.

-import xxxxx—This flag-value pair specifies that an import statement is to be generated for xxxxx. This flag-value may be used multiple times in the argument array.

-interface—This flag indicates that the output code is an interface instead of a class.

-notpublic—This flag indicates that the output class is to have package visibility. The default is for the output class to be public.

-output zzzzz—This flag-value pair specifies that the name of the output class is to be zzzzz. This name may be qualified. The name of the generated Java file is this name with .java appended. A C2CConstructor that is not a C2CTransformation must have this flag specified. (In the next section, we see that there is a default name for a C2CTransformation).

-package yyyyy—This flag-value pair specifies that the output class is to be in the package yyyyy.

Some of these flags conflict with one another because of the specification of Java. For example, -abstract and -final cannot be used together. Consistent with our pedagogical goals, there are no checks for these conflicts; instead, such checks manifest themselves as compilation errors.

Listing 7.4 The C2CConstructor class

```
package c2c;
import mopex.UQueue;

public abstract class C2CConstructor extends C2C {

    private   UQueue  cmdLineImports;

    protected String generateFlags() {
        return "[-notpublic] [-final] [-abstract] "
            + "[[-import name]...] [-package name] [-output name]";
    }

    protected String generateClassNamePrefix() { return ""; }

    protected void checkAndProcessArgs( Args args ) {
```

Produces a string for usage and help messages ❶

```
        outputClassName = args.getFlagValue( "-output" );      ❷
        if ( outputClassName == null )                          Sets
            if ( inputClassName == null ) {                     output
                throw new C2CException( "no output class name");  class
            } else {                                            name
                outputClassName = classNamePrefix + inputClassName;
            }


        packageName = args.getFlagValue( "-package" );      ❸ Sets the
        if ( packageName == null )                            qualified
            qualifiedOutputClassName = outputClassName;       output class
        else                                                  name
            qualifiedOutputClassName
                = packageName + "." + outputClassName;


        isNotPublic = args.hasFlag( "-notpublic" );      ❹ Sets modifiers for
        isFinal = args.hasFlag( "-final" );                 the output class
        isInterface = args.hasFlag( "-interface" );
        isAbstract = args.hasFlag( "-abstract" );


        cmdLineImports = args.getFlagValues( "-import" );  ❺ Enqueues import
                                                              package name
        if ( outputClassName.equals( inputClassName ) )
            throw new C2CException("outputClassName = inputClassName");
    }

    protected UQueue       generateImports() {return cmdLineImports;}
    protected String       getClassLevelJavadoc() {return "";}
    protected String       getSuperclass() {return "";}
    protected UQueue       generateInterfaces() {
        return new UQueue(String.class);
    }
    protected String       generateFields() {return "";}
    protected String       generateConstructors() {return "";}
    protected String       generateMethods() {return "";}
    protected String       generateNestedClasses() {return "";}
    protected void         checkPostconditions() {}
}
```

Let's examine C2CConstructor in more detail:

❶ The generateFlags method produces a string for usage and help messages. A subclass of C2CConstructor is obligated to add to this string if it has additional command-line arguments.

❷ If the -output flag is not present in the command line, this line uses the prefix and the input class name to generate the default output class name. Note that inputClassName is set in C2CTransformation.

❸ If -package appears in the command line, the qualified output class name is set differently from the output class name.

❹ The modifiers for the output class are set. Note that once set, these instance variables cannot be unset.

❺ Imports from the command line are used to initialized the queue from which import directives are generated. A subclass of C2CConstructor may add to this queue.

Now that we have programmed C2CConstructor, enough framework exists to present a different implementation of a "Hello world!" program. Listing 7.5 presents a subclass of C2CConstructor that generates a "Hello world!" program similar to what is presented in listing 7.1. The command line

```
java HelloWorldConstructor -output HelloWorld
```

produces a program equivalent to the one produced by the generator in listing 7.1.

Listing 7.5   The C2CConstructor for a "Hello world!" program

```
public class HelloWorldConstructor extends C2CConstructor {

    static public void main( String[] args ) {
        new HelloWorldConstructor().createClass( args );
    }

    protected String generateMethods() {
        return super.generateMethods()
            + "    public static void main( String[] args ) { \n"
            + "        System.out.println( \"Hello world!\" );\n"
            + "    }                                           \n";
    }
}
```

C2CConstructor provides a good base for generating classes when introspection on another class is not needed. When introspection is needed, we use C2CTransformation.

7.2.4   *C2CTransformation*

C2CTransformation is used to program a transformation that maps an input class to an output class. C2CTransformation extends C2CConstructor so that an input class can be specified as the last entry in the argument array. To do so, checkAndProcessArgs is overridden, as shown in listing 7.6. This override extracts the qualified input class name from the arguments array before making the super call to process the other arguments. Afterward, the input class is loaded with Class.forName, which also sets the field inputClassObject. Once the input class object is loaded, the transformation has its most important object upon which to apply Java reflection.

Listing 7.6 The C2CTransformation class

```
package c2c;

public abstract class C2CTransformation extends C2CConstructor {

    protected String generateFlags() {
        return super.generateFlags() + " inputClassName";        ◁──  Appends class
    }                                                               ❶ name parameter

    protected void checkAndProcessArgs( Args args ){
        qualifiedInputClassName = args.getLast();
        int i = qualifiedInputClassName.lastIndexOf(".");          ❷
        if ( i == -1 )                                           Strips away
            inputClassName = qualifiedInputClassName;       qualifier to set the
        else                                                 input class name
            inputClassName = qualifiedInputClassName.substring(i+1);

        super.checkAndProcessArgs( args );              Loads the input class  ❸

        try {
            inputClassObject = Class.forName( qualifiedInputClassName );  ◁──┘

            if ( inputClassObject.isArray()
                 || inputClassObject.getDeclaringClass() != null
                 || inputClassObject.isPrimitive() )
                throw new C2CException("illegal class");
        } catch (ClassNotFoundException e) {          Eliminates primitive  ❹
            throw new C2CException(e);              classes, array classes, and
        }                                            nested classes as inputs
    }
}
```

Let's examine C2CTransformation in more detail:

❶ The generateFlags method is overridden to add the input class to the description of the command line.

❷ The input class name on the command line is expected to be fully qualified. The qualifier is stripped away to get the class name. This is done in case a default output class name needs to be generated. Note that this must be done prior to the super call to checkAndProcessArgs in C2CConstructor.

❸ The input class is loaded. Note that if the input class is not present in the command line, this load fails (unless the last command-line argument happens to be a loadable class not intended to be the input class).

❹ This test eliminates primitive classes, array classes, and nested classes from being inputs. Experience has shown that the definition of transformations for nested classes is a complex topic and appears to have little benefit. (Note that forName in Java 1.4 fails when given the name of a primitive class, and the isPrimitive test is not necessary. However, this quirk of forName has generated enough complaints that it may be changed in some future release of Java.)

We have now defined enough of the C2C framework to present an interesting and useful transformation.

7.3 *Example: extent management*

Now that he has prepared the way with the C2C framework, George can easily create the code-generation tool that was promised in the negotiation with Wildlife Components' customer. The tool enables a class to compute its extent, which is the set of instances of that class or any of its subclasses. Computing the extent of a class is another extrinsic property of the Java reflection API. That is, there is no direct way to use the reflection API to find the extent of a class. However, a transformation can be written that generates a subclass that manages its extent.

Listing 7.7 contains C2ExtentManagedC, a subclass of C2CTransformation that has three essential parts:

- There is a private field named myExtent that is inserted into the class with a generateFields override. Note that a WeakReference is used to store each element of the extent so as to allow garbage collection of these elements.

- Each constructor of the input class is paralleled in the output class. In each of these new constructors, a weak reference to each new instance is stored in myExtent. These parallel constructors are generated in the override to generateConstructors. Note that if the input class has no declared constructors, a constructor with no parameters is generated in the output class.

- A new static method named getExtent is generated that allows the extent to be retrieved. This method is generated in the override to generateMethods.

In addition to the above, the output class is made a subclass of the input class.

Listing 7.7 The `C2ExtentManagedC` transformation

```
package c2c;
import java.lang.reflect.*;
import java.io.Serializable;
import mopex.*;

public class C2ExtentManagedC extends C2CTransformation {

    private int numberOfConstructors = 0;

    static public void main( String[] args ) {
        new C2ExtentManagedC().createClass( args );
    }

    protected UQueue generateImports() {
        return super.generateImports()
                    .add("java.util.Vector")
                    .add("java.lang.ref.*");
    }

    protected String generateClassNamePrefix() {
        return "ExtentManaged" + super.generateClassNamePrefix();
    }

    protected String getSuperclass() {return inputClassName;}

    protected void checkAndProcessArgs( Args args ) {
        super.checkAndProcessArgs( args );
        if ( Serializable.class.isAssignableFrom(inputClassObject) )
            throw new C2CException("refuse Serializable input classes");
        if ( Cloneable.class.isAssignableFrom(inputClassObject) )
            throw new C2CException("Cloneable and Singleton conflict");
    }

    protected String generateFields() {
        return super.generateFields()

            + "    static private Vector myExtent = new Vector();\n";
    }

    protected String generateConstructors() {
        String managementCode =
            "    myExtent.add( new WeakReference(this) );\n";
        String overriddenConstructors = "";
        Constructor[] cArray = inputClassObject.getDeclaredConstructors();
        if ( cArray.length != 0 ) {
            for (int i = 0; i < cArray.length; i++ )
                overriddenConstructors
                    += Modifier.toString( cArray[i].getModifiers() )
                    + " "
                    + Mopex.createRenamedConstructor( cArray[i],
                                                      outputClassName,
                                                      managementCode );
```

① Creates a transformation object and calls `createClass`

② Adds required packages to queue

③ Prepends the property name

④

⑤ Rejects Cloneable or Serializable input classes

⑥ Adds static field to track the extent

⑦ Generates constructors that add to the extent

```
                numberOfConstructors = cArray.length;
            } else {
                overriddenConstructors = outputClassName
                                + "()\n     {\n"
                                + managementCode
                                + "     }\n";
                numberOfConstructors = 1;
            }
            return super.generateConstructors() + overriddenConstructors;
        }
        protected String generateMethods() {
            return super.generateMethods()
                + "    static public " + outputClassName + "[] getExtent() {\n"
                + "        Vector extent = new Vector();\n"
                + "        for (int i = myExtent.size()-1, j = 0; i >= 0; i--) {\n"
                + "            " + outputClassName + " anObj = \n"
                + "              (" + outputClassName + ")\n"
                + "              ((WeakReference)myExtent.elementAt(i)).get();\n"
                + "            if ( anObj != null )\n"
                + "                extent.add(anObj);\n"
                + "            else\n"
                + "                myExtent.remove(i);\n"
                + "        }\n"
                + "        return (" + outputClassName + "[])\n"
                + "            extent.toArray( new " + outputClassName + "[1]);\n"
                + "    }\n";
        }

        protected void checkPostconditions() {
            super.checkPostconditions();
            if ( outputClassObject.getDeclaredConstructors().length
                != numberOfConstructors )
                throw new C2CException( "non-ExtentManaged constructors added"
        );
        }
    }
```

❽ **Generates method to retrieve the extent** *(annotation at `protected String generateMethods() {`)*

❾ **Ensures no other transformation has added constructors** *(annotation at `protected void checkPostconditions() {`)*

Now let's look inside of `C2ExtentManagedC`, which is shown in listing 7.7. This in-depth look is followed by an example of its use in listing 7.8.

❶ The main method creates a transformation object and calls `createClass` with the command-line arguments.

❷ Import directives need to be generated for `java.util.Vector` and `java.lang.ref.*`. The `add` operation on `UQueue` returns the queue object, which allows the succinct coding of the override of `generateImports`. The implementation of `UQueue` is presented in section 7.5.

❸ The override of generateClassNamePrefix establishes that the adjective ExtentManaged must appear in the default name of output classes. The default name may be changed with the -output flag in the arguments array.

❹ This ensures that the generated class is a subclass of the input class.

❺ For the sake of simplicity, we disallow the input class to be serializable or clone-able. Each of these interfaces permits instances of a class to be created without calling a constructor. This limitation can be eliminated by adding an override to clone (if the input class implements Cloneable) or an override to readObject (if the input class implements Serializable).

❻ A static field is added to track the extent.

❼ For each constructor of the input class, a similar constructor is generated that adds the newly constructed object to the extent. This is accomplished with the method createRenamedConstructor, which is defined in listing 7.9.

❽ The method to retrieve the extent is generated. This method is complicated by the fact that some entries may have been garbage collected, which results in weak references that are null. These are removed from the extent when get-Extent is called.

❾ This transformation has an override of checkPostconditions. If a subclass of the C2ExtentManagedC transformation were to generate additional constructors, these new constructors would not place instances in the extent vector, which would render the C2ExtentManagedC transformation ineffective. Note that because our transformations generate code, a transformation could sneak a constructor into an override of generateFields or generateMethods. For this reason, the override of checkPostconditions ensures that the number of constructors in the output has not increased. This is accomplished with the introspective call Class.getDeclaredConstructors on the output class object, which is loaded by the framework.

Let's look at an example of the use of C2ExtentManagedC. Figure 7.2 presents a class diagram that depicts the result of using C2ExtentManagedC on an input class named Squirrel. The code for Squirrel is not shown, but the two constructors declared by Squirrel are a copy constructor and a constructor with no parameters. The output class is named ExtentManagedSquirrel and is a subclass of Squirrel. The output class has corresponding constructors, a static private field to track the instances, and a static method for accessing the set of instances. Listing 7.8 shows the code generated by the execution of C2ExtentManagedC.

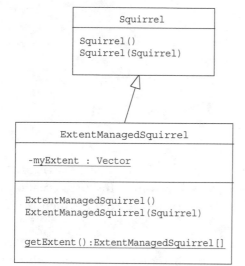

Figure 7.2
Class diagram illustrating the relationship between the input class Squirrel for the C2ExtentManagedC transformation and its output class ExtentManagedSquirrel

Listing 7.8   Output class for command: java C2ExtentManagedC Squirrel

```java
import java.util.Vector;
import java.lang.ref.*;
public  class ExtentManagedSquirrel
    extends Squirrel
{
//============= F I E L D S =====================
    static private Vector myExtent = new Vector();

//============= C O N S T R U C T O R S ==========
public ExtentManagedSquirrel()
{
    super();
    myExtent.add( new WeakReference(this) );
}
public ExtentManagedSquirrel(Squirrel p0)
{
    super(p0);
    myExtent.add( new WeakReference(this) );
}

//============= M E T H O D S ====================
    static public ExtentManagedSquirrel[] getExtent() {
        Vector extent = new Vector();
        for (int i = myExtent.size()-1, j = 0; i >= 0; i--) {
            ExtentManagedSquirrel anObj =
                (ExtentManagedSquirrel)
                ((WeakReference)myExtent.elementAt(i)).get();
            if ( anObj != null )
```

```
                    extent.add(anObj);
            else
                myExtent.remove(i);
        }
        return (ExtentManagedSquirrel[])
                extent.toArray( new ExtentManagedSquirrel[1]);
    }

  //============= N E S T E D   C L A S S E S ======
  }
```

A client must instantiate `ExtentManagedSquirrel` rather than `Squirrel`. So it is important to hide the `Squirrel` constructors if possible. Instance creation is best done by presenting an Abstract Factory pattern to the client, which is discussed in chapter 3.

The extent-managed property does extend to subclasses of `ExtentManagedSquirrel`. That is, all instances of a subclass are included in the extent of `ExtentManagedSquirrel`. This occurs because the only way for a subclass to create an instance is by going through a constructor defined in the extent-managed class. For example, in figure 7.3, instances of `UglySquirrel` are included in the extent of `ExtentManagedSquirrel`.

A second issue involving inheritance and the design of the `C2ExtentManagedC` transformation arises when both a class and its subclass are transformed. This leads to the problem depicted in figure 7.4, where `Squirrel` has a subclass, `UglySquirrel`. If the hierarchy can be arranged as is done on the left side, then instances of `ExtentManagedUglySquirrel` are included in the extent of `ExtentManagedSquirrel` as they should be.

If the class hierarchy must be arranged as is done on the right side of figure 7.4, the situation is problematic. When using the transformation presented in listing 7.7, instances of `ExtentManagedUglySquirrel` are not included in the extent of `ExtentManagedSquirrel`. This issue is usually a problem, because an ugly squirrel is a squirrel (subclasses should be subtypes). The problem can be solved with a more complex transformation

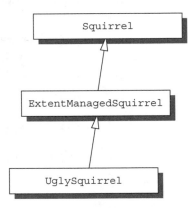

Figure 7.3 The instances of `Ugly-Squirrel` are included in the extent of `ExtentManagedSquirrel` because constructors of `Extent-ManagedSquirrel` must participate in creating instances of `UglySquirrel`.

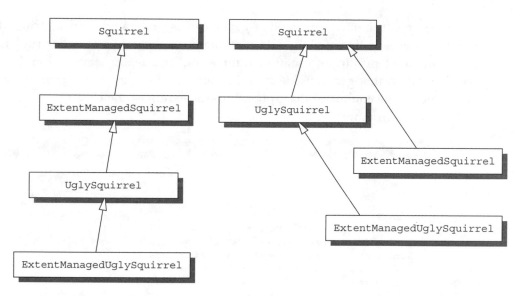

Figure 7.4   Two ways of subclassing with `C2ExtentManagedC`. The one on the left works well when it can be done. The one on the right is problematic because instances of `ExtentManagedUglySquirrel` are not included in the extent of `ExtentManagedSquirrel` when the classes are generated by the transformation presented in this chapter.

that analyzes the superclasses of the input class and what transformations have been applied to them. If a class has superclasses that have been transformed with `C2ExtentManagedC`, new instances are added to the extents of the transformed subclasses of those superclasses. George's problem falls into this latter category if the customer wishes to transform both a class and one of its subclasses that come from Wildlife Components' library. If the customer does wish this, George will have to produce the more complex transformation. However, we will not do so in this book.

Now let's look at the `Mopex` methods that support `C2ExtentManagedC`.

The implementation of the `generateConstructors` override employs an additional method of `Mopex`, the convenience facility that was first introduced in chapter 1. This method, `createRenamedConstructor`, is shown in listing 7.9. Note that `createRenamedConstructor` is defined in terms of the `Mopex` methods `formalParametersToString` (listing 7.10), `actualParametersToString` (listing 7.11), and `classArrayToString` (listing 7.12). Each of these uses `getTypeName` (listing 7.13) to get a Java-compilable name for a type from its corresponding class object.

The `createRenamedConstructor` method generates a constructor with the same parameters and exceptions as the specified constructor. In addition, the generated constructor is renamed, an explicit super call is generated, and a string (the parameter code) is inserted to add functionality to the generated constructor. In the context of our transformation framework, createRenamedConstructor is a handy method that gets reused often. In the case of C2ExtentManagedC, the code parameter is the command that appends to the extent of the class the weak reference to a new instance.

Listing 7.9 createRenamedConstructor, a static method of Mopex

```
public static String createRenamedConstructor( Constructor c,
                                               String name,
                                               String code )
{
    Class[] pta = c.getParameterTypes();
    String fpl = formalParametersToString( pta );
    String apl = actualParametersToString( pta );
    Class[] eTypes =  c.getExceptionTypes();
    String result = name + "(" + fpl + ")\n";
    if ( eTypes.length != 0 )
        result += "    throws "
                    + classArrayToString( eTypes )
                    + "\n";
    result += "{\n    super(" + apl + ");\n" + code + "}\n";
    return result;
}
```

The formalParametersToString method takes a class array and returns a comma-separated string of type names, each followed by a constructed formal parameter.

Listing 7.10 Implementation of Mopex.formalParametersToString

```
public static String formalParametersToString( Class[] pts ){
    String result = "";
    for ( int i = 0; i < pts.length; i++) {
        result += getTypeName( pts[i] ) + " p" + i ;
        if ( i < pts.length-1 )
            result += ",";
    }
    return result;
}
```

The actualParametersToString method works with formalParametersToString in that a comma-separated string of formal parameters is returned, one for each of the formal parameters generated by formalParametersToString.

Listing 7.11   Implementation of `Mopex.actualParametersToString`

```java
public static String actualParametersToString( Class[] pts ){
    String result = "";
    for ( int i = 0; i < pts.length; i++) {
        result += "p" + i ;
        if ( i < pts.length-1 )
            result += ",";
    }
    return result;
}
```

The `classArrayToString` method generates a comma-separated string of type names, one for each class object in the specified array.

Listing 7.12   Implementation of `Mopex.classArrayToString`

```java
public static String classArrayToString( Class[] pts ){
    String result = "";
    for ( int i = 0; i < pts.length; i++) {
        result += getTypeName( pts[i] );
        if ( i < pts.length-1 )
            result += ",";
    }
    return result;
}
```

The three preceding methods use `getTypeName` to generated individual type names for the specified class object. The `getTypeName` method adds brackets to the end of the type name of an array and traverses to its component type. It returns the name of any non-array class. Therefore, a two-dimensional `int` array class would be rendered as `int[][]` (which is compilable Java code). For this reason, `getTypeName` proves useful during code-generation tasks where `getName` alone is insufficient.

Listing 7.13   Implementation of `Mopex.getTypeName`

```java
public static String getTypeName( Class cls ){
    if ( !cls.isArray() ) {
        return cls.getName();
    } else {
        return getTypeName( cls.getComponentType() ) + "[]";
    }
}
```

Note that we encountered the problem of extent management in section 6.4, where `AbstractProduct` is required to account for `Product` instances. A transformation similar to the one presented in this section can be crafted to add extent management to `AbstractProduct`.

7.4 *C2IdentitySubclassOfC and its subclasses*

A common situation is the desire to create a subclass of a class that adds a property with some additional fields and methods. To do this, a programmer would start by subclassing the class to be augmented and then reintroducing all of the same constructors with super calls. From there, the additional functionality can be put into this subclass. `C2IdentitySubclassOfC` is a transformation that provides the starting point of the subclass with the constructors. It is named with the word `identity` because without any additional work, the class it produces has exactly the same functionality as the input class. Many of the later transformations subclass `C2IdentitySubclassOfC` and then add functionality. Listing 7.14 presents the implementation of the transformation `C2IdentitySubclassOfC`.

Listing 7.14   The `C2IdentitySubclassOfC` transformation

```
package c2c;
import java.lang.reflect.*;                    Allows the transformation to be  ❶
import mopex.*;                                  used from the command line

public class C2IdentitySubclassOfC extends C2CTransformation {

    static public void main( String[] args ) {
        new C2IdentitySubclassOfC().createClass( args );    Prepends
    }                                                       description
                                                          ❷ of transformation
    protected String generateClassNamePrefix() {
        return "SubclassOf" + super.generateClassNamePrefix();
    }                                                       Sets superclass
                                                            to be the
    protected String getSuperclass() {return inputClassName;}  ❸ input class

    protected void checkAndProcessArgs( Args args ){    ❹ Rejects interfaces as
        super.checkAndProcessArgs( args );                 input classes
        if ( inputClassObject.isInterface() )
            throw new C2CException("input class is an interface");
    }                                                       Mirrors each input-class
                                                            constructor with a
    protected final String generateConstructors() {    ❺ constructor having the
        String result = "";                                same parameters
        Constructor[] cArray = inputClassObject.getDeclaredConstructors();
        for (int i = 0; i < cArray.length; i++ )
            result += "public "
```

```
                    + Mopex.createRenamedConstructor( cArray[i],
                                                outputClassName,
                                                "" );
         return super.generateConstructors() + result;
      }
   }
```

Let's examine the methods defined by `C2IdentitySubclassOfC`:

❶ There is a `main` so that the transformation may be used from the command line. We use this feature later to generate the `C2CException` class.

❷ The adjectival phrase that describes the transformation is added to the prefix.

❸ The superclass is set to the input class.

❹ If the input class object represents an interface, the transformation fails with a `C2CException`.

❺ Each constructor of the input class is mirrored in the generated class by a constructor with the same parameters. The super call in the constructor body emulates constructor inheritance.

Despite its simplicity, `C2IdentitySubclassOfC` is an ideal base class from which to derive many transformations, because it is the place to start when you want the same class but with the addition of some particular property.

One class that is generated using `C2IdentitySubclassOfC` is `C2CException`. If a problem occurs during the execution of a transformation, a `C2CException` is thrown. This class is generated as a subclass of `RuntimeException` with the command line

```
java c2c.C2IdentitySubclassOfC -package c2c \
           -output C2CException java.lang.RuntimeException
```

when the class path is appropriately set. The importance of the `-output` and `-package` flags is also illustrated here. Listing 7.15 presents the code generated by this command line. Note that because `C2IdentitySubclassOfC` and its superclasses use `C2CException`, the first version of the framework was written with `RuntimeException`.

Listing 7.15   The `C2CException` class

```
package c2c;
public  class C2CException
    extends RuntimeException
```

```
{
//============= F I E L D S =====================

//============= C O N S T R U C T O R S ==========
public C2CException(java.lang.String p0)
{
    super(p0);
}
public C2CException(java.lang.Throwable p0)
{
    super(p0);
}
public C2CException(java.lang.String p0,java.lang.Throwable p1)
{
    super(p0,p1);
}
public C2CException()
{
    super();
}

//============= M E T H O D S ====================

//============= N E S T E D   C L A S S E S ======
}
```

C2IdentitySubclassOfC can be the basis of many transformations that add a property to a class by creating a subclass. Chapter 4 showed how proxies can be created for tracing and synchronizing properties. An alternative approach is to write a transformation (as a subclass of C2IdentitySubclassOfC) for each of these properties. Chapter 8 presents a transformation for another property, invariant checking, when discussing the Decorator pattern.

7.5 *UQueue*

Let's complete our presentation of the C2C framework by presenting the implementation of UQueue, which is a container class that implements a queue whose add operation does nothing if the object to be added is already in the queue. Containers such as UQueue are much easier to use when they are specialized for the type of objects to be contained. This way, if an attempt is made to add an object of the wrong type, the error can be detected, preferably at compile time, but if not, then at runtime.

The requirements for UQueue are as follows:

- Each constructor for UQueue has a parameter specifying the type of the container elements.

- The add operation is called, and the type of the object to be added is checked at runtime.

- If an object to be added to the queue is already there, the queue is not changed.

- At least one constructor must allow the specification of an equivalence operation for testing whether an object is in the queue. The default equivalence operation is the equals operation introduced by Object.

- UQueue must have a toArray operation that produces arrays of the proper type (rather than the Object arrays that are produced by the Java container classes).

These requirements are satisfied by the UQueue class as implemented in listing 7.16.

Listing 7.16 UQueue, a class in the mopex package

```java
package mopex;
import java.util.*;
import java.lang.reflect.*;

public class UQueue {

//============= F I E L D S =======================
    private List    myList = new ArrayList();
    private Object eltArray;
    private Class  eltType;
    private Method equalsMethod = null;

//============= C O N S T R U C T O R S ==========
    public UQueue( Class eltType ) {
        this.eltType = eltType;
        eltArray = Array.newInstance( eltType, 0 );
    }

    public UQueue( Class eltType, Method m ) {
        Class[] fpl = m.getParameterTypes();
        if (!(Modifier.isStatic(m.getModifiers())
            && m.getReturnType() == boolean.class
            && fpl[0] == eltType
            && fpl[1] == eltType
            && fpl.length == 2))
                throw new RuntimeException("illegal signature");
        equalsMethod = m;
        this.eltType = eltType;
        eltArray = Array.newInstance( eltType, 0 );
```

❶ **Parameter specifies the type of the queue elements**

❷ **Method parameter is used to determine equivalence in the add method**

```
        }
//============ M E T H O D S ====================
    public boolean isEmpty()         { return myList.size()==0 ; }
    public int      size()           { return myList.size(); }
    public Object   remove()         { return myList.remove(0); }
    public Object   elementAt( int i ) { return myList.get(i); }

    public UQueue add( Object element ) {
        if ( !eltType.isInstance( element ) )
            throw new RuntimeException("illegal arg type");
        if ( !contains(element))
            myList.add(element);
        return this;
    }

    public boolean contains( Object obj ) {
        if ( equalsMethod == null ) {
            return myList.contains(obj);
        } else {
            for ( int i = 0; i < myList.size(); i++ ) {
                try {
                    Object[] apl = {obj,myList.get(i)};
                    Boolean rv = (Boolean)equalsMethod.invoke(obj,apl);
                    if ( rv.booleanValue() )
                        return true;
                } catch (Exception e){
                    throw new RuntimeException(e);
                }
            }
            return false;
        }
    }

    public Object[] toArray() {
        return myList.toArray( (Object[])eltArray );
    }

    public String toString( String separator ) {
        String result = "";
        for ( int i = 0; i < myList.size(); i++ ) {
            result += myList.get(i);
            if ( i < myList.size()-1 )
                result += separator;
        }
        return result;
    }
}
```

Ensures that the element to be added is of the correct type and not already in queue ❸

Determines if the object is in the queue ❹

❺ **Ensures that the returned array can be cast to the proper array type**

Converts queue to string with specified separator ❻

Let's look at the implementation in detail:

❶ The first constructor has a parameter for specifying the type of the queue elements. The type is stored in the instance variable eltType. In addition, the constructor creates an empty array of that type, which is used in the toArray operation.

❷ The second constructor has an additional parameter that is a Method, which must be static, taking two parameters of the specified type and returning a boolean. This method is used to test equivalence in the add method.

❸ The add method ensures that the element to be added is of the correct type and adds the element if it not already in the queue (a condition that is determined by the contains method).

❹ If the first constructor created the queue object, the contains method of ArrayList is called to determine if the object is in the queue. That contains method uses equals. If the second constructor created the queue object, the queue is sequentially searched for an equivalent object using the static method specified at construction time.

❺ The toArray method ensures that the returned array can be cast by the caller to the proper array type.

❻ The parameter to the toString method specifies a separator to be inserted between the string representations of the queue elements.

UQueue is an example of a dynamically-typed container class. Alternatively, the C2C framework could have been used to create a transformation for a statically-typed container class. We do not present this alternative, because transformations that generate such container classes correspond to the generics that are added to Java 1.5 (a topic further discussed in chapter 10). This new Java feature should obviate most of the need to generate code for specialized container classes. However, you may not be able to use Java 1.5 or you may have a requirement that is beyond the limitations of Java 1.5 generics, in which case you may wish either to write a dynamically parameterized container class (as we present in this section) or to use the C2C framework to generate the container classes that you need.

7.6 *Using the framework*

This concludes the introduction to the class-to-class transformation framework. Figure 7.5 shows the framework presented in this chapter. This figure includes the example transformations that are presented in this chapter.

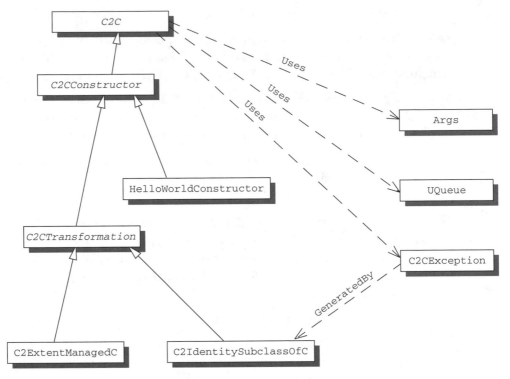

Figure 7.5   Class diagram showing the relationships among the classes of the C2C framework for writing class-to-class transformations[3]

We envision that the transformations built with the C2C framework can be used in three ways:

- A transformation may be used at runtime, when a class is dynamically constructed and loaded by a call to the static method createClass. This parallels what is done when getProxyClass is called. The difference is that the transformations are more flexible but slower in constructing classes.

- An application build process may use the main in the transformation to create class files, which become part of the application. This use treats the transformations as code-generator tools. The generated source files are not changed but are needed for debugging.

---

[3] The circularity in the figure implies that in order to begin the programming of the framework, the first version of C2CException had to be written manually (actually RuntimeException was used).

■ A transformation is used once to generate a source file that is subsequently edited. This eliminates much of the drudgery of many tasks. However, once the file is edited, the link between the generator and the source file is broken and the source file must be maintained manually. For this reason, this way of using a transformation is the least desirable of the three.

Whichever way transformations are used, they do contribute to improved flexibility and increased productivity.

7.7 Relation to Aspect-Oriented Programming

Aspects, features, facets, or properties have always been part of object-oriented programming. Their presence becomes most apparent when the addition of *one word* to a requirement causes small snippets of code to be added in scattered places all over an application. The kind of word that can have so great an impact is an adjective. For example, consider the adjective *thread-safe*. Requiring a class, library, or application to be thread-safe results in semaphore lock and unlock commands popping up all over the place. Just as dandelions disturb the beauty of a lawn, the semaphore commands disturb the readability of the code. Unlike dandelions, these scattered code snippets are so tangled in the application that they cannot be removed without destroying the application (in the sense that the requirement from which the snippets arise is no longer satisfied). Further, the available constructs of object-oriented programming cannot bring the snippets together in one place. Something seems to be missing.

The area of study for this problem (that identifies and finds ways to untangle the snippets, to separately express them, and then to reuse them) is called Aspect-Oriented Programming [50], which is the name invented by Gregor Kiczales and his team at Xerox PARC. The Aspect-Oriented Programming community rightfully uses the word *tangle* to emphasize that there is a problem here to be solved. When the aspect is successfully expressed as a separate entity, the verb *tangle* is better replaced with *weave* or *compose* (both of which have a positive connotation) when expressing the mixing of the aspect code with the application code.

Class-to-class transformations satisfy the most basic requirement of Aspect-Oriented Programming. Each transformation captures a class property independently of any class having that property. In addition, as we have defined them, class-to-class transformations may be applied at runtime. However, transformations of the C2C framework are a weak form of Aspect-Oriented Programming, because two features are missing:

- The result of a class-to-class transformation is a class with a new name rather than a modified class with the same name.

- Our class-to-class transformations must be explicitly applied rather than there being some general specification of when to automatically apply a transformation.

The transformations of the C2C framework create new classes rather than modifying the existing class by inserting code, because of the lack of intercessional power in the Java reflection API. Performing code insertion eliminates the problem depicted in figure 7.4 where the ExtentManagedUglySquirrel is not a subclass of ExtentManagedSquirrel even though we would like it to be so. This inconvenience can be mitigated with the use of interfaces and factory methods. However, a more powerful reflection API that permits class modification (even if only at load time) removes this weakness. The bottom line is that despite its power, Java reflection does not quite move us across the boundary into Aspect-Oriented Programming. Crossing that boundary requires a more powerful reflection API.[4]

The C2ExtentManagedC transformation is our first example of adding an aspect to a class in the sense of Aspect-Oriented Programming. The next chapter introduces other useful transformations in the context of design patterns. In addition, section 10.3 contains a brief introduction to some of the tools for Aspect-Oriented Programming.

7.8 *Summary*

Before we become too enamored with the potential of class-to-class transformations, let's remind ourselves that goal of this book is to teach Java reflection. The transformation framework is foremost a vehicle for demonstrating the use and effectiveness of Java reflection. This chapter demonstrated a number of features of Java reflection:

- Both the input class and the output class are loaded using forName, which is one of the five ways in Java to obtain a class object. The others are the get-

---

[4] This lack of intercessional reflective capability in Java has been mentioned several times in this book, which raises the question: is more reflective capability in Java really needed? The answer is yes. As evidence, we offer the fact that the builders of powerful tools (for example, Hibernate) are using cglib (cglib.sourceforge.net), Javassist, and the various toolkits for manipulating bytecodes such as Jikes or BCEL (jakarta.apache.org/bcel) to provide functionality that may also be achieved with a more capable reflection API.

`Class` method, the `.class` literal, various methods of `Class`, and the use of methods in the `ClassLoader`, which is covered in chapter 6.

- The class objects are examined with introspective methods such as `get-DeclaredConstructors` to obtain significant information for further use.

- Some simple methods (for example, `createRenamedConstructor`) in our Mopex class used additional introspective methods to generate code fragments that are easily combined to form complete classes.

The result of these uses of reflection is a small and understandable framework for writing class-to-class transformations. A class-to-class transformation adds code to a class that pertains to all instances of the class. Java reflection has limitations with respect to intercession. These limitations may be circumvented by generating code. Class-to-class transformations are the way we recommend that such code be organized.

A separate issue from the pedagogical value of the class-to-class transformation framework for teaching reflection is whether the framework is in itself a useful tool for programmers. The existence of the framework is scant support for the proposition that the framework is a useful tool. The next chapter presents additional transformations. We believe that at the end of these chapters you will agree that the framework is valuable for more than just illustrating reflection.

Design patterns

8

In this chapter

- The relationship between design patterns and reflection
- How to support the use of design patterns with reflection
- Examples of useful code generators

In the early 1990s, it became clear that object-oriented programming was not the panacea that all hoped it would be. There were many reasons for this disappointment. Among the most prominent was that the declining cost and increased capacity of computers led to the demand for larger and more capable software systems than the object-oriented programming of the early 1990s could easily produce. There were many responses to this situation. One successful response was the study of reflection. Another successful response was the revival of the study of the work on the design theories of the architect Christopher Alexander and their applicability to software design. This revival culminated in the book *Design Patterns* [38] by Gamma, Helm, Johnson, and Vlissides, which has become the primary reference for studying software design patterns.

A design pattern is intended to capture the experience of a successful designer. "Each design pattern systematically names, explains, and evaluates an important and recurring design in object-oriented systems" [38 p. 2]. A design pattern is *applied*, not implemented, because the pattern must be fit to the problem context before implementation. This is a subtle point; there is not just one way to apply a design pattern.

This chapter explores reflective implementation support for the some of the software design patterns described by Gamma, Helm, Johnson, and Vlissides. Patterns are part of the vocabulary of the software engineer expert in object-oriented software programming. If you are not familiar with these patterns, we suggest coming back to this chapter after reading *Design Patterns*.

As John Vlissides explains in *Pattern Hatching* [88], a pattern is more than a solution to a problem in context. A pattern is named, recurring, and teachable. In many cases, code generation can perform almost everything that a programmer does when applying the pattern. Despite the fact that there are many ways to apply a pattern, individual programmers working in a particular programming language develop a style of applying a pattern. It is this style of pattern application in addition to the pattern that is captured by the code generator. Once this style of application is fixed, code generation can relieve much of the drudgery of applying a pattern.

This chapter combines reflection with code generation using the class-to-class transformation framework from chapter 7 to address the issue of pattern application. Because these are specifically class-to-class transformations, this approach has a spectrum of effectiveness. At one end are patterns (and your authors' style of applying them) that are nearly completely described by a class-to-class transformation. At the other end are patterns that are not characterized by class-to-class transformations at all. In the middle are patterns that are partially described by a class-to-class transformation. For some patterns, the transformation is a useful tool, and for others, the parameterization of the transformation is so complex that you may as well write the Java code. This chapter presents several examples of transformations that can easily be programmed to aid the application of patterns.

8.1 *Singleton*

The Singleton pattern is applied to get a class that may have only one instance. This implies

> if x `instanceof` S and y `instanceof` S, then x and y are the same object

for all classes S created by applying the Singleton pattern. The Singleton pattern is at the end of the spectrum of patterns most amenable to capture with a class-to-class transformation. That is, a transformation can be programmed to apply the Singleton pattern to an input class such that the result is a class that may have at most one instance in its extent.

The context for applying the Singleton pattern is an individual class. The key to applying the Singleton pattern with a class-to-class transformation is controlling how instances are constructed. Given a class C, our design (as depicted in figure 8.1) is to subclass C and replicate each constructor with a private constructor that just calls its super constructor. Corresponding to each constructor is a `getInstance` method that invokes the constructor if necessary (because no instance exists) and returns the instance. In other words, `getInstance` is a factory method for the singleton class. This is the essence of the transformation `C2SingletonC`, which is presented in listing 8.1.

Although the `C2SingletonC` transformation is simple in concept, there are a number of special issues that must be addressed:

- *Interfaces may not be input classes*—Interfaces do not have constructors and, therefore, cannot be transformed into Singleton classes. The override of `checkAndProcessArgs` excludes interfaces.

- *Cloneable input classes may not be transformed*—The `clone` method in `java.lang.Object` creates an object without calling a constructor. In addition, the `clone` method has following output specification:

  > x == x.clone() is never true

  This implies that calling `clone` creates an instance distinct from the target of the call. This is in conflict with the specification of Singleton. Consequently, the transformation throws an exception in the override of `check-AndProcessArgs` for `Cloneable` input classes.

- *Serializable input classes may not be transformed*—In a `Serializable` class, objects may be created by `readResolve` without calling constructors. `readResolve` is a hook method that allows you to intercede during `read-Object` to override the returned object. To keep our `C2SingletonC` transformation simple, `Serializable` input classes are not part of its input domain.

- *Our `C2SingletonC` transformation allows the garbage collector to destroy the Singleton object*—This is accomplished by using a `WeakReference` to store the Singleton object. This design choice has the advantage of space conservation, but it implies that the Singleton object may not always exist, which can lead to other complications, as discussed later in this chapter.

Note that these issues are not just related to creating a transformation. These issues are inherent in applying the Singleton pattern in general.

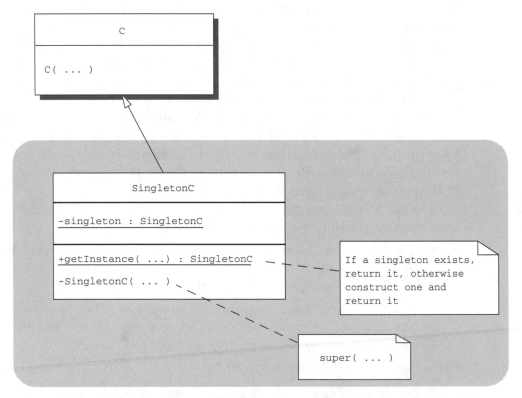

Figure 8.1 Design for the outcome of applying the Singleton pattern on the class C with the use of the C2SingletonC transformation. The resulting class SingletonC makes the constructor private while providing a factory method and a new private instance variable to hold the location of the singleton.

Listing 8.1 presents the implementation of the C2SingletonC transformation. For each constructor of the input class, C2SingletonC generates a constructor and a static getInstance method. The constructors are generated using the Mopex method createRenamedConstructor, which is defined in listing 7.9 on page 166. The complementary static method for each constructor calls the constructor to create a singleton, if none exists, and then returns the singleton.

Listing 8.1 The C2SingletonC transformation

```
package c2c;
import java.lang.reflect.*;
import mopex.*;
import java.io.Serializable;

public class C2SingletonC extends C2CTransformation {

    private int numberOfConstructors = 0;

    static public void main( String[] args ) {
        new C2SingletonC().createClass( args );
    }
```

❶ C2SingletonC may be called from command line

```
    protected void checkAndProcessArgs( Args args ) {
        super.checkAndProcessArgs( args );
        setFinal();
        if ( inputClassObject.isInterface() )
            throw new C2CException("cannot generate Singleton for interface");
        if ( Serializable.class.isAssignableFrom(inputClassObject) )
            throw new C2CException("cannot handle Serializable input classes");
        if ( Cloneable.class.isAssignableFrom(inputClassObject) )
            throw new C2CException("Cloneable and Singleton are conflicting");
    }
```

❷ Ensures output class is final and eliminates bad input classes

```
    protected UQueue generateImports() {
        return super.generateImports().add("java.lang.ref.*");
    }
```

❸ Ensures WeakReference is imported

```
    protected String generateClassNamePrefix() {
        return "Singleton" + super.generateClassNamePrefix();
    }
```

❹ Prepends prefix with Singleton

```
    protected String getSuperclass() {return inputClassName;}
```

❺ Sets superclass to be the input class

```
    protected String generateFields() {
        return super.generateFields()
            + "static private WeakReference singleton = null;\n";
    }
```

❻ Declares a static field

```
protected final String generateConstructors() {          ❼ Mirrors the constructors
    String result = "";                                       of the input class
    Constructor[] cArray = inputClassObject.getDeclaredConstructors();
    String code = "    if (singleton!=null && singleton.get()!=null)\n" +
                  "        throw new RuntimeException("
                            + "\"Singleton constructor failure\");\n" +
                  "    singleton = new WeakReference( this );\n";
    if ( cArray.length != 0 ) {
        for (int i = 0; i < cArray.length; i++ ) {
            result += "private "
                + Mopex.createRenamedConstructor( cArray[i],
                                                  outputClassName,
                                                  code);

        }
        numberOfConstructors = cArray.length;
    } else {
        result = "private " + outputClassName + "() {" + code + "}\n";
        numberOfConstructors = 1;
    }
    return super.generateConstructors() + result;
}
protected String generateMethods()          ❽ Generates a getInstance
{                                               method for each constructor
    String result = "";
    Constructor[] cArray = inputClassObject.getDeclaredConstructors();
    if ( cArray.length != 0 ) {
        for (int i = 0; i < cArray.length; i++ ) {
            Class[] pta = cArray[i].getParameterTypes();
            String fpl = Mopex.formalParametersToString( pta );
            String apl = Mopex.actualParametersToString( pta );
            Class[] eTypes =  cArray[i].getExceptionTypes();
            int modifiers = cArray[i].getModifiers();
            result += "static " + Modifier.toString( modifiers ) + " "
                + outputClassName + " getInstance(" + fpl + ")\n";
            if ( eTypes.length != 0 ) {
                result
                    += "    throws " + Mopex.classArrayToString( eTypes )
                    + "\n";
            }
            result += "{\n"
                + "    if (singleton==null || singleton.get()==null)\n"
                + "        new " + outputClassName + "(" + apl + ");\n"
                + "    return (" +outputClassName+ ")singleton.get();\n"
                + "}\n";
        }
    } else {
        result = "    static " + outputClassName + " getInstance() {\n"
            + "        if (singleton==null || singleton.get()==null)\n"
            + "            singleton = new " + outputClassName + "();\n"
            + "        return (" + outputClassName + ")singleton.get();\n"
            + "    }\n";
```

```
        }
        return super.generateMethods() + result;
    }
    protected void checkPostconditions() {
        super.checkPostconditions();
        if ( outputClassObject.getDeclaredConstructors().length
            != numberOfConstructors )
            throw new C2CException( "non-Singleton constructors added" );
    }
}
```

9 Ensures no other transformation has added a constructor

Let's examine each of the methods defined by C2SingletonC:

1 The presence of the typical main method indicates C2SingletonC may be called from the command line.

2 The checkAndProcessArgs override ensures that the input class is not an interface, serializable, or cloneable for reasons given previously.

3 The generated code uses WeakReference, which is imported from java.lang.ref.

4 The default prefix is prepended with Singleton.

5 The generated code is declared to be a subclass of the input class.

6 A static field is declared that contains a weak reference to the singleton.

7 Each constructor of the input class is replicated in the generated code with a private constructor that creates the singleton if it does not exist. If the constructor is called and a singleton exists, something has gone wrong (most likely, another transformation has added code that called a constructor rather than getInstance).

8 Corresponding to each constructor, a getInstance method is added that returns the singleton if it exists and returns a newly created one if it does not exist.

9 The number of constructors is counted both during the transformation process and after the generated class is loaded. If the counts are different, some other transformation has added a constructor that C2SingletonC has not seen. This is an incompatibility for which an exception is raised.

Suppose we have a Dog class defined as follows:

```
public class Dog {
    public Dog( Object obj ) {}
}
```

Listing 8.2 shows a class `SingletonDog` generated by `C2SingletonC`.

Listing 8.2   Example of the use of `C2SingletonC` on the class `Dog`

```
import java.lang.ref.*;
public final  class SingletonDog
    extends Dog
{
//============= F I E L D S =====================
static private WeakReference singleton = null;

//============= C O N S T R U C T O R S ==========
private SingletonDog(java.lang.Object p0)
{
    super(p0);
    if (singleton!=null && singleton.get()!=null)
        throw new RuntimeException("Singleton constructor failure");
    singleton = new WeakReference( this );
}

//============= M E T H O D S ====================
static public SingletonDog getInstance(java.lang.Object p0)
{
    if (singleton==null || singleton.get()==null)
        new SingletonDog(p0);
    return (SingletonDog)singleton.get();
}

//============= N E S T E D   C L A S S E S ======
}
```

`C2SingletonC` is not the only way to apply the Singleton pattern. Here are two variations:

- *You can create a Singleton class that can be extended*—This could be done by changing `C2SingletonC` to create protected constructors and to not make the generated class final. Some complications arise in doing so, because the Singleton property is inherited. This implies that if `Y` is a direct subclass of `SingletonX` and an instance of `Y` is created, that instance counts as the single instance of `SingletonX` and no other instance of `Y` is created. Further, if `Z` is another direct subclass of `SingletonX`, no instances of `Z` can be created while the instance of `Y` exists. This is because the instance of `Y` is the singleton for `SingletonX`, and if simultaneously an instance of `Z` exists, there would exist two instances of `SingletonX`. Note that enforcement is handled by having all constructors throw an exception in the case where they are called when an instance exists. That is, a call to a constructor when an instance exists could not come from a getInstance method.

- *In the version presented here, you can call a getInstance method with one set of parameters and receive an object constructed with another set of parameters or by a different constructor*—This arrangement may not always be reasonable. Rather than have a number of getInstance methods that call constructors, you could generate a Singleton class that creates the singleton in the initializer of the static field by calling a particular constructor (which would be specified in a command-line parameter). There would be only one getInstance with no parameters that returns this statically constructed instance. Note that while this resolves construction discrepancies, it removes the ability to have the instance garbage collected.

The point of presenting these two variations is that pattern application is not standard. If there were only one universal way to apply a pattern, the underlying concept would likely be incorporated into your programming language. On the other hand, if you or your group agrees about a standard way to apply a pattern, a transformation can be written to make applying the pattern easy.

8.2 Decorator class-to-class transformations

The Decorator pattern adds additional functionality to objects by having its code executed before or after method calls on the objects. Chapter 4 presented a number of examples of one style of applying the Decorator pattern in which the code for the additional functionality is part of the invocation handler of a proxy instance. Alternatively, the Decorator pattern may be applied with a subclass that cooperatively overrides methods with the appropriate decoration code. Class invariant checking qualifies as a good example, because the boolean method that encodes the class invariant is executed before and after every method execution. Section 5.5 explained the importance of class invariant checking and also showed how to properly code invariant checking to avoid infinite recursion. This section demonstrates how to write a class-to-class transformation for applying the Decorator pattern. In particular, the problem of class invariant checking is used again to permit you to contrast this technique with the earlier one.

Figure 8.2 depicts the basic notions implemented in the transformation C2InvariantCheckingC. Basically, an input class X is subclassed. Each instance method of X is overridden so that the invariant is checked before and after the super call to the instance method. In addition, a method is added to perform the check of the invariant while avoiding infinite recursion.

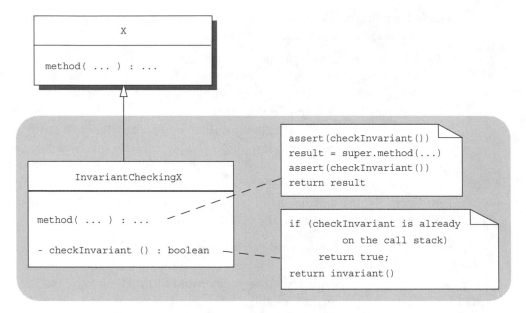

Figure 8.2 Design for the outcome of the use of the `C2InvariantCheckingC` transformation

Listing 8.3 contains the code for the transformation `C2InvariantCheckingC`. It is a subclass of `C2IdentitySubclassOfC`, which was introduced in chapter 7. As such, the output class generated by `C2InvariantCheckingC` has all of the constructors of the input class. Note that the transformation does not establish that the invariant is true after contruction is complete; doing so requires a small code change that is left to the reader.

Listing 8.3 The `C2InvariantCheckingC` transformation

```
package c2c;
import java.lang.reflect.*;
import mopex.*;

public class C2InvariantCheckingC extends C2IdentitySubclassOfC {

    protected Method  invMethod;

    static public void main( String[] args ) {
        new C2InvariantCheckingC().createClass( args );
    }

    protected String generateClassNamePrefix() {
        return "InvariantChecking" + super.generateClassNamePrefix();
    }
```

```
protected void checkAndProcessArgs( Args args ) {    ❶ Performs checks
    super.checkAndProcessArgs( args );                    on input class

    try {
        invMethod = inputClassObject.getMethod( "invariant", null );
    } catch(NoSuchMethodException e){
        throw new C2CException(e);
    }
    if ( invMethod.getReturnType() != boolean.class )
        throw new C2CException("invariant return not boolean");

    if ( inputClassObject.getPackage() != null ) {
        if ( !inputClassObject.getPackage().getName().equals(packageName) )
            throw new C2CException( "input class in different package" );
    } else if ( packageName != null ) {
        throw new C2CException( "Input class in different package" );
    }

    if (Mopex.getMethodsLackingImplementation(inputClassObject).length!=0)
        setAbstract();
}
                                              Overrides all methods
protected String generateMethods() {    ❷ that can be overridden

    int mods = Modifier.STATIC | Modifier.ABSTRACT
            | Modifier.FINAL | Modifier.PRIVATE;

    Method[] nsMethods = Mopex.selectMethods( inputClassObject,
                                              0,
                                              mods,
                                              Object.class );

    String result = generateCheckInvariant();

    String wrapperCode
        = "    assert checkInvariant() : \"invariant failure\";\n";
    for ( int i = 0; i < nsMethods.length; i++ ) {
        if ( !invMethod.equals( nsMethods[i]) ) {
            int mods2 = Mopex.getModifiersWithout( nsMethods[i],
                                                   Modifier.NATIVE );
            result += Modifier.toString(mods2) + " "
                    + Mopex.createCooperativeWrapper( nsMethods[i],
                                                      wrapperCode,
                                                      wrapperCode );
        }
    }
    return super.generateMethods() + result;        ❸ Uses call stack
}                                                      introspection to
                                                       avoid infinite
private String generateCheckInvariant() {  <──────┐   recursion
    return "private boolean checkInvariant() {\n"
        + "    StackTraceElement[] ste\n"
        + "        = (new Throwable()).getStackTrace();\n"
        + "    String className = this.getClass().getName();\n"
```

```
        + "    String mName = \"checkInvariant\";\n"
        + "    for ( int i = 1; i < ste.length; i++ ) {\n"
        + "        if ( ste[i].getClassName().equals(className)\n"
        + "             && ste[i].getMethodName().equals(mName) )\n"
        + "            return true;\n"
        + "        }\n"
        + "    return this.invariant();\n"
        + "}\n";
    }
}
```

The transformation in listing 8.3 has the following notable features:

❶ Three checks are performed in the override of checkAndProcessArgs.

- The transformation must check for the method named invariant that has no parameters and returns a boolean. Note that the use of getMethod implies that the invariant method must be public.

- The transformation assumes that the generated output class is in the same package as the input class. This reasonable assumption simplifies the code generation in several ways. For example, an import statement does not have to be generated.

- If any of the methods lack an implementation, the output class is declared abstract. The check is performed using getMethodsLackingImplementation, which is another method added to the Mopex class in listing 8.5.

❷ In generateMethods, selectMethods (listing 8.6) is used to identify all methods that can be overridden. That is, selectMethods finds all the methods that are neither static nor final nor abstract nor private. This criterion is adequate because the output class is in the same package as the input class (otherwise, methods with package visibility cannot be overridden). The overrides are generated by createCooperativeWrapper, which is defined in listing 8.10 as part of Mopex. This method, createCooperativeWrapper, creates an override for the method that is specified by the first argument. The second and third arguments specify code fragments that are placed before and after the super call. The variable wrapper-Code is initialized with the statement that checks the invariant using the private method checkInvariant. This code uses an assert statement to check the value returned by checkInvariant. Note that the -enableassertions (or -ea) switch must be set on the java command line to actually have the invariant checked. The methods introduced by Object are not overridden by the transformation because they are not expected to have side effects (that is, these methods should not invalidate class invariants). For efficiency purposes, the transformation does not override invariant with an invariant check. This is accomplished with a simple test in generateMethods.

❸ The generated checkInvariant method uses call stack introspection to avoid an infinite recursion if the invariant method calls another method defined by the input class. This pitfall is explained in chapter 5.

Note that C2InvariantCheckingC provides a best effort for checking invariants. For example, static methods cannot be overridden and, therefore, the transformation does not attempt to provide an invariant check when static methods are called. Invariants can involve static fields. Consequently, this transformation does not provide a complete solution to checking invariants.

There are several differences between this subclassing style of applying a pattern and the proxing style presented in chapter 4. The first and obvious difference is that the subclassing style adds the property to all instances of the class, while the proxing style adds the property to selective instances. A subtler difference involves the control over instance creation that is needed. With the proxing style, a programmer need not control the code that instantiates the target object. The programmer needs only the ability to intercede in the passing of the target reference to the client code (at which time a reference to the proxy instance may be substituted for the target reference). With the subclassing style, the programmer must be in control of the code for instance creation, because it is the subclass that must be used for instantiation. Without this level of control, the subclassing style loses much of its value (an interesting way to mitigate this situation is discussed in section 8.4).

The following listings define the new methods of Mopex that are used in the implementation of C2InvariantCheckingC. In total, the code for C2InvariantCheckingC plus the supporting Mopex method may seem large. Indeed, some of these methods are used only once in this book. However, our experience shows that the methods have broader applicability in other transformations or other tasks requiring reflection. This is why these methods are placed in Mopex rather than being a private method in the class that uses them.

In addition, several of the methods that follow use the unique queue class (UQueue) that was presented in section 7.5. Listing 8.4 presents a handy method that removes unwanted modifiers from a set of modifiers. When you generate an implementation for an abstract method, getModifersWithout is used to remove the abstract modifier, which would cause a compilation error if it were to remain.

Listing 8.4   getModifiersWithout, a method of Mopex

```
public static int getModifiersWithout( Method m, int unwantedModifiers )
{
    int mods = m.getModifiers();
    return (mods ^ unwantedModifiers) & mods;
}
```

Listing 8.5 contains the implementation of getMethodsLackingImplementation. In order for a method to lack an implementation, the method must be declared abstract (in a class or interface) and must not be subsequently defined (in a class). Basically, getMethodsLackingImplementation compiles two queues. The first is a queue of methods that are declared abstract. The second is a queue of methods that are not declared abstract (that is, have implementations). Then, if any method in the first queue does not appear in the second, that method lacks an implementation. Both queues are created by calls to selectMethods0, which is a private method of Mopex that is defined in listing 8.6. The identifier equalSignatures-Method refers to a static Method field that is defined and initialized in listing 8.7.

Listing 8.5   getMethodsLackingImplementation, a method of Mopex

```
public static Method[] getMethodsLackingImplementation( Class cls ) {
    UQueue imq = selectMethods0( cls,
                                 0,
                                 Modifier.ABSTRACT,
                                 null );
    UQueue amq = selectMethods0( cls,
                                 Modifier.ABSTRACT,
                                 0,
                                 null );
    UQueue rmq = new UQueue( Method.class, equalSignaturesMethod );
    for ( int i = 0; i < amq.size(); i++ ){
        Method rm = (Method)amq.elementAt(i);
        if ( !imq.contains(rm) )
            rmq.add( rm );
    }
    return (Method[])rmq.toArray();
}
```

Listing 8.6 shows the implementation of selectMethods. There are two public versions that each return a Method array and a private version for use within Mopex that returns a unique queue of method objects. The two int parameters hold Modifier bit vectors. The first (mustHave) specifies modifiers that the selected methods must have. The second parameter (mustNotHave) specifies modifiers that the selected methods must not have. For example, in getMethods-LackingImplementation, selectMethods0 is used twice: once to collect all of the abstract methods and once to collect all of the methods that are not abstract. The entire inheritance graph of both classes and interfaces is used to select methods. The fourth parameter (limit) is used to prune the upper part of the superclass chain. Usually, the limit parameter is used to eliminate the methods of java.lang.Object.

Listing 8.6   selectMethods, a method of Mopex

```
public static Method[] selectMethods( Class cls,
                                      int mustHave,
                                      int mustNotHave ) {
    return (Method[])selectMethods0( cls,
                                     mustHave,
                                     mustNotHave,
                                     null ).toArray();
}

public static Method[] selectMethods( Class cls,
                                      int mustHave,
                                      int mustNotHave,
                                      Class limit ) {
    return (Method[])selectMethods0( cls,
                                     mustHave,
                                     mustNotHave,
                                     limit ).toArray();
}

private static UQueue selectMethods0( Class cls,
                                      int mustHave,
                                      int mustNotHave,
                                      Class limit ) {
    UQueue mq = new UQueue( Method.class, equalSignaturesMethod );
    Class[] ca = selectAncestors(cls,0,0,limit);
    for ( int j = 0; j < ca.length; j++ ){
        Method[] ma = ca[j].getDeclaredMethods();
        for ( int i = 0; i < ma.length; i++ ) {
            int mods = ma[i].getModifiers();
            if ( ((mods & mustHave) == mustHave)
                && ((mods & mustNotHave) == 0) )
                mq.add( ma[i] );
        }
    }
    return mq;
}
```

The implementation of selectMethods requires a comparison of Method objects for signature equality. This comparison is performed with equalSignatures, a method of Mopex that is presented in listing 8.7. Note that a minor optimization is performed in listing 8.7. A static initializer is used to set the value of a static field equalSignaturesMethod, which selectMethods0 uses to construct the UQueue.

Listing 8.7   equalSignatures, a method of Mopex

```
static private Method equalSignaturesMethod;

static {
    Class[] fpl = { Method.class, Method.class };
    try {
        equalSignaturesMethod = Mopex.class.getMethod( "equalSignatures",
                                                        fpl );
    } catch(NoSuchMethodException e){
        throw new RuntimeException(e);
    }
}

public static boolean equalSignatures( Method m1, Method m2 ){
    if ( !m1.getName().equals(m2.getName() ) ) return false;
    if ( !Arrays.equals( m1.getParameterTypes(),
                         m2.getParameterTypes() ) )
        return false;
    return true;
}
```

The implementation of selectMethods also requires a list of all of the classes from which the specified class can inherit methods and all of the interfaces that contribute method declarations. The selectAncestors method in listing 8.8 provides that capability.

Listing 8.8   selectAncestors, a method of Mopex

```
public static Class[] selectAncestors( Class cls,
                                       int mustHave,
                                       int mustNotHave ) {
    return selectAncestors( cls, mustHave, mustNotHave, null );
}

public static Class[] selectAncestors( Class cls,
                                       int mustHave,
                                       int mustNotHave,
                                       Class limit ) {
    UQueue cq = new UQueue(Class.class);
    if ( !cls.isInterface() ) {
```

```
        for ( Class x = cls; x != limit; x = x.getSuperclass() ){
            int mods = x.getModifiers();
            if ( ((mods & mustHave) == mustHave)
                && ((mods & mustNotHave) == 0) )
                cq.add( x );
        }
    }
    Class[] ca = getAllInterfaces( cls, limit );
    for ( int i = 0; i < ca.length; i++ ) {
        int mods = ca[i].getModifiers();
        if ( ((mods & mustHave) == mustHave)
            && ((mods & mustNotHave) == 0) )
            cq.add( ca[i] );
    }
    return (Class[])cq.toArray();
}
```

Because the interfaces contributing to a class form a directed acyclic graph, the algorithm to find a unique list of these interfaces is more complex than that of finding all of the superclasses. Listing 8.9 shows a depth-first search for these interfaces.

Listing 8.9 `getAllInterfaces`, a method of `Mopex`

```
public static Class[] getAllInterfaces( Class cls, Class limit ) {
    assert( limit == null
            || (!limit.isInterface() && !limit.isPrimitive())) );
    UQueue cq = new UQueue(Class.class);
    if ( cls.isInterface() )
        cq.add( cls );
    for (Class x = cls; x != null && x != limit; x = x.getSuperclass())
        getInterfaceSubtree( x, cq );
    return (Class[])cq.toArray();
}

private static void getInterfaceSubtree( Class cls, UQueue cq ) {
    Class[] iArray = cls.getInterfaces();
    for ( int j = 0; j < iArray.length; j++ ) {
        cq.add( iArray[j] );
        getInterfaceSubtree( iArray[j], cq );
    }
}
```

Listing 8.10 presents the `Mopex` method `createCooperativeWrapper`. This method is handy for generating overrides that decorate a super call with actions before and after the call.

Listing 8.10 `createCooperativeWrapper`, a member of the `Mopex` class

```
public static String createCooperativeWrapper( Method m,
                                               String code1,
                                               String code2 ) {
    Class[] pta = m.getParameterTypes();
    Class retType = m.getReturnType();
    String fpl = formalParametersToString( pta );
    String apl = actualParametersToString( pta );
    Class[] eTypes =  m.getExceptionTypes();
    String result
        = retType.getName() + " " + m.getName() + "(" + fpl + ")\n";
    if ( eTypes.length != 0 )
        result += "    throws " + classArrayToString( eTypes ) + "\n";
    result += "{\n" + code1 + "    ";
    if (retType != void.class)
        result += retType.getName() + " cooperativeReturnValue = ";
    result += "super." + m.getName() + "(" + apl + ");\n";
    result += code2;
    if (retType != void.class)
        result += "    return cooperativeReturnValue;\n";
    result += "}\n";
    return result;
}
```

Now that we have presented the `C2InvariantCheckingC` transformation, there are several decision issues to ponder:

- *The solution implemented by the transformation uses inheritance rather than delegation*—This fails to capture one facet of the intent of the Decorator pattern, which is:

  "Attach additional responsibilities to an object dynamically. Decorators provide a flexible alternative to subclassing for extending functionality." [38]

  The solution fails to provide the ability to add or remove invariant checking dynamically. Of course, if you always want the invariant checked, the transformation provides an adequate solution. On the other hand, if Java supported dynamic reclassification (that is, the capability to dynamically change the class of an object, for example, see [24]), then the solution would fulfill the dynamic facet of the intent of the Decorator pattern.

- *Once an invariant checking subclass has been created, all of its subsequent subclasses also check invariants*—This implies that the same class invariant must hold down the inheritance hierarchy. In addition, `C2InvariantCheckingC` may be used to generate invariant checking subclasses further down in the inheritance hierarchy. This implies that class invariants may only be strengthened (which is a cornerstone of the Eiffel programming language; see *Eiffel: The Language* [70]).

This section showed how to create a transformation for a very specific decoration of a class. If you wish, a more general transformation that directly supports the Decorator pattern is possible. Such a transformation would have command-line parameters for the code to be executed before and after method invocations. The specification (and not the implementation) would follow the scheme described in [32] (which is repeated in chapter 8 of *Putting Metaclasses to Work* [33]).

8.3 Proxy (again)

Chapter 4 presented the use of `java.lang.reflect.Proxy` to implement a number of design patterns. This section presents a transformation that implements the Proxy pattern. That is, given an input class object (representing an interface), the transformation generates a class supporting that interface in which the implementation of each method forwards all calls to a target object. In effect, this

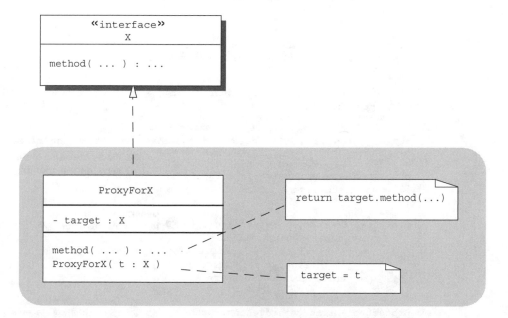

Figure 8.3   Design for the outcome of the use of the `C2ProxyForC` transformation

transformation replicates the workings of java.lang.reflect.Proxy. This transformation generates code to replace dynamic proxies (which forward calls with the invoke method of Method) with faster static proxies (which forward calls with compiled method invocations). For example, a good candidate for such replacement may be a scheme for dynamic class replacement similar to what is presented in section 6.4.

Figure 8.3 show the design for the transformation C2ProxyForC. The gray area highlights the result of the transformation. The basic concept is simple: have one constructor that sets the target of the proxy instance, and implement each method to forward the call to the target.

Listing 8.11 presents the code for the C2ProxyForC transformation, which follows the design in figure 8.3.

Listing 8.11 The C2ProxyForC transformation

```java
package c2c;
import java.lang.reflect.*;
import mopex.*;

public class C2ProxyForC extends C2CTransformation {

    static public void main( String[] args ) {
        new C2ProxyForC().createClass( args );
    }

    protected String generateClassNamePrefix() {
        return "ProxyFor" + super.generateClassNamePrefix();
    }

    protected void checkAndProcessArgs( Args args ) {        ❶ Ensures that the input
        super.checkAndProcessArgs( args );                     class is an interface

        if ( !inputClassObject.isInterface() )
            throw new C2CException( "input class is not an interface" );
    }                                                        ❷ Places the name of the input
                                                               class in the list for implements
    protected UQueue generateInterfaces() {    ←┘
        return super.generateInterfaces().add(inputClassName);
    }
                                                 Generates declarations
    protected String generateFields() {     ❸ for two private fields
        return super.generateFields()
            + "    private " + inputClassName + " target;\n"
            + "    private static final String targetClassName = \""
            + qualifiedInputClassName + "\";\n";
    }
                                                       Creates a constructor
    protected String generateConstructors() {    ❹ that initializes the target
        return super.generateConstructors()
```

```
            + outputClassName + "( " + inputClassName + " tgt ) {\n"
            + "        target = tgt;\n"
            + "}\n";
    }
    protected String generateMethods() {
        String result = "";
        Method[] methods = Mopex.selectMethods( inputClassObject,
                                                Modifier.PUBLIC,
                                                Modifier.STATIC,
                                                java.lang.Object.class );
        for ( int i = 0; i < methods.length; i++ ) {
            int mods = Mopex.getModifiersWithout( methods[i],
                                                  Modifier.NATIVE
                                                | Modifier.ABSTRACT );
            result += "    " + Modifier.toString(mods) + " "
                    + Mopex.headerSuffixToString( methods[i] ) + "{\n";
            Class[] fpl = methods[i].getParameterTypes();
            String apl = Mopex.actualParametersToString( fpl );
            if ( methods[i].getReturnType() == void.class ) {
                result += "        target."
                        + methods[i].getName()
                        + "(" + apl + ");\n";
            } else {
                result += "        return target."
                        + methods[i].getName()
                        + "(" + apl + ");\n";
            }
            result += "    }\n";
        }
        result +=
            "    public boolean equals( Object obj ) {\n" +
            "        return target.equals( obj );\n" +
            "    }\n" +
            "    public int hashCode() {\n" +
            "        return target.hashCode();\n" +
            "    }\n" +
            "    public String equals() {\n" +
            "        return target.toString();\n" +
            "    }\n";
        return super.generateMethods() + result;
    }
    protected void checkPostconditions(){
        if ( outputClassObject.getDeclaredConstructors().length != 1 )
            throw new C2CException("a proxy has only one constructor");
        super.checkPostconditions( );
    }
}
```

⑤ Creates an implementation for each method in the interface

⑥ Ensures that no other transformation adds a constructor

There is very little subtlety in this transformation. Let's look at the details:

❶ checkAndProcessArgs ensures that the input class is an interface.

❷ generateInterfaces places the name of the input class in the list for the imple-ments clause.

❸ generateFields ensures that there are two private fields. One is an instance variable for holding the target of the proxy object. The other is a static for conve-niently determining the type of the target objects.

❹ generateConstructors creates a one-parameter constructor that initializes the target.

❺ generateMethods creates an implementation for each method in the interface. In addition, overrides are generated for equals, hashCode, and toString, all of which are forwarded to the target; this parallels the workings of java.lang.reflect.Proxy. Each implemented the method forwards each call with a statically compiled invocation.

❻ The override of checkPostConditions ensures that no other transformation adds a constructor. Such a constructor is likely to cause an error, because it would not initialize the target instance variable.

This simple transformation has a limitation. It fails to produce compilable code if the input interface declares either equals, hashCode, or toString with the same signature as Object, because these methods become doubly declared. We leave it to you to correct this limitation.

The restriction that the input class file represents a Java interface steers us clear of many problems. For example, suppose the input class file represents a Java class. The generated output class must extend (subclass) that input class, because a proxy instance must be assignable to any entity of the type of the input class. But subclassing implies that the instance variables of the input class are inherited. These instance variables are vestigial in the sense that they have no meaning in the proxy. However, the fact that their initializers do get called in the context of the proxy instance can be a cause for concern.

The C2ProxyForC transformation is narrowly focused. It generates a class that applies the Proxy pattern for the purposes of hiding the location of the target object. Because the code that forwards method calls is a local method call, the hidden target must reside in the same address space as the proxy instance. This could, of course, be changed by using a different version of the transformation. Although C2ProxyForC is simple, it has its uses, for example, when you wish to dynamically change the implementation of an object (which is a problem that is addressed in chapter 6).

It is worthwhile to compare the C2C framework with java.lang.reflect.Proxy. As an example of the former, C2ProxyForC is a specific transformation with one purpose: to hide the location of the target. The latter, java.lang.reflect.Proxy, produces proxy instances that may do the job of a number of transformations (for example, invariant checking) depending on what the invocation handler does. This highlights the difference between the two facilities. With the C2C framework, variation is achieved with the implementation (and composition) of small transformations. With Proxy, variation is achieved through the implementation and composition of different invocation handlers. The C2C framework is more malleable (for example, the coding of a singleton is not a problem amenable to a solution with Proxy). On the other hand, Proxy usually requires less code. Each has its own performance advantages. The use of the invoke method of Method in the invocation handler is much slower than using a compiled method call (a fact that we demonstrate in chapter 9). But if proxy classes must be dynamically generated, Proxy can create proxy classes faster than code generation.

8.4 *Another composition feature*

The classes generated by C2ProxyForC create simple proxies. That is, their instances hide the reference to the target and forward method calls but add no new functionality. This is different from the use of java.lang.reflect.Proxy in chapter 4, where we demonstrated how proxy instances can add new functionality. On the other hand, section 8.2 demonstrates how to create a transformation that adds functionality via subclassing. This leads to a very pleasing composition feature. A class generated by C2ProxyForC may be decorated by a subclassing transformation. For example, given an interface Squirrel, C2ProxyForC can generate ProxyForSquirrel. Subsequently, you can use C2InvariantCheckingC to generate the InvariantCheckingProxyForSquirrel class (the -output parameter defined in section 7.2.3 may be used to give this class a more pleasing name). This composition feature mitigates the problem of having a great subclassing transformation but no ability to use it on a class declared to be final.

8.5 *Problematic issues in writing class-to-class transformations*

This chapter and the previous chapter are dedicated to reflective code generation—more specifically, class-to-class transformations. This extensive coverage is needed because code generation is the main tool used to circumvent the limitations of Java reflection with respect to intercessional features. But code generation does have its problems. Before leaving this topic, let's summarize the Java features that cause difficulty in code generation.

- *Final classes and final methods*—Some transformations (for example, `C2ExtentManagedC` in listing 7.7 on page 160) attempt to create a subclass of the input class. This cannot be done if the input class is declared `final`. Even if the input class is not final, some methods may be declared final, which may also make the transformation impossible to apply if a final method needs to be overridden. In some circumstances (for example, when applying the Decorator pattern), you may employ a delegation strategy that uses a proxy, as is done in chapter 4 or as alluded to in section 8.4.

- *Static methods*—Private instance variables may be accessed by a static method if it is passed an object reference. This kind of variable access breaks encapsulation in such a way that the reflective programmer has no opportunity to intercede. For example, a call to such a static method could violate an invariant. Our invariant-checking transformation does not generate code to quickly detect the violation.

- *Public fields*—When creating a subclass of the input class, public fields are very problematic for a transformation, because there is no way to intercede on access to a public field. Java correctly does not allow a subclass to reduce the access permissions of inherited methods, which means if the input class declares an instance variable public, a transformation that creates a subclass cannot change that declaration. However, public fields break encapsulation. The only way to reestablish encapsulation is with a delegation strategy that presents a proxy to a client.

- *equals*—A transformation must take care to handle `equals` properly. This is required even if the input is an interface. A change to `equals` requires a change to `hashCode` (proper Java programming requires that two equal objects have the same hash code). In addition, if `Comparable` is implemented, the implementation of `compareTo` must be consistent with `equals`.

- *RuntimeException and Error*—The handling of runtime exceptions and errors is also problematic, because they are not declared by the input class. The programmer of a transformation needs to understand whether to handle them or pass them on.

- *Constructors*—Generating constructors for a class is usually simple (as in `C2ExtentManagedC`), but there are times when it can get complex. For example, in the `C2SingletonC` transformation, a factory method is generated for each constructor, but it is unclear whether you should be allowed to call a factory method with arguments when a singleton exists.

- *Nested classes*—The `C2C` framework does not allow transformation of a nested class. The topic of nested classes by itself is complex. Trying to cope with nested classes makes the transformations so complex that there does not appear to be a reasonable return on investment.

- *Data inheritance*—Situations arise when you would prefer to transform an interface rather than a class or an abstract class. Such situations occur when you create a subclass where the inherited fields have no meaning. For example, `C2ProxyForC` restricts the input class to be an interface. There is a strong temptation to eliminate this restriction. You should resist this temptation because to be substitutable, the generated proxy class must be a subclass of the input class. This raises the nasty question of how to handle any inherited instance variables. For an object that must forward methods, these instance variables have no meaning, but they exist and there is no way to get rid of them.

- *Inheritable properties*—Various properties of an input class must also be properties of the output class if a transformation generates a subclass. For example, if the input class is `Cloneable`, then the output class must be `Cloneable`, too. The same is true for `Serializable`, `Runnable`, `Comparable`, and so on. At times, method inheritance takes care of the situation and there is nothing you need to do. At other times, the nature of the transformation dictates that you must consider issues specific to the transformation. For example, `C2SingletonC` does not subclass a `Cloneable` class, because the singleton property is in conflict with the cloneable property.

- *Multiple execution of code added by transformations*—In using class-to-class transformations, you must take care when transforming both a class and one of its subclasses. This can lead to undesired multiple executions of the code added by the transformation.

This is a good, but not comprehensive, list of the problematic issues. Many of them have the same underlying cause. The type checking of the compiler is programmed as if a subclass implements a subtype. This complex topic is covered excellently in Barbara Liskov and John Guttag's *Program Development in Java* [62].

Suffice it to say that the better transformations do not fool the compiler by generating subclasses that are not subtypes.

8.6 *Summary*

Understanding how to apply design patterns makes you a better designer of object-oriented applications. This chapter presented a set of code-generation tools, class-to-class transformations, for quickly applying a pattern. Such tools do not characterize the pattern as much as they capture a particular style of applying the pattern. Introspection is particularly important in this kind of code

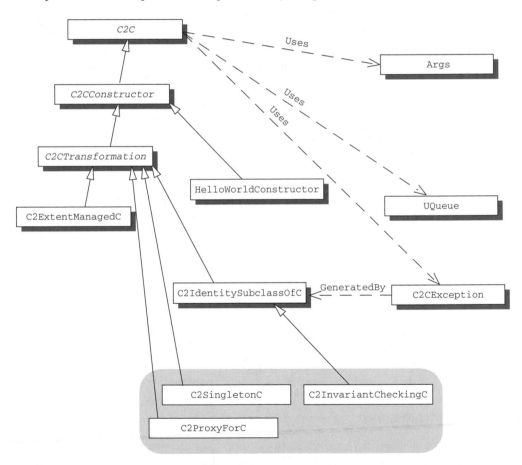

Figure 8.4   Complete class diagram for the class-to-class transformation framework. The classes added to the framework in this chapter are displayed in the gray area.

generation because introspection allows the code generator to examine the context in which the pattern is applied and properly adapt the code to be generated.

We chose to present transformations for Singleton, Decorator, and Proxy, because they are among the easiest patterns to support with transformations. Six other of the twenty-three presented in *Design Patterns* [38] have the potential to be supported with a class-to-class transformation. Of these, five—Flyweight, Memento, Prototype, Chain of Responsibility, and Builder—have effective support with a transformation (see [34]). The sixth, Adaptor, requires so much ancillary information to apply the pattern that writing a transformation does not produce a useful tool. There are many software design patterns; in fact, there is *The Patterns Almanac 2000* [77]. How many of these are amenable to being supported with class-to-class transformations is an open question.

This concludes the two-chapter sequence on class-to-class transformations. Figure 8.4 contains the class diagram for the framework as presented in this book. After two chapters, it is easy to forget that there are two primary reasons for introducing class-to-class transformations. First, they are a concrete problem that allows us to exercise our understanding of the Java reflection API. Second, code generation is the main tool for circumventing the limitations of the Java reflection API.

Evaluating performance

9

The flexibility achieved by reflection in Java is attained to a large extent by delaying the binding of names. That is, the binding of names (of methods, fields, and so on) that is normally done by the compiler is delayed until runtime. This delayed binding has a performance impact in the form of searches and checks executed at runtime. As an example of the former, getMethod must search the inheritance hierarchy for the appropriate method object. An example of the latter is Method.invoke,[1] which must check accessibility. This is not a negative statement; it is merely an observation of the trade-off involved in the use of reflection.

The purpose of this chapter is to show you how to measure the performance of reflection. As Java evolves, as computer architecture progresses, and as circuit features contract, the performance trade-offs will change. Understanding how to make the design decisions is a skill that outlasts memorizing the performance numbers for a particular platform.

In chapter 5, George was assigned to write an invariant-checking facility. George is now interested in refactoring the checkInvariant calls into one place. This refactoring will improve readability, which lowers maintenance costs. His understanding of reflection gives him two design alternatives:

1 He can use java.lang.reflect.Proxy with an invocation handler that wraps the Method.invoke that forwards the method with calls to check-Invariant.

2 He can use the C2InvariantCheckingProxyForC transformation (see section 8.4) that calls checkInvariant before and after forwarding the method. (Note that he does not want to use C2InvariantCheckingC directly, because he cannot rearrange the inheritance hierarchy to avoid duplicate calls to the invariant method.)

In the application, classes that check invariants have interfaces and have instances created only in factory methods. This means that the refactoring will be relatively easy. George also knows that the application currently satisfies its performance requirements.

George prefers the first alternative because there is less code to write. Before he performs this refactoring, George would like to have some idea that, after the refactoring, his application will still satisfy its performance requirements. This

---

[1] Because both Method and InvocationHandler have an invoke method, just writing invoke is confusing and can be ambiguous. The phrase "the invoke method of Method" leads to some ugly sentences. In this chapter, we use Method.invoke to mean "the invoke method of Method." Unqualified uses of invoke denote the invoke method of an invocation handler.

chapter shows how to write programs to make the measurements required for such design decisions and how to go about the analysis.

9.1 Categorizing performance impact

The impact on performance associated with the use of Java reflection can be divided into three categories. It is important to understand these categories because each impacts the performance of an application at different times. Consequently, each may matter more or less in design decisions depending on the application. Let's define the categories:

- *Construction overhead*—The time it takes to perform modifications to a class object during its construction. This may manifest itself in extra latency for constructing a proxy class or instance. It may also take place during dynamic loading and reflective construction of a delegate. For our transformation framework, construction overhead takes place during the running of the transformation and the compilation of the new class, in addition to dynamic loading and construction. Normally, this is just a one-time cost.

- *Execution overhead*—The extra time added to the services supplied by an object/component because of its reflective features. For example, this is the extra time it takes to call a method using `Method.invoke` compared to a compiled call. Another example is the added latency of forwarding method calls through a proxy. Generally, execution overhead, of course, is incurred more frequently than construction overhead.

- *Granularity overhead*—Added latency resulting from reflective code that applies to more of an object/component than was intended or necessary. Sometimes, when using a proxy (either generated with `Proxy` or with our framework), the change need not apply to the entire interface. For example, consider the synchronized proxy of section 4.6.2 It may not be necessary for all methods to be synchronized. The extra synchronization may result in a decrease in attainable concurrency, which in turn may slow an application.

These categories enable us to make some quick decisions. For example, construction overhead may not be an issue for a very long-lived application because all classes are loaded when the application begins execution. In the following section we concentrate on the execution overhead because, in general, it has the highest impact. Our goal is to demonstrate how to measure the performance of a reflective feature and how to make inferences about a design from such measurements.

9.2 *Using microbenchmarks*

A **benchmark** is a test used to assess the performance of hardware or software. A **microbenchmark** [2] is a performance measurement of a short piece of code. Deciding how short a piece of code must be to qualify is subjective. However, the intent is the desire to obtain a measurement of some small identified capability that can be used as a parameter to a performance model. This section shows you how write microbenchmarks. Later in the chapter, we write another microbenchmark to help George with his design decision.

A program for a microbenchmark has the basic form of the following pseudo code:

```
Perform setup
m0 = get first measurement
for (int i=0; i<repCount; i++)  {
        Run code to be measured
}
m1 = get second measurement
report (m1-m0)/repCount
```

The metric may be time or space or some other quantity that is important enough to deserve this special attention. Determining a sufficient number of repetitions is a tactical decision based on issues such as clock resolution, the need to amortize overhead, and so on. Listing 9.1 shows a real program for a microbenchmark to measure the time it takes to print "Hello world!"

Listing 9.1 `HelloWorldBenchmark`

```java
public class HelloWorldBenchmark {
    public static double aDouble = 123456789.0;
    public static void main(String args[]) {

        int numberOfIterations = 15000;

        // Loop to measure the overhead
        long time0 = System.currentTimeMillis();
        for ( int j = 0; j < numberOfIterations; j++ ) {
            aDouble /= 1.000001;
        }
        long time1 = System.currentTimeMillis();

        aDouble = 123456789.0;
        System.out.println("Hello world!");

        long time2 = System.currentTimeMillis();
        for ( int j = 0; j < numberOfIterations; j++ ) {
            aDouble /= 1.000001;
            System.out.println("Hello world!");
```

```
      }
      long time3 = System.currentTimeMillis();

      double timeForOverheadLoop = (time1 - time0);
      double timeForHelloWorld = (time3 - time2) - timeForOverheadLoop;
      System.out.println( "HelloWorldBenchmark: " + timeForOverheadLoop
                        + " milliseconds for basic loop." );
      System.out.println( "HelloWorldBenchmark: " + timeForHelloWorld
                        + " milliseconds for " + numberOfIterations
                        + " iterations." );
      System.out.println( "HelloWorldBenchmark: "
                        + (timeForHelloWorld/numberOfIterations)
                        + " milliseconds per print command" );
   }
}
```

Here are some general guidelines for writing microbenchmarks properly.

- *Account for overhead*—This is the code for loop control and obtaining the metric. In listing 9.1, the loop is timed without the code to be measured in order to compute the overhead, which subsequently can be subtracted from the timing of the code to be measured.

- *Warm up the code*—The code to be measured may need to be executed (possibly more than once) to eliminate variance due to special events (for example, the loading of a dependent class). The microbenchmark in listing 9.1 executes the print command once outside the main timing loop for this reason.

- *Know the clock resolution*—The program in listing 9.1 uses System.current-TimeMillis to get the time in milliseconds. However, the reporting of the timing of the overhead clearly showed the clock resolution be 10 milliseconds. The main timing loop is executed for sufficient iterations to make the resolution an insignificant issue. You should not make judgements based on measurements that differ by less than twice the clock resolution.

- *Understand the effect of compiler optimizations*—A common pitfall is for optimization to remove the overhead loop. In listing 9.1, we avoid this pitfall by having the overhead loop change the field, aDouble, that is static and public with a divide command (the change cannot be eliminated because access from outside the class is possible). Another optimization is in-line expansion, or in-lining, in which the compiler substitutes the body of a method at the method call site in place of the method call. The technique used later to prevent in-lining works for Java 1.4.1—a different technique may be required for other versions of Java.

- *Eliminate interference*—With a modern operating system, much is going on asynchronously that can potentially interfere with obtaining accurate measurements. Some examples of possible sources of interference are network communications, garbage collection, maintenance tasks such as defragmentation, and so on. To properly run a microbenchmark, you must ensure that these interfering activities are shut down.

- *Apply proper statistical methods*—Running a microbenchmark is an experiment, and so you can expect different results from run to run. This is where the elementary statistics that you were required to study comes in handy. Bill Alexander [2] recommends repeating your benchmark measurements until the *t*-test indicates .95 confidence that the true value is within 5% of the mean of the measurements. (If you need a good statistics book, try *Statistics: The Exploration and Analysis of Data* [20].)

- *Use common sense*—You should examine your measurements for patterns. If you find one, you may have to redesign your microbenchmark. For example, the distribution may look bimodal—the measurements seem to form two clusters. In the bimodal case, you should redesign the microbenchmark to measure each modality separately.

- *Expect uncertainty*—Modern processors are exceedingly complex. At times the microbenchmark code itself affects the measurement (for example, by affecting the content of the various caches). No matter how hard you try, there is no way to eliminate this source of uncertainty (short of using the simulators used by the microprocessor designers).

Each of these guidelines has a Java interpretation that you must understand. For example, garbage collection in Java happens asynchronously, and you probably do not want to count the time used for garbage collections. If your microbenchmark creates few objects, garbage collection is usually not a problem. On the other hand, if many objects are created, it would be prudent to study the rules for garbage collection in your Java runtime environment.

We ran the simple microbenchmark on an IBM T20 Thinkpad (750 MHz Pentium III with 256MB RAM running Java 2 Platform, Standard Edition, version 1.4.1 for Windows 2000). For 10 runs of the microbenchmark, we obtained a mean of 327.4 microseconds to print "Hello world!" to a command window. The standard deviation was .326. The *t*-test indicates that a .95 confidence interval would be 327.15 microseconds to 327.65 microseconds, which is well within 5% of the mean.

The reason for running the simple microbenchmark was to get an idea of the time required for a common operation, System.out.println. We need to know this when we look at the times for some reflective operations later in this chapter. Intuitively, we know that System.out.println is an expensive operation. In addition, we need to time an inexpensive operation.

Now let's do one more microbenchmark to calculate the time required to call a nonstatic method. Listing 9.2 presents an interface, DoNothingInterface, with one method, doNothing. This interface is implemented by the DoNothing class in listing 9.3. A microbenchmark CallBenchmark (listing 9.4) measures the time for calling the method. Oddly, doNothing does something. The code in the body of doNothing is written to prevent the compiler from in-lining the method. For 20 runs of the microbenchmark on our Thinkpad, we obtained a mean of 8.89 nanoseconds to call doNothing. The standard deviation was .71. The *t*-test indicates that a .95 confidence interval would be 8.46 nanoseconds to 9.31 nanoseconds, which is just within 5% of the mean.

Listing 9.2 DoNothingInterface

```
interface DoNothingInterface {
    void doNothing();
}
```

Listing 9.3 DoNothing, which implements DoNothingInterface

```
public class DoNothing implements DoNothingInterface {
    public void doNothing( ) {
        CallBenchmark.aDouble
            = CallBenchmark.compute(CallBenchmark.aDouble);
    }
}
```

Listing 9.4 CallBenchmark

```
public class CallBenchmark {

    public static double aDouble;
    public static double aDouble1;
    public static double aDouble2;
    public static double aDouble3;

    public static double compute( double x ) {
        aDouble1 = aDouble1 + aDouble;
```

```
        aDouble2 = aDouble2 + 2 * aDouble;
        aDouble3 = aDouble3 + 3 * aDouble;
        return x / 1.000001;
    }
    public static void main(String args[]) {
        int numberOfIterations = 100000000;
        DoNothing target = new DoNothing();
        long time0 = System.currentTimeMillis();
        aDouble = 123456789.0;
        aDouble1 = 0;
        aDouble2 = 2;
        aDouble3 = 3;
        for ( int j = 0; j < numberOfIterations; j++ )
            aDouble = compute(aDouble);
        long time1 = System.currentTimeMillis();
        aDouble = 123456789.0;
        aDouble1 = 0;
        aDouble2 = 2;
        aDouble3 = 3;
        for ( int j = 0; j < numberOfIterations; j++ )
            target.doNothing( );
        long time2 = System.currentTimeMillis();

        double timeForCall = (time2 - time1) - (time1 - time0);
        System.out.println( "CallBenchmark: " + (time1 - time0)
                            + " milliseconds for basic loop executing "
                            + numberOfIterations + " iterations." );
        System.out.println( "CallBenchmark: "
                            + timeForCall + " milliseconds for "
                            + numberOfIterations + " calls." );
    }
}
```

9.3 *Benchmarking two ways to use Proxy*

Next, we present a microbenchmark that addresses George's design decision. This microbenchmark measures both the time to forward a call to a Java proxy with a compiled method call and the time to forward a call to a Java proxy using `Method.invoke`. Listing 9.5 shows the microbenchmark. It times the invocation of the method named `doNothing` in the `CallBenchmark` class by first calling the method on a proxy where the invocation handler, `DoNothingCaller`, implements the forwarding of the call with a compiled method call. The microbenchmark also uses a second class named `DoNothingInvoker`, which also implements the `InvocationHandler` interface. The `invoke` method in this class uses `Method.invoke` to forward the call to `doNothing`. Listing 9.6 contains the `DoNothingCaller` and `DoNothingInvoker` classes.

Listing 9.5 `InvokeBenchmark`

```java
import java.lang.reflect.*;

public class InvokeBenchmark {

    public static DoNothing target = new DoNothing();
    public static Class[] interfaces = { DoNothingInterface.class };

    public static Object newProxy( InvocationHandler obj ) {
        return Proxy.newProxyInstance( obj.getClass().getClassLoader(),
                                       interfaces,
                                       obj );
    }
    public static void main(String args[]) {
        int numberOfIterations = 5000000;
        DoNothingCaller caller = new DoNothingCaller();
        DoNothingInterface proxyForCaller
            = (DoNothingInterface)newProxy( caller );
        DoNothingInvoker invoker = new DoNothingInvoker();
        DoNothingInterface proxyForInvoker
            = (DoNothingInterface)newProxy( invoker );

        long time0 = System.currentTimeMillis();
        CallBenchmark.aDouble = 123456789.0;
        for ( int j = 0; j < numberOfIterations; j++ )      Direct call
            InvokeBenchmark.target.doNothing();             to method
        long time1 = System.currentTimeMillis();
        CallBenchmark.aDouble = 123456789.0;
        for ( int j = 0; j < numberOfIterations; j++ )      ❶ Call thru a proxy
            proxyForCaller.doNothing( );                       using a compiled call
        long time2 = System.currentTimeMillis();
        CallBenchmark.aDouble = 123456789.0;
        for ( int j = 0; j < numberOfIterations; j++ )      ❷ Call thru a
            proxyForInvoker.doNothing( );                      proxy using a
        long time3 = System.currentTimeMillis();               Method.invoke

        double timeForProxyCall = (time2 - time1) - (time1 - time0);
        double timeForProxyCallPlusInvoke = (time3 - time2) - (time1 - time0);
        System.out.println( "InvokeBenchmark: " + timeForProxyCall
                            + " milliseconds for "
                            + numberOfIterations + " proxy calls." );
        System.out.println( "InvokeBenchmark: " + timeForProxyCallPlusInvoke
                            + " milliseconds for " + numberOfIterations
                            + " proxy calls using invoke." );
    }
}
```

Listing 9.6 Classes used by `InvokeBenchmark`

```java
import java.lang.reflect.*;

public class DoNothingCaller implements InvocationHandler {

    public Object invoke( Object t, Method m, Object[] args )
        throws Throwable
    {
        InvokeBenchmark.target.doNothing();
        return null;
    }
}

-----------------------------------------------------------------

import java.lang.reflect.*;

class DoNothingInvoker implements InvocationHandler {

    public Object invoke( Object t, Method m, Object[] args )
        throws Throwable
    {
        return m.invoke( InvokeBenchmark.target, args );
    }
}
```

Figure 9.1 presents three sequence diagrams that each depict one of the intervals timed in the benchmarks. The top sequence diagram represents the situation programmed in `CallBenchmark` (listing 9.4). The bottom two sequence diagrams represent the situations programmed in `InvokeBenchmark` (listing 9.5). Keep in mind that the last one is an abstraction of the reality depicted in figure 4.2.

For nine runs of the microbenchmark on our Thinkpad, we obtained the following results:

- For calling `doNothing` through the proxy with a method call, the time to use a proxy had a mean of 25.0 nanoseconds. The standard deviation was 1.34. The *t*-test indicates that a .95 confidence interval would be 23.99 nanoseconds to 26.01 nanoseconds, which is just within 5% of the mean.

- For calling `doNothing` through the proxy that uses `Method.invoke`, the time to use a proxy had a mean of 2928.0 nanoseconds. The standard deviation was 12.57. The *t*-test indicates that a .95 confidence interval would be 2918.5 nanoseconds to 2937.5 nanoseconds, which is well within 5% of the mean.

Both cases measure the time required to get the method into control and return. These measurements are consistent with what we learned from `CallBenchmark`.

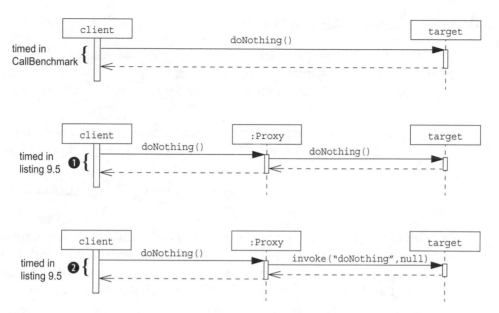

Figure 9.1   The three cases timed in the program `InvokeBenchmark`

The `InvokeBenchmark` program provides basic measurements that directly apply to the issue of replacing a method call with either a dynamic proxy that forwards calls using `Method.invoke` or a proxy that forwards calls using a compiled method. This is not quite George's design problem. However, if the dynamic proxy that forwards calls with compiled methods is sufficient, then so is a static proxy generated by the `C2InvariantCheckingProxyForC` transformation (because it forwards the method call without marshalling the arguments into an array). Rather than taking a direct approach to George's problem, we presented the `InvokeBenchmark` program because it provides more valuable insight into the performance of Java reflection, namely, the performance of dynamic proxies in the absence of `Method.invoke`.

The measurements show that calling a method (that has no parameters) through a proxy is about 2.29 times as expensive as executing a directly compiled call. Further, calling the method through a proxy that uses `Method.invoke` is about 331 times as expensive as directly calling the method. This certainly does not mean that an application will run either 2.29 or 331 times slower if it uses these features. Applications do much more than call methods.

Next we consider how such raw performance measurements can be used to analyze software design decisions.

9.4 *Understanding Amdahl's Law*

We know that the use of reflection will slow our application in exchange for greater adaptability, increased reuse, and higher quality. All software engineers face the question of whether to pay the price for these benefits. There are two viable strategies:

- Use the features that yield maximum adaptability and higher quality. If the resulting application is too slow, then it is easier to speed up a high-quality program than correct a low-quality program.

- Analyze the impact of the reflective features and know beforehand which to use.

Rarely is the software engineer in a position to adopt the first strategy. For this reason, we now focus on how to perform analyses required by the second strategy.

When designing an enhancement to a microprocessor, computer architects use Amdahl's Law to compute speedup [43] where speedup is expected to be a number greater than 1. The basic idea is

$$Speedup \quad = \quad \frac{Performance\ of\ task\ without\ using\ the\ enhancement}{Performance\ of\ task\ using\ the\ enhancement}$$

In this formula, the enhancement is the use of the reflective feature, which we expect to be slower. If speedup is computed, we would deal with numbers less than 1.

However, in general, the design problem that most interests us is using reflective features to gain flexibility. For this reason, it is better to use the inverse of this formula to calculate slowdown. This has the additional advantage of yielding numbers greater than 1, which makes for a more understandable presentation. The formula to compute slowdown is

$$Slowdown \quad = \quad \frac{Performance\ of\ task\ using\ the\ enhancement}{Performance\ of\ task\ without\ using\ the\ enhancement}$$

Amdahl's Law is quite general and can be applied at various levels of granularity. For example, it can be applied to an entire application, a thread, a method, or a short code sequence. Amdahl's Law recognizes that slowdown (or speedup) depends on the proportion of the work affected by the enhancement. The following equation is the version of Amdahl's Law that is used in the remainder of this chapter.

$$Slowdown = \frac{RTime + Work}{NTime + Work}$$

where *RTime* is the microbenchmark measurement of a reflective feature and *NTime* is the microbenchmark measurement for its nonreflective alternative. *Work* is the relative amount of time spent doing other things. For example, *RTime* may be the time to call a method through a proxy that executes a compiled call (as in `DoNothingCaller`) with the corresponding *NTime* being the time to simply execute a compiled call (the measurement obtained with `CallBenchmark`).

It is usually convenient to express *Work* in terms of multiples of *NTime*, that is,

$$Work = NTime * x$$

where *x* is the scaling factor that dictates how much more time is spent doing other things. Making this substitution yields

$$Slowdown = \frac{RTime + NTime * x}{NTime + NTime * x}$$

which can be rewritten as

$$Slowdown = \frac{\dfrac{RTime}{NTime} + x}{1 + x}$$

This form of Amdahl's Law allows us to make design decisions for a range of processors. For example, the *RTime/NTime* ratio should be about the same for all Pentium IIIs no matter the speed at which the clock is running. That is, once the ratio *RTime/NTime* is established, the slowdown is about the same for all Pentium IIIs. A design decision that is appropriate for a slow processor of a particular family is in general also appropriate for a faster processor, but the converse is not true.

Before using this form of Amdahl's Law with the data gathered in section 9.3, let us study the properties of the previous slowdown function with *x* as an independent parameter. Knowing the properties of such an important function is important for building intuition and accurate decision making. The following properties are derived using some elementary calculus:

- The *y*-intercept is *RTime/NTime* (derived by setting $x = 0$).

- For positive *x*, the function is greater than 1 (because *RTime/NTime* is greater than 1).

- The limit as *x* approaches infinity is 1 (that is, the line *y*=1 is an asymptote).

- The function is monotonically decreasing for positive *x* (the first derivative is $(1-RTime/NTime)/(1+x)^2$, which is negative for positive *x*).

- The shape of curve appears as shown in figure 9.2. The knee of the curve is the point at which the rate of decrease falls below -1 (this is found by solving for *x* when the value of the first derivative is -1).

The properties aid in making better design decisions. Consider knowing the knee of the curve. If you believe that the value of *x* for your application is much, much larger than the *x* value of the knee, then your calculation of slowdown is not going to be sensitive to how accurately you measure *x* (the amount of other work the application does). On the other hand, slowdown is very sensitive to the workload, if it is estimated to be to the left of the knee.

It is now time to combine our microbenchmark results with Amdahl's Law to calculate the slowdown curves for two kinds of enhancements. The first is using dynamic proxies that forward with compiled method calls as in `DoNothingCaller`. The second is using dynamic proxies that forward methods with `Method.invoke` as in `DoNothingInvoker`.

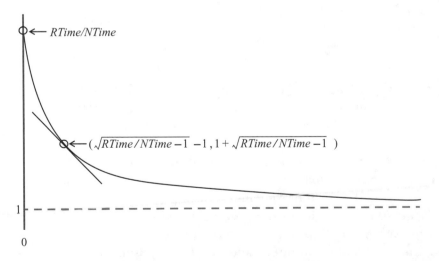

Figure 9.2   The shape of the slowdown curve

9.5 *Applying Amdahl's Law*

First, let us examine the use of `Proxy`. Figure 9.3 shows the slowdown curve for use of `Proxy` where *NTime* is 8.89 nanoseconds and *RTime/NTime* is 2.81. (If the position of the knee of the curve at x = .346 looks odd, remember that the axes are not uniform.) The slowdown curve shows us that if *Work* is 10 times *NTime* (88.9 nanoseconds for our T20 Thinkpad), the overhead for using a proxy is just under 17%. If *Work* is 20 times *NTime*, the overhead decreases to just under 9%. Executing a compiled method call in Java 1.4.1 is highly efficient, which means that 10 or 20 times *NTime* is not very much work. For example, a side effect of `CallBenchmark` is the timing of that code added to suppress in-lining of the `doNothing` method. Those few additions, multiplications, and the loop control take between 10 and 20 times *NTime*. In addition, the `HelloWorldBenchmark` demonstrated that the `println` is about 32,000 times *NTime*. Slowdown goes below 1% at about 190 times *NTime*. So the slowdown due to the use of `Proxy` at miniscule levels (below 5%) should be quite tolerable in most applications.

In general, should the software engineer be concerned about this level of overhead from the use of `Proxy`? This is a highly context-dependent issue. On one hand, microprocessor performance is improving at about 3.9% per month (which is the monthly growth rate that is implied by Moore's Law). On the other hand, the global context set by Moore's Law provides little solace to the software

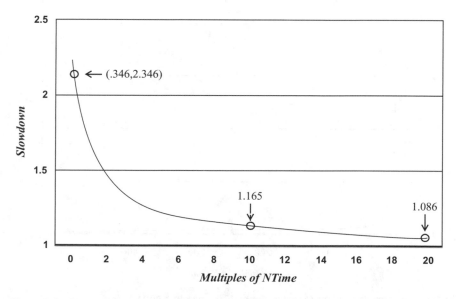

Figure 9.3 The slowdown curve for calling a method on a proxy

engineer whose product fails because of performance issues. The use of Amdahl's Law arms the software engineer to objectively address the performance issues.

Now let's turn our attention to `Method.invoke`. Figure 9.4 shows the slowdown curve for the use of `Proxy` where *NTime* is 8.89 nanoseconds and *RTime/NTime* is 329.4. The curve shows a very rapid decrease of slowdown when work is less than 17 times *NTime* where the overhead is 1900%. The slowdown curve shows us that if *Work* is 250 times, the overhead for using a proxy is about 131%. If *Work* is 500 times *NTime*, the overhead decreases to about 66%. Slowdown goes below 10% at about 3,500 times *NTime* and below 5% at 6,000 times *NTime*.

If these numbers seem high, consider the following. The `HelloWorldBench-mark` measured the time to print "Hello world!" as 327.4 microseconds. This is over 36,000 times *NTime*, which implies a slowdown of under 1%. It does not take

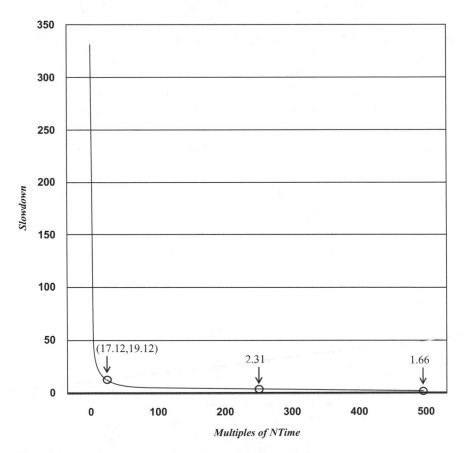

Figure 9.4   The slowdown curve for using `Method.invoke` in a proxy

much programming to overwhelm the execution overhead of `Method.invoke` and make it inconsequential. In addition, in a user interface, the execution overhead of `Method.invoke` (2.93 microseconds on our 750 MHz laptop) cannot be detected by its human user. In cases where you have discretion in using `Method.invoke`, the previous results dictate that you must exercise care in making the decision but should not dismiss its use out of hand.

As a reader of this book, you are interested in questions of the form, "Can reflective feature <blank> be used in the design while still satisfying the performance constraints?" We chose to present the measurements in figures 9.3 and 9.4 because of their relevance to two important design questions:

- Can `Proxy` alone be used while satisfying performance constraints?
- Can `Proxy` and `Method.invoke` be used while satisfying performance constraints?

This second question is exactly the one George is asking with respect to his desire to use the first design alternative. In this case, the situation is depicted in figure 9.4, where *RTime* is 2928.0 nanoseconds (the measurement for a proxy that forwards with `Method.invoke`) and *NTime* is 8.89 nanoseconds (the measurement for a compiled call). George needs to determine the value of x using the formula

$$Work = NTime * x$$

Because George has a running application that he wishes to refactor, he can instrument his application to determine *Work* for each applicable performance requirement. Note that the execution time of the `checkInvariant` method must be included in his determination of *Work*.

At this point, we need to leave George to finish this task. However, we must emphasize that when performing this kind of analysis, the granularity of the *Work* measurements must be the same as that of the performance requirements. That is, for each performance requirement, you must do a separate analysis with a commensurate *Work* measurement.

9.6 *Summary*

Runtime performance is often cited as a disadvantage that renders reflection APIs impractical. Don't be taken in by this argument. Reflection is not slow! Over the first 50 years of software engineering, similar arguments were made against the move to high-level languages, against the move to virtual memory, against the move to object-oriented programming, and, most recently, against the move to garbage collection.

Historically, the tide in software engineering favors those abstractions offering the best return on investment. Return on investment is a complex issue dealing with time to market, flexibility, availability of programmers, quality, and maintainability as well the performance of the software. As a software engineer, you should be making design decisions based on satisfaction of requirements and maximizing return on investment.

The speed of your software is not a measure of your competency as a software engineer. Most applications have no performance constraints other than "if possible, don't let any human user perceive any latency." This constraint is not changing. Meanwhile, ubiquitous multigigahertz multiprocessor laptops with ever-increasing amounts of storage are just around the corner. In addition, improved compilation of reflection APIs will further mitigate performance concerns associated with the use of reflection.

This progress increases the likelihood that software engineers can profitably apply reflection. However, you, as the software engineer, are not relieved of the obligation concerning performance requirements. You now have the tools to address these concerns when circumstances require it.

Reflecting on the future

10

In this chapter

- Future developments in Java reflection
- Concepts to remember

By now, you have probably thought of many places in your own applications where reflection can increase flexibility. This newfound flexibility has benefits in two dimensions:

- *Adaptation to change in both requirements and platform*—These adaptations allow an application to better serve the needs of its human users and keep pace with technology.
- *Reuse of components*—Flexible components programmed with reflection can be used in many contexts.

This improvement in flexibility has been brought about by a steady evolution in the reflective facilities in Java. This is clearly illustrated in figure 10.1. Java started from sound theory by representing classes as objects and instances of `Class`. Upon this base, metaobjects were added in `java.lang.reflect` to provide introspective capability. This was augmented in Java 1.3 with `Proxy` to provide something that approximates an intercessional capability. This augmentation continued in Java 1.4 with the addition of the `StackTraceElement`, which is essential for call stack introspection.

This timeline illustrates the Java community's commitment to evolving and augmenting Java's reflective capabilities. Following this trajectory and our understanding of reflection, we can reasonably expect more metadata and more intercessional capabilities in future versions. Let's see what is just over the horizon.

10.1 Looking forward: Java 1.5

There are several areas of Java 1.5 that will have a direct impact on programming with reflection. Among these are the addition of generics, the Annotation Facility, and a set of Java language extensions that include enumerated types and

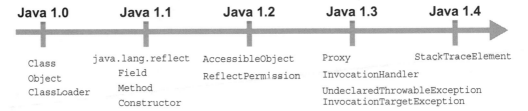

Figure 10.1   The timeline represents the evolution of Java reflection by matching features to the release in which they first appeared.

autoboxing. The web site for the Java Community Process (www.jcp.org) is the best place to preview what may be in Java 1.5.

The Java Community Process (JCP) is an organization that develops and revises the Java technology specifications, reference implementations, and test suites. The main process of the JCP is one that evolves a Java Specification Request (JSR) into a specification that is used to change a particular Java technology. The three JSRs of interest to us as reflective programmers are 14, 175, and 201. The overview in this chapter represents our best guess at how these JSRs will impact reflective programming in Java 1.5.

None of the new features of Java 1.5 invalidate any technique presented in this book. Just prior to the completion of this book, J2SE 1.5.0 Beta 1 became available. The code in this book does compile with Java 1.5. All of our test cases run without error. Of course, none of these test cases use the new features of Java 1.5, which may require some changes to code that we have presented. We identify some such changes later in this chapter.

10.1.1 *JSR 14—Generics*

Java 1.5 will have generic types and methods [8]. A generic type allows you parameterize a class with a type. This is very useful when you want a container that is specialized. Consider UQueue, which was introduced in chapter 7. That class gets specialized at runtime by having the user identify the type of queue entries in the constructor. A more elegant concept is to have a language that allows the specialization at compile time. Java 1.5 will have such a facility. For example, here is an overly simple way to define UQueue in Java 1.5:

```
class UQueue<T> extends ArrayList<T> {
   public boolean add( T m ) {
      if ( this.contains( m ) )
         return false;
      super.add( m );
      return true;
   }
}
```

The syntax <T> indicates that UQueue has a parameter T that must be a type name. A unique queue of Method is constructed with new UQueue<Method>() and a unique queue of String is constructed with new UQueue<String>(). Note that the Java 1.5 containers in java.util will become genericized.

There are several facets of the JSR 14 specification that can impact reflective programming. One such facet is that type erasure is used to implement generic types. Type erasure maps a generic type to a suitable non-generic type for implementation. In our previous example, although a program may declare both UQueue<Method> and UQueue<String>, there will be only one class object that represents both. That is, the following will be true:

```
UQueue<Method>.class == UQueue<String>.class
```

In this case, that class object may be thought of as the one associated with UQueue<Object>. Consequently, the first impact of Java 1.5 on reflection is that different types do not necessarily associate with different class objects.

Another change is that the declarations of Class and Constructor will become generic. This means you may see type expressions such as Class<Dog>, which can be used to declare that a method returns a class object whose instances are of type Dog. One advantages of making Class and Constructor generic is that the calls to newInstance no longer require a cast, which make reflective code more readable. With respect to backward compatibility, type erasure ensures that there is still one class object associated with Class<T> and one class object associated with Constructor<T>.

A third change due to JSR 14 is the addition of new interfaces needed for generic types. Five new interfaces will be added to java.lang.reflect, as shown in figure 10.2. The addition of Type as an interface implemented by Class (where none existed before) may add complexity to some reflective programming tasks. However, with respect to compatibility, it is hard to imagine a reflective Java 1.4 program that fails because Class.class.getInterfaces() does not return an empty array.

Generic types will be a great benefit to Java programmers. However, generic types in Java 1.5 will have a number of limitations as a result of the type erasure technique used for implementation. Among these are:

- Generic type parameters cannot be instantiated with primitive types.
- Enclosing type parameters should not be used in static members.
- A type parameter by itself cannot be used in a cast, in an instanceof operation, in a new operation, in an extends clause, or in an implements clause.

Various techniques that we have presented may prove useful, if you need to go beyond these limitations. For example, reflective code generation may be used to generate a container class for primitive types.

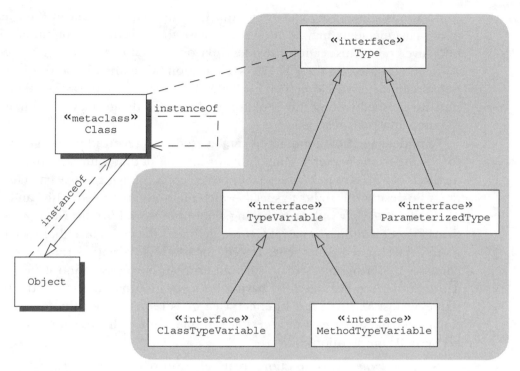

Figure 10.2 The gray area represents the new interfaces that are being added to
`java.lang.reflect` **in Java 1.5 for supporting the generic types in the JSR 14 specification.**

10.1.2 JSR 175—Annotation Facility

An annotation is a note attached to a program element (a method, a class, and so on) that expresses some additional information about the element. An annotation expresses some intention of the programmer with respect to the element. For example, a programmer may wish to mark a method to indicate that it should never appear in a trace. In this sense, an annotation is similar to a modifier, but Java has only 11 modifiers, and programmers have vastly many more intentions that they wish to express. In the past, comments have been used for this purpose. But there are important differences between annotations and comments:

- Comments appear only in the source code of a program (typically, a compiler deletes comments during lexical analysis), while annotations may remain in the compiled code.

- Comments are unstructured text (which is difficult to process), while annotations are structured and highly amenable to automated processing.

Annotations allow programmers to attach additional metadata to their applications. This metadata may be used to increase the effectiveness of either tools or reflective code. This section provides a flavor of what can be accomplished with annotations based on the JSR 175[1] specification, which first became available for public comment on November 11, 2003. This specification was not final at the time we finished writing this book, so the following details may have changed by the time Java 1.5 is released.

To understand how annotations can be used, let's reconsider George's solution for tracing from chapter 4. One of the weaknesses of that solution is that all of the methods of a class must be traced. Suppose George's tracing proxy has a user Martha, who desires the ability to specify which methods are traced. This can be done in Java 1.4, but only with an annoying amount of work for both George and Martha. Let's look at one scenario: George defines a data structure that specifies the methods exempted from being traced, for example, a static string array named notTraced. Martha must create such an array in her classes, and George's code can then discern her intent by having his invocation handler check the method name against Martha's list. In effect, George is requiring Martha to create additional metadata that he can access at runtime. Although this sounds easy, there are several complications:

- *Granularity*—This solution treats all overloaded methods with identical names the same. If Martha needs to distinguish between overloaded methods, George must define a more complex data structure that is more difficult for her to fill in.

- *Consistency*—The method definition and the data structure are separated in the source text. This increases the difficulty of keeping the two consistent, especially during maintenance.

- *Inheritance*—George's code must search up the inheritance hierarchy when dealing with inherited methods. In addition, George must answer some tricky questions: Should interfaces be allowed to declare notTraced arrays? If so, how should such declarations be merged?

Problems such as these arise for all reflective code when the reflective programmer needs to know more about the intent of the application programmer.

---

[1] JSR 175 began its life titled "Metadata Facility." The JSR 175 committee chose to retitle the work "Annotation Facility." That title more precisely characterizes the facility in that Java already has much metadata accessible through the Reflection API.

This is where annotation saves the day. In Java 1.5, George can proceed as follows. First, George declares the following annotation type for Martha to use:

```
@Retention(RetentionPolicy.RUNTIME)
@Target(ElementType.METHOD)
public @interface NotTraced { }
```

The `@interface` statement on the third line declares an annotation type.[2] The first line declares that the annotation is available at runtime. The second line declares that the annotation may be applied to a method declaration. The declaration can be imported into Martha's code where individual methods can be declared as not to be traced. Such a method declaration would look like this:

```
public @NotTraced toString( String separator ) { ... }
```

The introduction of annotations makes the job of both George and Martha easier.

Martha's job is easier because declaring a method not to be traced is done by simply writing a new modifier in the method declaration. In addition, maintenance is easier because the new modifier is located within the method declaration.

George's job is easier for a number of reasons. First, he does not have to design a data structure to store this information for all the methods of a class. The information is stored with the method objects and is accessible through new reflective methods (described later in this section). Second, the granularity problem is solved because the information is stored with the method objects. Third, the annotation facility defines a set of policies for annotation inheritance, which relieves George of having to program such policies.

The `NotTraced` annotation is a marker annotation; a method either has it or does not have it. Annotations may be defined to have structured values. The Annotation Facility is much more extensive in that an annotation type may be declared to have members. For example, you could define the annotation type

```
public @interface TraceParams { int level(); boolean stderr(); }
```

which allows each of its annotations to be given a pair of values, one for the level of the trace and one for whether the trace is to be integrated into the standard error stream. This annotation type may be used in a declaration like this:

---

[2] A new keyword like `annotation` cannot be used in the design of the Annotation Facility, because keywords in Java are reserved, which means a keyword cannot be used as an identifier. Adding a new keyword to Java 1.5 would imply that all of the existing classes that use the new keyword as an identifier would not longer be valid Java code.

```
@TraceParams(level=3,stderr=true)
public toString( String separator ){
    ...
}
```

More complex annotation types are possible, as is explained in the "JSR 175 Public Draft Specification," but we do not address them because the specification is not final.

An annotation is a new concept in the Java language. At runtime, an annotation is represented by an object (which is a metaobject, because it is information about the program rather than the problem domain). Figure 10.3 depicts our interpretation of how the Annotation Facility draft specification envisions the implementation of our example annotation, NotTraced. There is the interface Annotation, which all annotation types extend to declare their members. That interface in our example is also named NotTraced. This interface is implemented with a proxy class, whose corresponding invocation handler contains the metadata for the annotation and whose invoke method returns the proper value for each member of the annotation.

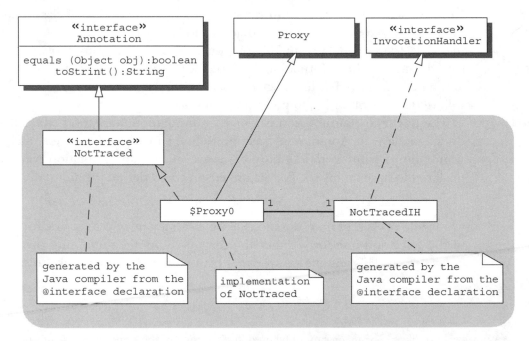

Figure 10.3   The gray area shows the classes generated by the @interface declaration of annotation type NotTraced. There is a generated interface that is implemented by a dynamic proxy class. Corresponding to the proxy class is an invocation handler that implements the content of the annotation. The use of NotTraced causes instances of the proxy class and invocation handler to be created.

Figure 10.4 depicts the interfaces for reflective access to annotations. For the reflective programmer, an annotation is a metaobject. The presence of an annotation may be discerned from a metaobject (for example, a `Method` object) using the `isAnnotationPresent` method. For example, if the field `method` contains a `Method` object declared in one of Martha's classes, George may write

```
boolean exemptFromTrace = method.isAnnotationPresent(NotTraced.class);
```

to query if the method should not be traced. Table 10.1 briefly describes the new reflective methods for annotations. If an annotation is retrieved, its member values may be queried using the members specific to that annotation. In addition, there is a `getParameterAnnotations` method for use with method objects and constructor objects.

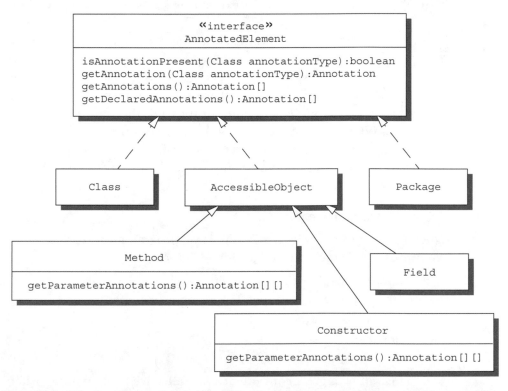

Figure 10.4 This class diagram depicts the additions to Java to support reflective access to annotation. The interface's `AnnotationElement` is being added. As the diagram implies, there are several new methods available for the classes that implement `AnnotationElement`. Further, both `Method` and `Constructor` will have `getParameterAnnotations` methods.

Table 10.1 New methods defined by `AnnotationElement` and its descendents

Method	Description
isAnnotationPresent(Class annotationType)	Returns `true` if the target element was annotated with an instance of the specified annotation type.
getAnnotation(Class annotationType **)**	Returns an annotation of the target element that is of the specified annotation type.
getAnnotations()	Returns an array of all annotations for the specified annotated element.
getDeclaredAnnotations()	Returns the array of annotations declared by the specified annotated element.
getParameterAnnotations()	For a method or constructor, returns an array of annotation arrays. Each annotation array represents the annotations of the corresponding parameter for the method or constructor.

One way to view the Annotation Facility is as a convenient new communication channel between application programmers and those who supply them with tools, which includes reflective programmers. The tool providers declare annotation types; application programmers use these annotation types to declare their intentions about a program element, and, in the end, the tools take action on those extra declared intentions. This section is merely a brief overview of the "JSR 175 Public Draft Specification," which defines a rich facility. Once Java 1.5 is released, the specifics of the Annotation Facility are likely to change, and this section may become out of date.

10.1.3 JSR 201—Language extensions

Language extensions will make reflective programming easier. Five language extensions will be included in Java 1.5.

- *Autoboxing*—this is the automatic coercion of a primitive value to an object of the appropriate wrapper. For example, you may write

  ```
  new Object[] { 1 }
  ```

  instead of

  ```
  new Object[] { new Integer(1) }
  ```

  This will be a great convenience for reflective programming when creating argument lists for use with `Method.invoke` and `Constructor.newInstance`.

- *Enumerations*—You will be able to write a declaration like

  ```
  public enum Flavors {vanilla, chocolate, strawberry}
  ```

In general, enumerations will make Java programming much better. However, there may be some complexity added to reflective code when dealing with the cases of parameter types or return types. For example, listing 4.12 in section 4.7.3 will need to be changed to handle enumerations.

■ *Enhanced for loop*—You will be able to write `for` loops of the form

```
for ( String s : c ) { ... }
```

where c has type *Iterable* or is an array type. Because this is a control structure enhancement, it should not have an impact on reflective code.

■ *Static imports*—A new form of the import statement that allows static methods and fields to be imported. For example, if you write

```
import static java.lang.reflect.Modifier.*;
```

then instead of writing `Modifier.FINAL`, you can write just `FINAL`. This makes all code that uses `Modifier` easier to write and simpler to read.

■ *Variable-arity methods*—The last formal parameter of a method may be declared with an ellipsis to indicate that the method may be called with a variable number of arguments. For example, `getMethod` in `Class` has been redefined as

```
public Method getMethod( String name, Class ... parameterTypes)
```

which means that you can now write

```
Object.class.getMethod( "wait", long.class, int.class )
```

as well as

```
Object.class.getMethod( "wait",
                        new Class[]{long.class,int.class})
```

Variable-arity methods makes the writing of many reflective calls easier.

10.1.4 *Impact of Java 1.5 on reflective code*

The previous brief description of reflection in Java 1.5 makes evident that the transition to Java 1.5 implies a major increase in the expressiveness and the complexity of the Java language. This increase in complexity must be reflected (literally) in the metaobject classes by increasing their number and the number of methods of their interfaces. Some reflective code will have more cases with which to deal, as with a field representing an enumeration or a method that returns an enumeration. Java 1.5 reflective programming will not be easier, but it will be more challenging and more rewarding.

10.2 *Looking forward: competition for Java reflection*

Reflection in general (with the ability to modify classes dynamically) can make applications hard to maintain. Java avoids this problem by constraining reflection to be introspective (for example, you cannot add new members to a class after it is loaded, as reflection in general might allow). This Java language design decision trades flexibility for more maintainability. Every reflective programming language must address this trade-off. As reflection is more widely used, language designers will better understand how to balance maintainability and flexibility. The main competitors listed here will influence the evolution of Java reflection and vice versa. The list consists of languages that have effective commercial support as well as a reflection API.

10.2.1 *C#*

C# will be the cause of an increase in the pace of Java evolution. Microsoft clearly intends C# to usurp Java's dominant position among object-oriented programming languages. Like Java, C# has introspective facilities. Each ordinary object has an associated `Type` object that contains the expected metadata about fields, methods, and constructors of the class of the ordinary object. There are no intercessional features in C#. However useful the delegates and events of C# may be for simulating intercession, they do not qualify as intercessional features. On the other hand, the code-generation techniques discussed in chapter 7 are applicable to C# programming.

10.2.2 *Python*

Python is an interpreted, functional language with an object-oriented extension. With Python 2.2, that object-oriented extension has been enhanced to have a reflection API in which `Class` is permitted to be subclassed to create additional metaclasses. This follows the theory advanced in *Putting Metaclasses to Work* [33] in which metaclasses are the embodiment of class-to-class transformations (see [69]). Python is open source technology supported by the Python Software Foundation (www.python.org), which is a place to start if you're seeking commercial support.

10.2.3 *Smalltalk*

Xerox Corporation's Palo Alto Research Center developed Smalltalk in the 1970s, but it never achieved the commercial success of other languages. Smalltalk has an intercessional reflection API from which there is still much to learn. Those interested in Smalltalk might start with the Smalltalk Industry Council (www.stic.org), which includes IBM as a corporate member.

10.2.4 CLOS

Common LISP Object System (CLOS) contains the reflection API that was published in *The Art of the Metaobject Protocol* [49]. The reflection API is highly intercessional. CLOS has multimethods rather than being class-based, which makes an interesting difference to study. Commercial support for CLOS may be found through the Association of LISP Users (www.lisp.org).

10.2.5 Ruby

Ruby is an interpreted object-oriented scripting language. The reflective features appear to be simpler than Java but with some novel features. For example, there is a hook method with which a class can keep track of its subclasses as they are dynamically created. More information may be found on Ruby at www.ruby-lang.org.

10.2.6 Perl

As of version 5, Perl supports object-oriented programming only by convention. However, this makes a Perl class dynamically modifiable because its symbol table is accessible to programs. Therefore, though there is no formal reflection API, reflective tasks can be accomplished using Perl. Perl 6 is expected to contain a formal object model and with it a reflection API and metaclasses. This will be an exciting evolution for a dynamic language with such a broad mainstream user base.

10.3 Looking forward: Aspect-Oriented Programming

In *A Discipline of Programming* [22], Edsgar Dijkstra essentially asserts that an important goal of programming language design is to facilitate the separation of concerns that burden a programmer. Such separation permits a programmer to focus on her many and varied problems one at a time.

One of the observed shortcomings of object-oriented programming languages is the tangling of concerns in the declaration of a class and its methods. A concern is an area of interest. Ensuring that a class has just a single instance, enabling a class to be traced, or establishing a proper proxy for an instance of a class are all examples of concerns that in the mind of the programmer exist independently of any class in which the concern is manifest. The examples in this book are largely based on using reflection to separate concerns into reusable modules.

In addition to reflection, there are other ways to achieve separation of concerns. Aspect-Oriented Programming [50] is the name given to this area of study that identifies and finds ways to untangle concerns and separately express them. There are three projects that commonly cited as examples of Aspect-Oriented Programming:

- *AspectJ (www.eclipse.org/aspectj)*—AspectJ is a language that permits the organization of common fragments into a coherent module and then facilitates the insertion of those fragments into the proper classes. This means that AspectJ has an insertional component (which specifies where in a class code the fragment is to be inserted) and a quantification component (which specifies which classes are to receive particular insertions). AspectJ is available as a plug-in for Eclipse.

- *Hyper/J (www.research.ibm.com/hyperspace)*—Our object-oriented world view dictates that the class hierarchy is the dominant decomposition. Hyper/J takes the position that a software application can organized into multiple dimensions that represent features. The components of the application can be declared as points in this hyperspace. Hyper/J provides a tool to assemble the features into components and the components into the application.

- *Composition Filters (trese.cs.utwente.nl/composition_filters)*—A composition filter is a wrapper for a class that intercedes on method invocation both into and out from the class. The code-generation techniques of this book do not cover intercession on method invocations out from the class.

Note that each of these projects is focused on a tool to support Java programmers by inserting code that embodies a concern in an aspect. We believe that Aspect-Oriented Programming will have a large impact on the evolution of Java. However, aspect code must use introspective methods in order to adapt to the surrounding code (that is, the code into which the aspect is inserted). This leads us to the conclusion that Aspect-Oriented Programming will increase the importance of reflection, and what you learned in this book will have enduring value.

10.4 *Looking forward: your career*

The software marketplace is increasing its demand for flexibility (in both code that is easily adapted to changing requirements and code that can be reused flawlessly in many applications). Your ability to produce flexible code increases your value in that marketplace. Reflection is the technology of flexibility. Introspection

—the ability of your code to examine itself and its context—is the required first step for all flexibility. The final step occurs when your code changes its behavior based on introspectively gathered information.

We have taught you how to use introspection in Java. We have demonstrated how to use the existing Java reflective facilities to change application behavior. When these Java facilities appeared to be limiting, we have shown you how to transcend these limitations by generating code. You are prepared—we wish you good fortune.

Reflection and metaobject protocols

Reflection and metaobject protocols are topics with greater breadth than you would surmise from the facilities available in Java. This appendix elaborates on the earlier explanation of both reflection and metaobject protocols and the relationship between the two. This appendix does define some additional terminology, which is also defined in the glossary. All terminology is consistent with *The Java Language Specification* (Second Edition) [41] by Gosling, Joy, Steele, and Bracha. In cases in which such terminology conflicts with UML, *The Java Language Specification* is given precedence.

A.1 *Reflection*

Reflection empowers a program to examine itself and make changes that affect its execution. Early debugging systems and interpreted programming languages (especially LISP) took large steps in this direction. However, the beginning of reflection in programming languages is marked by Brian Cantwell Smith's 1982 doctoral dissertation [80]. Smith asserts three requirements for a system to be reflective:

1. A system must have a representation of itself.

2. There must be a causal connection between the system and its representation.

3. The system must have an "appropriate vantage point" [81] from which to perform its reflective work.

Let us examine each of these requirements.

Smith's first requirement is that a system have a representation of itself. This representation must be present or else there is nothing to examine. The representation should be convenient and complete. If the representation is not convenient, examination becomes unwieldy, slow, and cumbersome. If the representation is not complete, examination is not effective for what the representation does not cover.

As an example of something that is neither convenient nor complete, consider the text of a program residing in the file system. The text of a program is not convenient because it has to be parsed to be examined. It is not complete because it is not a representation of the running program (it is missing a representation of the location counter, the values of variables, and so on).

All LISP programs are constructed from list structures in the same way as LISP data. The unification of program and data in LISP provides a convenient representation. This representation made it possible for LISP to provide the base for the early research in reflection, which focused on completeness and Smith's other two requirements.

Second, Smith requires causal connection between a system and its representation. **Causal connection** between a system and its representation means that a change to the representation implies a change to the system and vice versa. To illustrate his intent, Smith offered the following baking analogy where recipes and cakes represent programs and their running instances. With causal connection, when you change the cake, the recipe changes accordingly, and if you change the recipe, the cake changes, too.

With recipes and cakes, causal connection would appear somewhat magical. However, programs and their running instances are simply electronic ones and zeros within the same system. Therefore, there is really nothing magical about programmatic causal connection.

Again we present program text as an inadequate representation for reflective programming because it lacks causal connection to its compiled and running instances. Change the program text, and the behavior of the in-memory instances stays the same. It is clear that a different representation is necessary for successful reflective programming.

The dangers of modifying a running program lead to the Smith's third requirement. The program requires a safe "place to stand" while executing reflective code, just as a cyclist needs to dismount a bicycle before changing a tire. Attempting to change a bicycle tire while riding it might cause damage to the rider, the bicycle, or other parts of the riding system. In the same way, executing incomplete changes can damage the executing software.

We can satisfy Smith's above three requirements for a reflective system the way Friedman and Wand [37] did, as shown in figure A.1. This model introduces the operations of reification and reflection. The base program must be *reified*, or rendered into its representation, before a metaprogram can operate. The base level, the running program, has available a reify operation that turns the running program (including stack frames, control registers, and so on) into a data structure that is passed to a metaprogram. The metaprogram queries the base program for information and makes changes using these data structures. These changes are reflected in the behavior of the base program, when it continues execution. The metaprogram invokes a reflect operation to continue the execution of the base program.

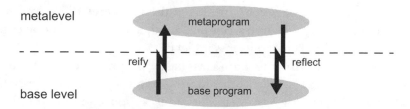

Figure A.1   Friedman and Wand's model for execution of a reflective system

Metaprograms basically do the same things we do as programmers. As programmers, we write code that queries the values of fields and invokes methods. We create and transform classes, adding properties and aspects as we go. Metaprograms have available many of these operations and are algorithmic expressions of these activities. If such activities need to repeated, an algorithmic description can enhance productivity, alleviate tedium, and remove human error.

Smith's vision is not totally fulfilled by figure A.1. According to that vision, both the base program and the metaprogram are part of the same program and are written in the same language for which the metaprogram is an interpreter. Further, the metaprogram may be considered a base program for an even higher-level metaprogram. This stacking is continued to form an infinite tower of interpreted programs. Exploring Smith's model and its philosophical implications is interesting (see [82]) but not one of our goals for this book. For this reason, we move our story along to the impact of reflection on object-oriented programming.

A.2 Reflective object-oriented programming

The self-representation required by reflection meshes very nicely with object-oriented programming. A collection of objects, called **metaobjects,** can be used to represent the program as well as a situation in the application domain. Reflective object-oriented programming systems generally do not have a reify operation. Instead, the metaobject representation exists when the program begins running and persists throughout the execution of the program.

The notion of having metaobjects in the programming system is present in Smalltalk-80 [39], where at runtime there exists a class object (a metaobject) to represent each class of a running program. The late 1980s were abundant with research in the relationship of reflection to object-oriented programming; notable examples are the work of Maes [63], Cointe [17], and Foote and Johnson [29].

However, the most notable work is *The Art of the Metaobject Protocol* [49] by Kiczales, des Rivieres, and Bobrow, which introduced the term **metaobject protocol** to describe a system's reflective facilities. Simply stated, a system's metaobject protocol is contained in the interface to its metaobjects.

We present reflection with respect to class-based programming (a term introduced by Peter Wegner [91]). In class-based programming, an object responds to the methods that its class supports. A class is said to **support** a method if the class declares or inherits the method. An object is said to **respond** to a method if the method can be invoked on the object. Java is a class-based programming language, which is one reason for our bias. A second reason is our belief that the formal modeling inherent in class-based languages is the better of the alternatives for professional programming. Other models, such as prototype-based programming (as in Self [87]), are not addressed in this book.

Class-based programming means that an object has the structure specified by its class and responds to the methods either inherited or introduced by its class. A simple, uniform way for a class-based programming language to introduce a metaobject protocol is to have **class objects** that can be queried and possibly changed. A reflective class-based programming language should obey the following three postulates:

1. There exists a nonempty finite set of objects, each identified by a value called an **object reference**.
2. Every object has a uniquely associated entity called a **class**.
3. Every class is reified with (represented by) an object.

Note the distinction between class and class object. A class is a notion that is part of the programming language, while a class object is a reification of that notion. This distinction explains why you must use the Java .class literal to obtain the class object from the class name.

Figure A.2 illustrates the object-oriented organization for reflection. The metaobjects are in the metalevel because they are the reification of the program. Reflective computation occurs when method calls are made on class objects. The difference between this situation and the one envisioned by the Friedman and

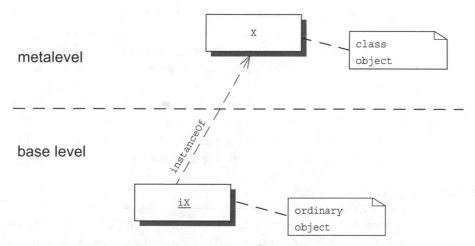

Figure A.2   The object-oriented organization for reflection

Wand model is that the reification exists continuously throughout the execution of the program.

The simplicity and uniformity of object-oriented reflection derives from treating classes as objects. However, the combination of postulates 2 and 3 leads to the circularity that the objects that represent classes must themselves have classes. These classes must also be represented by objects that have classes, and so on. This circularity is the key concern for organizing a model that satisfies all three postulates.

Figure A.2 illustrates that the relationship between objects and their class representations can be viewed as a graph. The vertices of the graph are objects and its edges are instanceOf relations. Given that graphical framework for analysis, the following theorem from graph theory motivates a successful organization that satisfies the postulates.

> THEOREM: *Every finite acyclic directed graph must have a vertex with no arrows leaving it.*
>
> PROOF: ([42] page 200)—Because the graph is finite and acyclic, the paths can be listed. Consider any maximal path P. The last vertex of P can have no successor because P is maximal. Therefore, the graph has a vertex with no arrows leaving it.

The graph is directed because of the nature of the instanceOf relation. The graph cannot be infinite, because of Postulate 1 and because it is to be realized in the finite memory of a computer. Postulate 2 states that every object has a class; therefore, every vertex has an arrow leaving it. Consequently, the graph must have a cycle.

This theorem implies that any programming language that obeys the three postulates must have a cycle in its graph of the instanceOf relation. This is true of Smalltalk-80 [39], where this notion of an instanceOf cycle was introduced. Smalltalk-80 had more than one class in the cycle, but in more recent programming languages such as Java, it has become standard to have a single class (named Class) that has a self loop, as shown in figure A.3. Notice that this level of sophistication is reached without yet introducing inheritance.

A.3 Inheritance

Some programming languages, such as Java and Smalltalk, have a single top to the inheritance hierarchy. It is customary to name this class Object, as depicted in figure A.4. It not necessary to have such a class (C++ gets by without one). However,

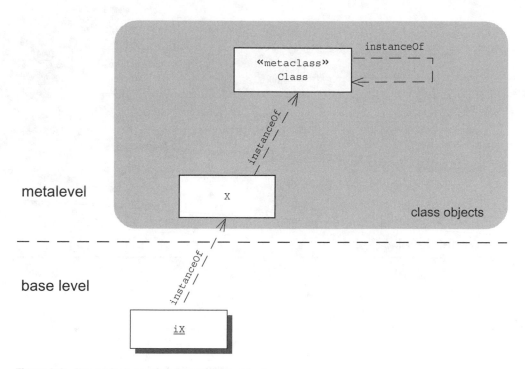

Figure A.3   The typical arrangement of class objects

having such a class is very convenient for defining methods to which all objects must respond. For example, as Java programmers, we appreciate the fact that all objects respond to `toString`. As we transition to Java metaprogramming in this book, we equally appreciate that all objects respond to `getClass`.

There are two kinds of circularities in figure A.4. `Class` is an instance of itself, and that forms a self loop in the graph. `Class` is also a subclass of `Object`, which is an instance of `Class`. It is natural to look at this graph and be wary of the possibility of circular definitions. However, as Java developers, we leverage a system that is arranged like this every time we program. We know that this arrangement works from our experiences, even if it has not been explained to us. The circularities of figure A.4 are handled by equations that govern the flow of method and field definitions, a topic that is beyond the scope of this book. For a more detailed discussion of why and how reflective class-based object models work, see *Putting Metaclasses to Work* [33].

Let's take a moment to review standard Java terminology for inheritance. A **direct superclass** is the one named in the extends clause of a class declaration. A

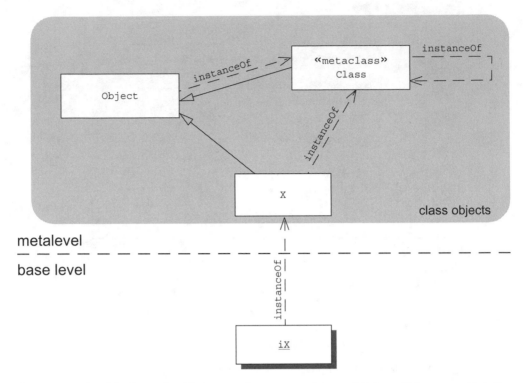

Figure A.4 When inheritance is added, `Class` becomes a subclass of `Object`. This ensures that all classes are objects.

class X **is a superclass of** a class Y if there is a sequence of one or more direct superclass links from Y to X. There is a set of corresponding statements defining **direct superinterface** and **is a superinterface of**.

A.4 *Metaobject protocols*

Reflection empowers a program to examine and modify itself, where modifications are causally connected to the behavior of the program. The metaobjects comprise a representation of the program, and the metaobject protocol is the interface to the metaobjects. It is time to consider what sort of operations you would like to perform with a metaobject protocol.

Introspection is the act of examining the structure and state of a program. Listing the names of the instance variables in an object is an example of an introspective use of a metaobject protocol. Here are some examples of introspective operations:

- Examining instance variable values
- Listing the methods of a class

Intercession refers to the ability of the metalevel to intercede in the operation of a program and change its behavior. Typically, intercession occurs by the metalevel changing the structure of the program. These structural changes subsequently manifest themselves as behavioral changes. Changing the binding (in a method table) of a method to the code that implements the method is an example of intercession. Equivalently, intercepting a method call and rerouting it is also an example of intercession. Here are more examples of intercessional operations:

- Adding new methods to a class
- Adding new instance variables to a class
- Changing the set of parent classes of a class
- Redefining methods
- Controlling method dispatch

All metaobject protocols have limitations. An **intrinsic property** (of a metaobject protocol) is a (computable) property that can be programmed with the metaobject protocol. An **extrinsic property** is a (computable) property that is not intrinsic. For example, in Java, computing the class object of an object is an intrinsic property; you simply use the getClass method. On the other hand, computing the instances of a class object is an extrinsic property of the Java metaobject protocol.

The Java metaobject protocol is almost totally introspective. Consequently, there are many useful reflective tasks that cannot be accomplished directly with the Java metaobject protocol. One of the goals of this book is to show you how to recognize such situations and show you what to do when they arise.

A.5 *Metaclasses*

In figures A.3 and A.4, we introduced Class with very little explanation. It is time to address that issue, because it is an additional important feature of reflective object- oriented programming. Class is a **metaclass**. Metaclasses are a set of classes that produce classes when instantiated. We know this set of classes exists because our postulates tell us that as objects, classes must themselves have instantiating classes. The class named Class is a metaclass that arises naturally from the three postulates and the desire to have minimal structure that satisfies them.

At this point, it is important to review some facts in order to ensure that you understand the structure of reflective object-oriented programming:

- A class is a metaobject.
- A metaclass is a (special) kind of class, whose instances are classes.

It is also important to understand these two points:

- Not all classes are metaclasses.
- Not all metaobjects are metaclasses.

We know the first point to be true because we have programmed with classes that instantiate objects that are not classes. The second point is illustrated by classes like `Field`, `Method`, and `Constructor`. These metaobjects do not produce classes by instantiation and are therefore, by definition, not metaclasses.

Because a metaclass is a class, there exists both the metaclass as written in the programming language and the metaclass object in the implementation of the programming language. Although precision in writing dictates that we distinguish between the terms *class* and *class object*, we avoid the awkward term *metaclass object* in favor of using the term *metaclass* for both cases (the class and the class object). Context will easily disambiguate the uses of metaclass.

Figure A.5 illustrates the relation between the set of objects, the set of classes, and the set of metaclasses. That is, all classes are objects and all metaclasses are classes. A class that is not a metaclass is called an **ordinary class**. An object that is not a class object is called an **ordinary object**.

For an object-oriented programming model design, as shown in figure A.5, the metaobject protocol includes both the methods introduced by `Class` and the methods introduced by `Object` (because `Class` inherits from `Object`). In addition, subclasses of `Class` also have the interface for class objects, which leads to the following little theorem.

THEOREM: *Any subclass of a metaclass is a metaclass.*

PROOF: A subclass of a metaclass inherits the interface for examining and modifying a class object. The instances of the subclass must be a class object.

This theorem addresses the issue of creating new metaclasses. You create a metaclass by subclassing `Class` or another metaclass. You cannot subclass `Class` in Java because `Class` is final. This means that a Java programmer cannot create new metaclasses. This topic is included in this book for two reasons. First, there is the

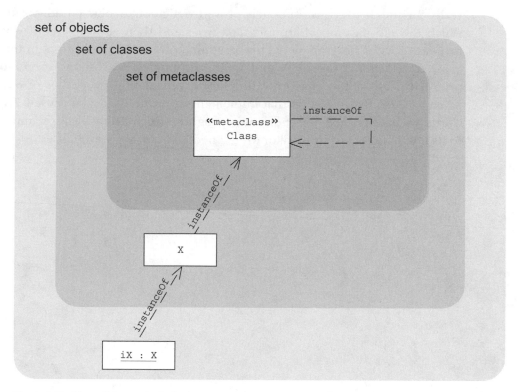

Figure A.5 Venn diagram depicting the containment of the set of metaclasses in the set of classes, which is contained in the set of objects

desire to convey a complete discussion of the topic of metaobject protocols. Second, metaclasses are the natural entry to the topic of class-to-class transformations.

A.6 *Class-to-class transformations*

The important issue is not *how* you create a metaclass but *why* you would want do to so. Because each class object has a metaclass, the construction of a class object is controlled by its metaclass. Furthermore, during the construction, the metaobject protocol may be used to change the class in a programmatic way. That is, a metaclass is the natural and proper modularity concept of a class-to-class transformation in reflective object-oriented programming.

To better understand why class-to-class transformations are valuable, consider the following linguistic interpretation of the evolution of computer programming. In the 1950s and 1960s, programming was about commanding the computer—

verbs. In the 1970s, this approach proved deficient. A new paradigm arose in which the specification of abstract data types and then classes—nouns—became foremost for the programmer. This paradigm, object-oriented programming, has evolved throughout the 1980s and 1990s. Although powerful and useful, object-oriented programming has proved deficient in isolating properties of objects—adjectives—so that the code that implements a property can be reused. In other words, we have pushed object-oriented programming with only classes and objects to its limit, and out of its breakdown the need for the metalevel arises.

Handling compilation errors in the "Hello world!" program

The "Hello world!" program in chapter 7 is a fine generator if there are no compilation errors in the generated code. However, on some platforms (including Windows 2000), if there are compilation errors, the `waitFor` statement misses the termination signal from the compilation process. The result is that generator program hangs and the error stream is not displayed. The Java documentation on `Process` states:

> The `Runtime.exec` methods may not work well for special processes on certain native platforms, such as native windowing processes, daemon processes, Win16/DOS processes on Microsoft Windows, or shell scripts. The created subprocess does not have its own terminal or console. All its standard io (i.e. `stdin`, `stdout`, `stderr`) operations will be redirected to the

parent process through three streams (`Process.getOutputStream()`, `Process.getInputStream()`, `Process.getErrorStream()`). The parent process uses these streams to feed input to and get output from the subprocess. Because some native platforms only provide limited buffer size for standard input and output streams, failure to promptly write the input stream or read the output stream of the subprocess may cause the subprocess to block, and even deadlock.

The problem seems to be that the reading of the error stream occurs after the `waitFor`, but the compilation process is blocked waiting for the error stream to be read before terminating.

Presented in listing B.1 is a version of the "Hello world!" program that does not use `waitFor`. Instead, the program polls the compilation process using `exitValue`. While the compilation process is running, `exitValue` throws an `IllegalThreadStateException`. Each time the exception is caught, the process is checked for a nonempty error stream whose size has stabilized. Once the error stream has stabilized, the compilation process has effectively terminated, and the error stream may be drained and displayed. Note that error stream is also displayed if the process terminates with a nonzero exit value.

This solution is used to test the C2C framework on Windows 2000 using Java 1.4.1. Other platforms may require different solutions.

Listing B.1   `HelloWorldGenerator2`

```
public class HelloWorldGenerator2 {

    public static void main( String[] args ) {

        try {
            FileOutputStream fstream = new
    FileOutputStream("HelloWorld.java");
            PrintWriter out = new PrintWriter( fstream );
            out.println( "class HelloWorld {                          \n"
                    + "    public static void main( String[] args ) { \n"
                    + "        System.out.println( \"Hello world!\" );\n"
                    + "    }                                           \n"
                    + "}                                               " );
            out.flush();
            Process p = Runtime.getRuntime().exec( "javac HelloWorld.java"
    );

            // The following section substitutes for p.waitFor( )
            int exitValue = -1;  // compilation failure is not -1
            int errStreamAvailable = 0;
            while ( exitValue == -1 ) {
```

```
        Thread.sleep( 10 );
        try {
            exitValue = p.exitValue();
        } catch(IllegalThreadStateException e){
            InputStream errStream = p.getErrorStream()  ;
            if ( errStream.available() > 0
                && errStream.available() == errStreamAvailable ) {
                for ( int j = errStream.available(); j > 0; j-- )
                    System.out.write( errStream.read() );
                p.destroy();
                throw new RuntimeException("compile failed" );
            }
            errStreamAvailable = errStream.available();
            exitValue = -1;
        }
    }

    if ( p.exitValue() == 0 ) {
        Class outputClassObject = Class.forName( "HelloWorld" );
        Class[] fpl = { String[].class };
        Method m = outputClassObject.getMethod( "main", fpl );
        m.invoke( null, new Object[]{ new String[] {} } );
    } else {
        InputStream errStream = p.getErrorStream();
        for ( int j = errStream.available(); j > 0; j-- )
            System.out.write( errStream.read() );
    }
} catch(Exception e){ throw new RuntimeException(e); }
}
}
```

UML

Table C.1 summarizes the UML conventions used to diagram reflective programs.

In UML, boxes represent classes and objects. The style of the name in the box indicates whether it is a class or not. The name of an object that is not a class is underlined. The name of a class object is never underlined. This book uses class diagrams, object diagrams, and sequence diagrams.

In UML, you typically draw class diagrams showing only classes or object diagrams showing only non-class objects. Modeling reflection calls for combining the two and using the `instanceOf` dependency to connect an object with its instantiating class. UML defines the `instanceOf` dependency with same meaning as the Java `instanceof` operator. However, this book uses the instanceOf dependency only to show that an object is a direct instance of a class. Figure 1.4 on page 19 is such diagram.

Sequence diagrams depict the interactions of an object with other objects. Figure 4.1 on page 75 is such a diagram. It depicts three objects: a client, a proxy, and a target. The lifeline of each object is drawn below the object. The long thin rectangles represent periods when the object is active. Between the active periods, arrows that represent method calls and the returns are drawn.

Table C.1 UML conventions for this book

Diagram Feature	Description
Dog	A class is drawn as a box with the name of the call written centered at the top of the box. The members of the class are written in compartments below the class name.
<<metaclass>> Class	A metaclass is drawn similarly to a class with the addition of the stereotype name <<metaclass>>.
<<interface>> Runnable	An interface in drawn similarly to a class with the addition of the stereotype name <<interface>>.
fido : Dog	An ordinary object is drawn as a box with the name of the object underlined. The name of the object may be followed by a clause giving the type of the object.
	A note box contains a comment that elaborates on some other model element.
label	This arrow represents a dependency between two model elements. It is labeled with the kind of dependency being depicted. Typical dependencies are imports from, uses, and calls.
	This arrow represents the extends dependency. The arrow points from a subclass to its direct superclass (or from an interface to a superinterface).
	This arrow represents the implements dependency. The arrow points from an implementing class to an interface.
instanceOf	This dependency is drawn from an object to a class. In general, the dependency indicates that the object may be typed by the class. In this book, we draw this dependency only to the class that instantiates the object.
	This arrow indicates a method call in a sequence diagram.
	This arrow indicates a return from a method call in a sequence diagram.

glossary

causally connected.   A computation is causally connected to its representation if a change to one causes a change in the other.

class invariant.   A logical condition that is true for each instance of the class after the instance is constructed and whenever no method of the class is executing.

class loader.   An instance of a subclass of `ClassLoader`.

class object.   A metaobject that is the representation of a class.

extrinsic property.   A computable property that is not intrinsic.

header of a method.   Consists of the method modifiers, the return type, the name of the method, the number and types of formal parameters to the method, and the throws clause.

instance variable.   A field that is not static.

intercession.   Those aspects of a reflection API that allow you to change the structure or behavior of a program.

intrinsic property.   A computable property that can be programmed with the reflection API.

introduces.   A class or interface introduces a member if it declares the member and that member is not declared by any of its superclasses or superinterfaces.

introspection.   Those aspects of a reflection API that allow you to examine the structure and state of a program.

invariant.   A logical condition of the state of a program that is always true, or always true except if control is in some particular piece of code.

marker interface. An interface that declares no methods or variables but when used indicates that an implementing class has some property. `Cloneable` is a marker interface.

metacircular interpreter. An interpreter that is written in the same language that it interprets.

metaclass. A class or class object whose instances are class objects.

metaobject. An object that represents part of the program.

metaobject protocol. The interface to the metaobjects.

metaprogrammer. A programmer who uses the reflection API.

microbenchmark. A performance measurement of a short piece of code.

ordinary class. A class object that is not a metaclass.

ordinary object. An object that is not a class object.

reflection. The empowerment of a program to examine and modify itself in a causally connected manner.

reify operation. An operation that renders an executing program into a data structure.

respond. An object responds to a method if the method can be invoked on the object.

self-representation. The data structures of an executing program that represent that program.

signature of a method. Consists of the name of the method and the number and types of formal parameters to the method.

support. A class supports a method if the class declares the method or inherits the method.

type error. A type error occurs when code accesses an object as if it belongs to a type to which it does not in fact belong.

type safety. A property of a program or a programming language. A program is type safe if it contains no type errors; a language is type safe if its complier is able to recognize and reject all programs containing type errors at compile time.

references

[1]   Agesen, O., S. N. Freund, and J. C. Mitchell. "Adding Type Parameterization to the Java Language." OOPSLA '97 Conference Proceedings, October 1997, 49–55.

[2]   Alexander, B. "The Art of Writing and Running Microbenchmarks." Unpublished.

[3]   Alpert, S. R. "Primitive Types Considered Harmful." In *More Java Gems*, edited by D. Duego, 435–54. Cambridge, UK: Cambridge University Press, 2000.

[4]   Back, R. J. R. and R. Kurki-Suonio. "Superimposition and Fairness in Reactive System Refinements." Jerusalem Conference on Information Technology, Jerusalem, Israel: October 1990, 22–25.

[5]   Bawden, A. "Reification without Evaluation." Proceedings of the 1988 ACM Conference on LISP and Functional Programming, 1988, 342–349.

[6]   Beck, K. and E. Gamma. "Test-Infected: Programmers Love Writing Tests." In *More Java Gems*, edited by D. Duego, 357–376. Cambridge, UK: Cambridge University Press, 2000.

[7]   Bloch, J. *Effective Java.* Reading, MA: Addison-Wesley, 2001.

[8]   Bracha, G., N. Cohen, C. Kemper, S. Marx, M. Odersky, S.-E. Panitz, D. Stoutmire, K. Thorup, and P. Wadler. "Adding Generics to the Java Programming Langauge: Participant Draft Specification." April 27, 2001 (http:/ /java.sun.com/Download4).

[9]   Brooks, F. P., Jr. *The Mythical Man-Month.* Reading, MA: Addison-Wesley, 1995.

[10] Cartwright, R. and G. L. Steele, Jr. "Compatible Genericity with Run-time Types for the Java TM Programming Language." OOPSLA '98 Conference Proceedings, October 1998, 201–215.

[11] Cazzola, W. "Evaluation of Object-Oriented Reflective Models." Proceedings of ECOOP Workshop on Reflective Object-Oriented Programming and Systems, July 1998.

[12] Cazzola, W. "SmartMethod: An Efficient Replacement for Method." SAC'04, March 2004.

[13] Chan, P., R. Lee, and D. Kramer. *The Java Class Libraries*, 2d ed., vol. 1. Reading, MA: Addison-Wesley, 1998.

[14] Chandy, K. M. and L. Lamport. "Distributed Snapshots: Determining Global States of Distributed Systems." *ACM Transactions on Computer Systems*, 3(1), 63–75 (February 1985).

[15] Chiba, S., "Load-time Structural Reflection in Java." ECOOP 2000—Object-Oriented Programming, 313–36, LNCS 1850. Berlin: Springer-Verlag, 2000.

[16] Cohen, G. A., J. S. Chase, and D. L. Kaminsky. "Automatic Program Transformation with JOIE." USENIX 1998 Annual Technical Conference, 1998.

[17] Cointe, P. "Metaclasses Are First Class: The ObjVlisp Model." OOPSLA '87 Conference Proceedings, October 1987, 156–165.

[18] Copeland, G. Personal communication.

[19] Czarnecki, K. and Eisenecker, U. W. *Generative Programming: Methods, Tools, and Applications*. Reading, MA: Addison-Wesley, 2000.

[20] Devore, J. and R. Peck. *Statistics* (4th ed.). Pacific Grove, CA: Duxbury, 2001.

[21] Dijkstra, E. W. "Go to Statement Considered Harmful." In *Communications of the ACM*, 147–48, vol. 11 (March 1968).

[22] Dijkstra, E. W. *A Discipline of Programming*. Englewood Cliffs, NJ: Prentice-Hall, 1976.

[23] Driver, C. "Evaluation of Aspect-Oriented Software Development for Distributed Systems." Master's thesis, University of Dublin, 2002.

[24] Drossopoulou, S., F. Damiani, M. Dezani-Ciancaglini, and P. Giannini. "Fickle: Dynamic Object Re-classification" (extended abstract). Presented at The Eighth International Workshop on Foundations of Object-Oriented Languages, January 2001.

[25] Drossopoulou, S., F. Damiani, M. Dezani-Ciancaglini, and P. Giannini. "More Dynamic Object Reclassification: Fickle$_{II}$." *ACM Transactions of Programming Languages and Systems*, 153–91, 24(2), (March 2002).

[26] Elnozahy, E. N., L. Alvisi, Y.-M. Wang, and D. B. Johnson. "A Survey of Rollback-Recovery Protocols in Message-Passing Systems." *ACM Computing Surveys*, 375–408, 34(3), (September 2002).

[27]   Elrad, T., R. E. Filman, and A. Bader (editors). "Aspect-Oriented Programming." *Communications of the ACM*, 29–97, 44(10), (October 2001).

[28]   Erradi, M., G. v. Bochmann, and I. A. Hamid. "Type Evolution in a Reflective Object-Oriented Language." University of Montreal Technical Report 827 (April 1996).

[29]   Foote, B., and R. E. Johnson. "Reflective Facilities in Smalltalk-80." OOPSLA '89 Conference Proceedings, October 1989, 327–35.

[30]   Foote, B. and J. Yoder. "Evolution, Architecture, and Metamorphosis." In *Pattern Languages of Program Design 2*, edited by J. M. Vlissides, J. O. Coplien, and N. L. Kerth. Reading, MA: Addison-Wesley, 1996.

[31]   Forman, I. R. "On the Time Overhead of Counters and Traversal Markers." Proceedings of the 1981 International Conference on Software Engineering, 164–69.

[32]   Forman, I. R., S. H. Danforth, and H. H. Madduri. "Composition of Before/ After Metaclasses in SOM." OOPSLA '94 Conference Proceedings, October 1994, 427–39.

[33]   Forman, I. R. and S. H. Danforth. *Putting Metaclasses to Work*. Reading, MA: Addison-Wesley, 1999.

[34]   Forman, N. B. *Metaclass-Based Implementation of Software Patterns*. Master's report, University of Texas at Austin (December 1999).

[35]   Forman, I. R. "Declarable Modifiers: A Proposal to Increase the Efficacy of Metaclasses." In *Reflection and Software Engineering*, edited by W. Cazzola, R. Stroud, and F. Tisato. LNCS 1826, Berlin: Springer-Verlag, (June 2000).

[36]   Francez, N. and I. R. Forman. *Interacting Processes: A Multiparty Approach to Distributed Systems Design*. Reading, MA: Addison-Wesley, 1996.

[37]   Friedman, D. P. and M. Wand. "Reification: Reflection without Metaphysics." Conference Record of the 1984 ACM Symposium on LISP and Functional Programming, 1984, 348–55.

[38]   Gamma, E., R. Helm, R. Johnson, and J. Vlissides. *Design Patterns: Elements of Object-Oriented Programming*. Reading, MA: Addison-Wesley, 1995.

[39]   Goldberg, A. and D. Robson. *Smalltalk-80: The Language and Its Implementation*. Reading, MA: Addison-Wesley, 1983.

[40]   Gong, L., G. Ellison, and M. Dageforde. *Inside Java 2 Platform Security* (2d ed.): *Architecture, API Design, and Implementation*. Reading, MA: Addison-Wesley, 2003.

[41]   Gosling, J., B. Joy, G. Steele, and G. Bracha. *The Java Language Specification* (2d ed.). Reading, MA: Addison-Wesley, 2000.

[42]   Harary, F. *Graph Theory*. Reading, MA: Addison-Wesley, 1972.

[43]   Hennessy, J. L. and D. A. Patterson. *Computer Architecture: A Quantitative Approach* (2d ed.). San Francisco, CA: Morgan Kaufmann Publishers, 1996.

[44] Herrington, J. *Code Generation in Action*. Greenwich, CT: Manning Publications, 2003.

[45] Hilsdale, E. and G. Kiczales. "Aspect-Oriented Programming in Aspect/J." 2002 (www.parc.com/groups/csl/projects/aspectj/downloads/PARC-Workshop-2002.pdf).

[46] Hoare, C. A. R. *Communicating Sequential Processes*. Englewood Cliffs, NJ: Prentice Hall, 1985.

[47] IBM. Jikes Bytecode Toolkit. (http://www.alphaworks.ibm.com/tech/jikesbt).

[48] Keller, R. and U. Holzle. "Binary Component Adaptation." Proceedings of ECOOP'98, 1998.

[49] Kiczales, G., J. des Rivieres, and D. G. Bobrow. *The Art of the Metaobject Protocol*. Boston, MA: The MIT Press, 1991.

[50] Kiczales, G., J. Lamping, A. Mendhekar, C. Maeda, C. Lopes, J.-M. Loingtier, and J. Irving. "Aspect-Oriented Programming." Proceedings of ECOOP'97, June 3–13, 1997. Also in *Lecture Notes in Computer Science* 1241, Berlin: Springer-Verlag, 220–42.

[51] Kirby, G., R. Morrison, and D. Stemple. "Linguistic Reflection in Java." *Software—Practice and Experience*, 28(10), 1998.

[52] Kniesel, G., P. Constanza, and M. Austermann. "JMangler—A Framework for Load-time Transformation of Java Classes." Proceedings of First International Workshop on Source Code Analysis and Manipulation (SCAM 2001).

[53] Knuth, D. E. *The Art of Computer Programming: Sorting and Searching*, vol. 3. Reading, MA: Addison-Wesley, 1973.

[54] Laddad, R. *AspectJ in Action*. Greenwich, CT: Manning Publications, 2003.

[55] Lamport, L. "Time, Clocks, and the Ordering of Events in Distributed Systems." *Communications of the ACM*, 558–65, 21(7) (July 1978).

[56] Ledru, P. "Smart Proxies for Jini Services." *ACM Sigplan Notices*, 36–44, 37(4) (April 2002).

[57] Liang, S. and G. Bracha. "Dynamic Class Loading in the Java Virtual Machine." OOPSLA '98 Conference Proceedings, October 1998, 36–44.

[58] Lieberherr, K. J., I. Silva-Lepe, and C. Xaio. "Adaptive Object-Oriented Programming Using Graph Customization." *Communications of the ACM*, 94–101, 37(5) (May 1994).

[59] Lieberherr, K. J. *Adaptive Object-Oriented Software*. Boston, MA: PWS Publishing, 1996.

[60] Lindholm, T. and F. Yellin. *The Java Virtual Machine Specification* (2d ed.). Reading, MA: Addison-Wesley, 1999.

[61] Linger, R. C., H. D. Mills, and B. I. Witt. *Structured Programming: Theory and Practice.* Reading, MA: Addison-Wesley, 1979.

[62] Liskov, B. and J. Guttag. *Program Development in Java.* Reading, MA: Addison-Wesley, 2001.

[63] Maes P. "Concepts and Experiments in Computational Reflection." OOPSLA '87 Conference Proceedings, October 1987.

[64] Malabarba, S., R. Pandey, J. Gragg, E. Barr, and J. F. Barnes. "Runtime Support for Type-Safe Dynamic Java Classes." University of California, Davis TR-CSE-2000-7 (earlier version in the Proceedings of the 14th European Conference on Object-Oriented Programming, June 2000).

[65] Massol, V. and T. Husted. *JUnit in Action.* Greenwich, CT: Manning Publications, 2003.

[66] Mätzel, K.-U. and W. R. Bischofberger. "Designing Object Systems for Evolution." TAPOS'97.

[67] Mems, T. "A Formal Foundation for Object-Oriented Software Evolution." Ph.D. dissertation, Vrije Universiteit Brussel (August 1999).

[68] *Merriam-Webster's Collegiate Dictionary,* version 2.5. 2000.

[69] Metz, D. and M. Simionato. "Metaclass Programming in Python." *IBM developerWorks.* February 2003 (www-106.ibm.com/developerworks/library/l-pymeta.html?ca=dnt-48h).

[70] Meyer, B. *Eiffel: The Language.* Englewood Cliffs, NJ: Prentice Hall PTR, 1991.

[71] Myers, A. C., J. A. Bank, and B. Liskov. "Parameterized Types for Java." Conference Record of POPL '97: The 24th ACM SIGPLAN-SIGACT Symposium on Principles of Programming Languages, 1997, 132–45.

[72] Neward, T. *Server-based Java Programming.* Greenwich, CT: Manning, 2000.

[73] Ourosoff, N. "Primitive Types in Java Considered Harmful." *Communications of the ACM,* 105–6, 45(8) (August 2002).

[74] Parnas, D. L. "Software Aging." Proceeding of the 16th International Conference on Software Engineering, 1994, 279–87.

[75] Portwood, M. T. "Using Java Technology Reflection to Improve Design." (ftp://ftp.oreilly.com/pub/conference/java2001/Portwood_Reflection.ppt).

[76] Riehle, D. and K.-U. Mätzel. "Using Reflection to Support System Evolution." 1998 (http://www.riehle.org/papers/1998/oopsla-1998-ws-28-pp.html).

[77] Rising, L. *The Patterns Almanac 2000.* Reading, MA: Addison-Wesley, 2000.

[78] Roubstov, V. "Cracking Java Byte-Code Encryption." *Java World.* May 2003 (javaworld.com/javaworld/javaqa/2003-05/01-qa-0509-jcrypt.html).

[79] Shavit, N. and N. Francez. "A New Approach to Detection of Totally Indicative Stability." Proceedings of 13th ICALP, LNCS 226, Springer-Verlag, July 1986.

[80] Smith, B. "Reflection and Semantics in a Procedural Language." Ph.D. thesis, Massachusetts Institute of Technology, 1982 (also published as technical report LCS TR-272).

[81] Smith, B. "Reflection and the Semantics of LISP." Conference Record of Symposium on Principles of Programming Languages, 1984, 23–35.

[82] Smith, B. C. *The Origin of Objects.* Boston, MA: The MIT Press, 1996.

[83] Steele, G. L., Jr., D. R. Woods, R. A. Finkel, M. R. Crispin, R. M. Stallman, and G. S. Goodfellow. *The Hacker's Dictionary.* New York: Harper and Row, 1983.

[84] Sun Microsystems. "From Mantis to Tiger." (http://java.sun.com/features/2002/03/totiger.html).

[85] Tatsubo, M., T. Sasaki, S. Chiba, and K. Itano. "A Bytecode Translator for Distributed Execution of 'Legacy' Java Software." ECOOP 2001—Object-Oriented Programming, 236–55, LNCS 2072. Berlin: Springer Verlag, 2001.

[86] Tel, G., R. B. Tan, and J. van Leeuwen. "The Derivation of Graph Marking Algorithms from Distributed Termination Detection Algorithms." Technical report, University of Utrecht (August 1986).

[87] Ungar, D. and R. B. Smith. "Self: The Power of Simplicity." OOPSLA '87 Conference Proceedings, October 1987, 227–242.

[88] Vlissides, J. *Pattern Hatching: Design Patterns Applied.* Reading, MA: Addison-Wesley, 1998.

[89] Wand, M. and D. Friedman. "The Mystery of the Tower Revealed: A Non-reflective Description of the Reflective Tower." Proceedings of the 1986 ACM Conference on LISP and Functional Programming, 1986, 298–307.

[90] Warren, I. *The Renaissance of Legacy Systems.* Berlin: Springer, 1999.

[91] Wegner, P. "Dimensions of Object-Based Language Design," OOPSLA '87 Conference Proceedings, October 1987, 168–82.

[92] Welch, I. and R. Stroud. "Kava—A Reflective Java Based on Bytecode Rewriting." In *Reflection and Software Engineering*, edited by W. Cazzola, R. Stroud, and F. Tisato, 155–68. LNCS 1826, Berlin: Springer-Verlag (June 2000).

[93] World Wide Web Consortium. *Extensible Markup Language (XML)* 1.0 (2d ed.). (www.w3.org/TR/2000/REC-xml-20001006).

[94] World Wide Web Consortium. "Web Services Architecture." W3C Working Draft 8, August 2003, (http://www.w3.org/TR/ws-arch).

index

A

Abstract Factory pattern 51, 54, 134
AccessibleObject
  isAccessible 39
  setAccessible 39, 41, 65, 67, 86, 139
active class 132
Amdahl's Law 218
AnnotationElement
  getAnnotation 234
  getAnnotations 234
  getDeclaredAnnotations 234
  getParameterAnnotations 234
  isAnnotationPresent 234
Apache 50, 100, 109
Args 152–153
  complete 153
  getFlagValue 152
  getFlagValues 152
  getLast 153
  hasFlagValue 153
  toString 153
Array
  get 40
  getBoolean 41
  getLength 40
  newInstance 40, 65, 171
  set 41, 67
  setBoolean 41
array types 14
arrays
  class objects 56
  name encoding 56
AspectJ 238
Aspect-Oriented Programming 175–176
assert statement 151

atomic class 74
attributes 29
Axis 100

B

base level 9, 19, 243
Base level object 9
base program 9
BCEL 176
benchmark 210
Builder pattern 54, 205
bytecode verifier 139

C

C# 236
C++ 246
C2C 148, 150
  command line flags 155
  command line processing 152
C2CConstructor 155, 157
C2CException 147, 169
C2CTransformation 158
C2ExtentManagedC 160
C2IdentitySubclassOfC 168, 188
C2InvariantCheckingC 188
C2ProxyForC 198, 208
C2SingletonC 183, 186
call stack introspection 108, 111–112, 191, 226
Castor 70
cglib 176
Chain of Responsibility pattern 205
checkAndProcessArgs 151
checkPostconditions 152

Class
    forName 53, 61–62, 65, 67, 84, 146, 158
    getClassLoader 81, 88, 96, 136
    getComponentType 13, 41, 65, 67
    getConstructor 58, 61
    getConstructors 58
    getDeclaredConstructor 58, 65
    getDeclaredConstructors 58, 183
    getDeclaredField 32, 67, 87
    getDeclaredFields 32, 38
    getDeclaredMethod 11, 20, 134
    getDeclaredMethods 11, 193
    getDeclaringClass 158
    getExceptionTypes 166
    getField 32
    getFields 32
    getInterfaces 22
        getAllInterfaces and 82
        uses 81, 88
    getMethod 6, 11, 146
    getModifiers 194
    getName 13, 167, 188
    getSuperclass 20, 22, 32, 38
    isArray 13, 158
    isAssignableFrom 22, 86, 183
    isInstance 22, 86
    isInterface 13, 183, 198
    isPrimitive 13, 44, 158
    newInstance 62, 84, 94, 130
class diagram 256
class invariant 116
Class literals 11
class loader
    delegation model 123, 126
    dynamic class replacement and 132
    security and 139
class object 10
ClassCastException 56–57, 83
ClassLoader
    defineClass 125, 127
    findClass 125
    findLoadedClass 125
    getParent 125
    getSystemClassLoader 125
    loadClass 125
ClassNotFoundException 55–56, 125
class-to-class transformation 144, 251
    Decorator pattern 187
    extent management 159
    Proxy pattern 197
    Singleton pattern 181

class-to-class transformations
    problematic language features 201
clone 80, 96, 116, 162, 181
Cloneable 14, 19, 160, 162, 181, 185, 203
    proxies and 80
CLOS 237
code generation
    class management 159
    Decorator pattern 187
    HelloWorld.java 145
    Proxy pattern 197
    reflection and 143
    Singleton pattern 181
com.sun.tools.javac 146
command line argurment processing 152
Composition Filters 238
construction overhead 209
ConstructOnce 131
Constructor
    getDeclaringClass 58
    getExceptionTypes 58, 183
    getModifiers 58, 65, 183
    getName 58
    getParameterTypes 59, 166
    newInstance 59, 61, 65
constructor objects 57
ConstructorgetParameterTypes 183
convenience facility 40, 48, 59, 165
cooperative method 148
createClass 151
createCooperativeWrapper 190, 196
createDBFacade 53
createRenamedConstructor 166, 183

D

Decorator pattern 170, 187, 197, 202, 205
delegation 51
deserialization 63
    assignFieldValues 67
    createInstances 65
    deserializeObject 65
    deserializeValue 68
design patterns
    Abstract Factory 54, 134
    Builder 54, 205
    Chain of Responsibility 205
    Decorator 170, 187, 197, 202, 205
    Facade 51
    Factory Method 51, 54, 181
    Flyweight 205

design patterns *(continued)*
  Memento 205
  Null Object 93
  Prototype 205
  Proxy 136, 197, 205
  Singleton 181, 205
  Strategy 133
  Template Method 148
direct superclass 22, 247
direct superinterface 22, 248
document 29
dynamic class replacement 132
dynamic invocation 7, 26, 142
  latency of 8
  using primitives with 16
dynamic loading 9, 31, 34, 48, 53, 105, 122
  array classes and 56
  construction overhead 209
  delegation and 71
  designing for 60
  disadvantages of constructors with arguments
    and 61
  no argument constructors and 70
  reflective construction and 54, 60, 71

E

element 29
encryption of class files 141
endorsed standard 142
equalSignatures 194
Error 202
exception
  C2CException 147, 169
  ClassCastException 56–57, 83
  ClassNotFoundException 55–56, 125
  IllegalAccessException 18, 21, 35, 57, 59
  IllegalArgumentException 8, 17–18, 35, 77
  IllegalStateException 117, 130–131
  IllegalThreadStateException 254
  InstantiationException 57
  InvocationTargetException 18
  NoSuchFieldException 31, 88
  NoSuchMethodException 12, 21, 58
  NullPointerException 83
  RuntimeException 169, 202
  SecurityException 31, 39, 58, 125
  UndeclaredThrowableException 83
  WrappedException 92, 96
execution overhead 209

extent of a class 145, 159
extrinsic property 138, 159

F

Facade pattern 51
Factory Method 54, 181
Field
  get 33, 86
  getBoolean 33
  getDeclaringClass 33, 41
  getModifiers 33, 38, 41, 67
  getName 33
  getType 33, 41
  set 34, 67
  setBoolean 34
finalize 96
findField 87
flexibility 28, 48, 69, 71, 105, 108, 218, 224, 226,
    238
  class loaders and 142
  delayed binding and 208
  delegation and 51
  dynamically linked libraries and 50
  in use of C2C framework 175
Flyweight pattern 205
forName 53, 55–56, 122, 128, 130, 144, 152
  primitives and 56

G

generateClassNamePrefix 151
generateConstructors 151
generateFields 151
generateImports 151
generateInterfaces 151
generateMethods 151
generateNestedClasses 151
getAllInterfaces 195
getInstanceVariables 38
getMethodsLackingImplementation 190, 192
getModifiersWithout 192
getSecurityManager 139
granularity overhead 209

H

Hacker' s Dictionary, The 122
HelloWorldBenchmark 210
Hibernate 176
Hyper/J 238

I

IBM 140, 237
identity class-to-class transformation 168
IllegalAccessException 18, 21, 35, 57, 59
IllegalArgumentException 8, 17–18, 35, 77
IllegalStateException 117, 130–131
IllegalThreadStateException 254
infinite recursion 108, 118, 187, 191
initiating loader 125
instance variables 35
instanceOf dependency 19, 23, 256
InstantiationException 57
intercession 74
  class loading and 122
introspection 7, 26
  accessing constructors 57
  accessing fields 31
  argument interfaces and 105
  dynamic invocation and 9
invariant 116
invariant checking 187
InvariantChecker 119
InvariantSupporter 117
InvocationHandler
  invoke 79
InvocationHandlerBase 86
InvocationTargetException 18

J

Java 1.5 226
  annotation facility 229
  generics 173, 227
  impact on reflective code 235
  language extensions 234
Java Community Process 227
Java compiler dynamically invoked 146, 148, 150
Java Language Specification 22, 37, 241
Java reflection
  limitations 144
Java Specification Requests 227
Javassist 140, 176
JDOM 30, 46, 71
Jikes 140, 176
JSR 14 227
JSR 175 229
JSR 201 234
JUnit 129

K

Kiczales, Gregor 175

L

LISP 242
loaded class 132
Logger 110
logging 108–109

M

Member 36
  getDeclaringClass 36
  getModifiers 36
  getName 36
Memento pattern 205
memory leaks 28
metaclass 23
metadata 48
metalevel 9, 19, 245, 252
metaobject 48, 57–58, 71
metaobject class 9, 15, 26, 59, 235
metaobject protocol 250
metaobjects 9
Method
  getDeclaringClass 15
  getExceptionTypes 15, 196
  getModifiers 15, 171, 192–193
  getName 15, 81, 194, 196, 198
  getParameterTypes 15, 100, 171, 194, 196, 198
  getReturnType 15, 94, 171, 196
  invoke 6, 15, 21, 81, 88, 96, 134, 136, 146
method invocation intercession 74
method objects 14
Microsoft 236
Modifier
  isAbstract 37
  isFinal 37
  isInterface 37
  isNative 37
  isPrivate 36
  isProtected 36
  isPublic 36, 41, 65, 67
  isStatic 36, 38
  isStrict 37
  isSynchronized 37
  isTransient 37, 41

Modifier *(continued)*
  isVolatile 37
  isStatic 171
modifying bytecodes 140
Monkey 118
Moore's Law 221
Mopex 20, 165, 191
  actualParametersToString 166–167, 183, 198
  classArrayToString 166–167, 183
  createCooperativeWrapper 188, 196
  createRenamedConstructor 160, 166, 168, 183
  equalSignatures 193–194
  findField 86–87
  formalParametersToString 166, 183
  getAllInterfaces 82, 194–195
  getInstanceVariables 38, 41
  getMethodsLackingImplementation 188, 192
  getModifiersWithout 188, 192, 198
  getSupportedMethod 21
  getTypeName 166–167
  headerSuffixToString 198
  selectAncestors 193–194
  selectMethods 188, 193, 198
multithreading 80, 89, 108, 119, 138, 175, 218

N

namespaces 130, 137
NoSuchFieldException 31, 88
NoSuchMethodException 12, 21, 58
NTime 219
Null Object pattern 93
NullPointerException 83

O

Object
  clone 116
object diagram 256

P

parent class loader 123
pattern application 180
Perl 63
persistence 75
pitfalls
  class-to-class transformation 201
  infinite recursion 118, 191
  of call stack introspection 114
  of dynamic invocation 17
  of dynamic proxy 103
  of interface introspection 37
  of microbenchmarking 211
property sheets 28
Prototype pattern 205
Proxy
  getInvocationHandler 77, 86, 134
  getProxyClass 77, 174
  isProxyClass 77
  newProxyInstance 77, 81, 88, 96, 100, 136
  use of 208
proxy 74, 134, 142
  clone and 80
  for tracing 81
  invocation handlers and 79
proxy classes 78
proxy instance 78
proxy interfaces 78
Proxy pattern 136, 197, 205
Python 236
Python Software Foundation 236

R

readObject 69, 162, 182
referent 136
reflection
  call stack introspection 111
  class loading 122
  code generation and 140, 143
  dynamic loading 50
  evolution in Java 226
  flexibility and 8
  introspection and 8
  reflective construction 50, 57
reflective access 26, 34, 69
  setAccessible and 38
  to annotations 233
  to array elements 40
reflective construction 48, 53–54, 209
  delegation and 71
  disadvantages of constructors with
    arguments 61
  dynamic loading and 54, 60, 71
  factory method and 54
reflective programming 9–10, 23, 227–228
regression testing 122
reify operation
  getStackTrace 111

reusability 226
root element 29
RTime 219
Runtime.exec 253
RuntimeException 169, 202

S

SecureClassLoader 139
security manager 31, 39, 58, 139
SecurityException 31, 39, 58, 125, 139
selectAncestors 194
selectMethods 193
Self (programming language) 245
self-representation 9
sequence diagram 256
Serializable 182
serialization 28
  limitations 69
  serializeObject 41
  serializeVariable 44
Servlets 50
setProperty 128
Simple Object Access Protocol 99
SimpleClassLoader 127, 139
SimpleClassLoaderTest 130
Singleton pattern 181, 205
slowdown 218
Smalltalk 236–237, 244, 246
SOAP 99
software rot 122
stack frame 108, 112, 114, 243
StackTraceElement 226
  getClassName 112–113, 119, 188
  getFileName 112
  getLineNumber 112–113
  getMethodName 112–113, 119, 188
  isNativeMethod 112
Strategy pattern 133
SynchronizedInvariantChecker 119
system class loader 122

T

target of a proxy 74
Template Method 148
test stub 90
Throwable
  getStackTrace 111, 113, 119, 188
  printStackTrace 111

Tomcat 50, 109
tracing 74, 76, 81, 89, 109, 170, 230
types, represented as class objects 12

U

UML 9, 19, 256
  class diagram 18, 92, 232
    annotations 233
    C2C framework 148, 174, 204
    CustomerDatabase facade 52
    Decorator pattern 188
    dynamic class replacement 133
    example of C2ExtentManagedC 163
    java.lang.reflect 59
    Parrot example 61
    Proxy pattern 197
    Singleton pattern 182
    Squirrel example 164–165
    support for generics 229
    zoo application 45
  class/object diagram 10, 19, 84
    class loader delegation model 124
    metalevel boundary 24–25, 245, 247–248
    set of metaclasses 251
  object diagram
    zoo application 45
  sequence diagram
    actual objects in method forwarding 80
    class loader delegation model 126
    intervals timed 217
    proxy chaining 90
    proxy definition 75
    use of getMethod and invoke 17
UndeclaredThrowableException 83
unit testing 90
unloaded class 132
UQueue 151
  definition 171
  uses
    Args 153
    C2CConstructor 155
    getAllInterfaces 195
    getMethodsLackingImplementation 192
    selectAncestor 194
    selectMethod 193
URLClassLoader 139
URLStreamHandler 139

V

Venn diagram
  set of metaclasses 251

W

WeakReference 136, 159, 182, 185
Web services 29, 99, 101, 103
Web Services Description Language 102
WrappedException 92, 96
writeObject 69
WSDL 99, 102

X

Xerox PARC 175, 236
XMethods 99, 102
XML 29–30, 99
  illegal characters 70

Z

ZooTest 46
  output 46